GETTING FOOD FROM WATER

GETTING FOOD FROM WATER
A Guide to Backyard Aquaculture

by GENE LOGSDON

Rainbow Trout

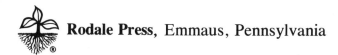 **Rodale Press**, Emmaus, Pennsylvania

Grateful acknowledgement is made to the National Audubon
Society for permission to reprint material from ''The Oxbow'' by
Ed Bry, which originally appeared in the May 1969 issue of
Audubon magazine. Copyright © 1969 by the National Audubon
Society.

Printed in the United States of America on recycled paper, containing a high percentage of de-inked fiber.

Library of Congress Cataloging in Publication Data
Logsdon, Gene.
  Getting food from water.

  Bibliography: p.
  Includes index.
  1. Aquaculture. 2. Farm ponds. 3. Fish
ponds. I. Title.
SH135.L63   630'.9169   78-16415
ISBN 0-87857-232-5

2 4 6 8 10 9 7 5 3 1

CONTENTS

Contents

Getting Food from Water

INTRODUCTION

We gardeners and homesteaders are inclined, at first, to dismiss aquaculture as a pursuit too impractical for us. The word has a sophisticated, foreign ring to it, and we automatically connect its practice with the dilettante or the business entrepreneur. We are surprised to learn that aquaculture has been a traditional family occupation in various parts of the world, including our own, for hundreds of years. But we are not surprised to find out that families involved in "cultivating the water" prefer to call themselves fishermen or fish farmers rather than aquaculturists. Most of us prefer to be called gardeners, not horticulturists, for about the same reason.

But fish farming is too narrow a definition for all the kinds of food and fiber production that aquaculture encompasses. Bardach, McLarney, and Ryther, in their book, *Aquaculture: The Farming and Husbandry of Freshwater and Marine Organisms*, define, with that title, much broader boundaries and it is this broader definition that I adhere to in this book. Aquaculture, then, includes the production not only of fish, but of plants like rice, crustaceans like crayfish, waterfowl, and even mammals like muskrats whose life cycle is intimately tied to streams or pools of water.

But where most books on aquaculture concentrate on commercial ventures in which strict economics call all the shots, I will concentrate on small-scale, part-time, or hobby aquaculture regardless of whether it is "efficient" enough to make a profit for the practitioner. I call this "backyard aquaculture" or "homestead aquaculture." McLarney, in the book already mentioned, calls it "subsistent aquaculture." The term bears the same relationship to commercial aquaculture that gardening and homesteading do to commercial agriculture. The professional trout producer, for example, is technically more of an aquaculturist than the gardener who raises only a few trout in a backyard pool, or the homesteader who increases the natural population of trout by improving the fish's habitat in his stream. But the latter are nonetheless practicing aquaculture, and it is for them that this book is especially intended.

Aquaculture can be practiced in a sort of seminatural state, using existing bodies of water, or it can be domesticated into a totally man-made environment. You can raise wild trout in a natural stream with proper management, or you can raise hybrid trout in completely artificial raceways. Sometimes the distinction is not so clear-cut. The Japanese "seed" and harrow natural clam beds much like a farmer planting a grain field. Salmon "ranchers" on our West Coast raise large numbers of silver salmon in saltwater or freshwater holding pens along the coast, release the fish at the proper age to "graze" the ocean, then "harvest" them when they return to spawn.

The first part of this book will concentrate on the more natural aquaculture as it is or can be practiced in existing bodies of water; the second part on aquaculture in man-made ponds, streams, and tanks. The first kind of aquaculture is far easier, cheaper, and less time-consuming for the gardener and homesteader, and seems to me a necessary first step before going on to more artificial methods. If a person will first study the amazingly varied ecosystem of a natural pond, he will then be prepared to manage an artificial pond better. Too often, the farm-pond builder thinks he is building a sterile swimming pool, and he will persist until he has chemicalized his pond to death in a vain effort to make it one.

There is no better way to study ecology or to appreciate the wisdom of organic husbandry than to observe how dependent marine organisms are on each other in the vital food chain of their existence—and, by extension, how dependent all of nature is on a proper balance and variety of food. Water organisms absorb or react to poisons and imbalances much more quickly than land organisms do. We recognize that shellfish on our polluted coasts are too loaded with harmful industrial chemicals to be eaten safely much more quickly than we recognize the same danger in meats and grains.

Growing food in water is remarkably like growing it in or on land. Water needs to be managed for fertility much like soil and much the same stratagems that make organic gardening successful can be used to pursue small-scale aquaculture. So closely do agriculture and aquaculture resemble each other that they seem to me to be basically inseparable. For the organic gardener and/or homesteader, the two can be considered two sides of the same coin, part and parcel of the same activity. If I talk about farm ponds for rearing fish, I will talk in the same breath about the increased value of that pond water for irrigation because of its increased fertility from fish wastes. If I discuss rearing fish in a tank enclosed by solar-heated plastic panels, I will quickly point out that in this greenhouse-like enclosure, you can also be raising vegetables.

But one does not live by bread alone, or even by a diet varied with frog legs, trout, and watercress. Sometimes this book will wander a bit from the straight path of utilitarian information just to talk about *enjoying* creeks and ponds and springs and the wondrous variety of life drawn to a body of unpolluted water. To stand beside a farm pond on a May morning, or sit beside a secluded garden pool in your yard, or walk along a clear stream through a pasture; to stand in awe before the life-giving power and beauty of clear clean water—surely that's the greatest use for it of all.

THE MEANING
OF WATERSHED 1

To practice aquaculture intelligently, particularly less intensive forms in naturally existing bodies of water, or in ponds built to catch run-off water, it helps to understand the various manifestations of watershed. Just as the formations of earth—hilltop, slope, valley, plain, hollow—each have characteristics more suitable for some agricultural uses than for others, so also do the various forms water takes in your watershed. Swift mountain streams are better for trout, gently running springs for watercress, warm-water streams for bass and catfish, shallow marshes for crayfish and muskrat, potholes for waterfowl, bogs for cranberries. Knowing the natural propensities of water in these various forms and their potential for aquacultural production can guide you in selecting a homestead most appropriate for your purposes. Or, if you have already settled in, the same knowledge can help you realize the full potential of what you already have in the way of water or what you can build.

DRAWING NATURE'S BOUNDARIES

The meaning of watershed is not difficult to grasp once we forget our usual way of dividing land by property lines or by arbitrarily drawn boundaries between national and political subdivisions. All the land from which water drains to the same outlet comprises a watershed. All the land draining into the Mississippi River forms the huge Mississippi Valley watershed, but that system is composed of countless smaller watersheds, some as mighty as the Ohio River Valley, some as tiny as the rivulet running out of a southern Illinois woodlot.

Because man would like to ignore natural divisions of land in

1

favor of his own arbitrary property lines, humans have always had problems implementing wise land use. Neighborhood feuds without number have been fought over who must pay what and how much for drainage and flood control and over the question of how far one owner's right of private property extends when poorly designed land development causes water run-off damage. Were the mistake not so serious, the Fates would surely laugh at man's stubborn insistence on building houses on flood plains, or his more modern habit of building flood plains by paving poorly designed parking lots that collect tons of water in heavy rains and dump them on hapless houses downstream. Man straightens creeks to rid himself of excess water faster, only to cause more violent flooding downstream. He builds levees to protect rich parts of cities, increasing flood damage beyond the levee. He throws up huge dams below heavily farmed watersheds and is surprised when the lakes fill up with mud in a decade.

The Hydrological Cycle

The Meaning of Watershed

When I try to grasp the concept of watershed both in its immense and in its minute manifestations, I relate it to my own region. The Killdeer Plains Wildlife Area, a few miles from my little farm, is a large wetland marsh (aquacultural practices are being used there to increase wildlife populations) straddling two great watersheds. Water on the south side of the Killdeer Plains flows out eventually into the Scioto River and south down the Ohio and Mississippi rivers. Water on the north side flows north, eventually into the Sandusky River and on into Lake Erie. Technically, if I stand in exactly the right spot in the Plains, one foot would be in the Mississippi watershed, the other in the Great Lakes watershed. If I stretch out my arms in the rain, water falling from my left hand lands, by and by, in the Gulf of Mexico; that from my right hand in the North Atlantic.

Such a telescopic view of watershed oversimplifies it, of course. If that water falling from my hand is not absorbed by plant or animal or evaporated back into the atmosphere as it very well might be, it first sinks into the soil and when that soil is saturated, gathers on the surface and begins to flow. In Killdeer, the soil is so flat and tight the water collects into marshes first. But given enough rain, by and by the water finds its way into sluggish creeks which eventually wend their way to larger creeks like the Tymochtee, the Little Sandusky, or St. James Run on the north-flowing watershed. All the while, these water droplets are joining with others all along the way, being renewed and enlarged by rain and from springs welling up from groundwater sources. As the water runs through my land on the St. James Run, I use some of it along with the rainwater runoff. I use it, that is, as long as it is fit to use. My cattle drink it, "my" fish and wildlife live in and on it, my gardens grow on its moisture, we swim in it. But it is not my water. I have no right to pollute it beyond another man's use farther down the line. I have no right to stop its flow, no right to alter its direction to the detriment of others.

The water must—or at least should—move on down the Tymochtee, the Sandusky, into the Great Lakes, and eventually out of the St. Lawrence; free for man's and nature's good purposes; free to form life-sustaining wetlands, streams, running springs, forest bogs, lowland swamps, rivers, lakes, saltwater marshes, tidal pools, seashores, oceans; then back to the clouds to fall again in a continuing cycle of perpetual motion.

3

MANIPULATING WATER

You can play with a tiny rivulet running down a hill after rain and learn all there is to know about the mechanics of manipulating water. Water is ruled by gravity; it always flows downward, seeking its own level. Block one path and it will find another. Level its path, and it will stand still. Increase the grade, and you increase the speed of its flow in direct proportion.

All these simple observations are the basic lessons of water manipulation in aquaculture. If you dam water, you must provide an overflow—a safety valve. If you wish to control water level in a tidal pool, it is a simple matter to use sluice gates that open and close with the tide. If you wish water to flow faster in a raceway, you have but to tilt the raceway to a steeper grade. If you wish to erode soil and fill pools with mud and turbid water, merely remove the vegetation that slows water's downward rush from the hillsides, and straighten the creek beds, and ditch the swamps out, and you shall have your wish.

One way or the other, aquaculture will make you aware of the dynamic, life-sustaining power of water and its natural system of watersheds, an appreciation that knowledge of artificial lines on paper maps can't give you. If a man tells you he is French or German or American, that he hails from California or Pennsylvania, he tells you very little. When he calls himself a mountain man or a plainsman or a river rat or a beachcomber, then you begin to know him.

BEGINNINGS: 2
THE NEVER-FAILING SPRING

The first and usually preferred source of water for homestead aquaculture is the running spring. Of all existing bodies of water, the spring has the best chance of being unpolluted. It is also the easiest and cheapest to control and manipulate since it flows at a relatively steady, predictable rate. Moreover, the law considers you the owner of a small spring that rises entirely on your property and gives you more or less exclusive right to its use. The use of waters that are defined as "public" is restricted by law, a problem that sometimes can be insurmountable for an aquaculturist seeking ocean shore locations for his business.

Therefore, property containing a good ever-flowing spring—or the potential of having one developed—is, for the self-reliant homesteader, worth something more than property not so blessed. No particular parts of the humid regions of this country necessarily have more springs than any other, though intensive farming, land clearing, and housing development are decreasing the number of them dramatically, where they were once common. A hundred years ago, every good farm in the East, by definition, had its spring and springhouse for a reliable water supply and for keeping perishable food cool. It goes without saying that, for the aquaculturally minded, that kind of water system could be invaluable.

I'm reminded of a remarkable spring I visited on a farm near Yellow Springs, Ohio, last summer. The sight of it would make any homesteader drool. The spring welled up on a hillside shelf—nearly at the top of a hill, actually—in such volume that it immediately formed a small stream. The stream ran through an ancient but very substantial and sophisticated springhouse, then spread out into a small pool on the rocky shelf before plunging steeply into a gorge beyond. I did not have to know too much about flow rates and

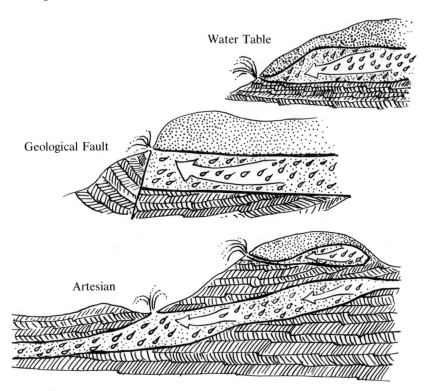

Springs generally have one of three sources. A water-table spring emerges when groundwater completely fills the pore space over a layer of impervious rock. A shift along a geological fault may expose a groundwater reservoir, creating a geological fault spring. An artesian spring develops when groundwater, usually under great pressure, breaks through the surface of the earth.

electric generating capacity to realize there was enough water and plenty of head for the installation of a turbine to generate all the electricity one household, at least, would need.

The pool below the springhouse was a water gardener's delight. How many water lilies might one raise easily in this never-failing, never-freezing water? But an even better use of the water had already been realized: The stream pools were overgrown with the lushest stand of watercress I have ever seen. Years before, the owner informed me, his family had derived a hefty part of its income cutting and harvesting the delicious salad green. "We never had to worry about it growing. Just harvest it every year. It made good money, but the cutting and packaging for sale was hard work."

GROWING WATERCRESS

Watercress is an aquatic perennial that in clean, slow-moving water grows easily and without help. It derives its nutrition more from the minerals in the water than from the soil or gravel beneath. Watercress should not be confused with other forms of garden or upland cress that are annual and that can be grown easily in moist gardens or flats. Seedhouses that sell watercress seed (Burpee does, among others) say the plant can also be grown in moist garden soil in shady places, but you will rarely find such culturing satisfactory. First of all, watercress really prefers a sunny location when it grows in water. Second, if you live in the North, you will find it will hardly ever overwinter in your garden.

If, however, you have a garden pool through which well water circulates, watercress should do well. Commercially, it is grown in greenhouses in flats kept nearly constantly watered, as well as outdoors in natural springs. Indoor crops should be eaten about fifty days after seeding, while that grown outdoors in spring water gets better flavored on into fall and winter. On watercress grown in spring water, stems as well as leaves are succulent and flavorful. I harvest them by cutting with a clipper or old scissors about 4 to 6 inches back from the tips or about 2 inches below the water surface. The plants like about 3 to 6 inches of water, and will grow to 6 inches or more above water level.

Seed can be planted on the soil surface or just beneath it, on the bank of a flowing spring. You can start the seed in wet sand, and transplant into the stream bed or at the shoreline. Once it gains a footing, watercress will spread of its own accord. Don't harvest it too hard the first year or so.

Watercress won't grow in swift streams or in muddy, polluted streams, especially if they flood with surface run-off water. I've tried to establish it in our creek, but the spring floods sweep it away. Experts caution not to eat watercress from polluted streams, though in my experience, the plant doesn't grow where water is dangerously polluted. Still, better safe than sorry. At any rate, watercress will always need careful washing and cleaning in the kitchen.

All the people I have questioned about marketing watercress give the same advice. Even though no demand for it exists in most areas, you will have little trouble selling any and all you want to

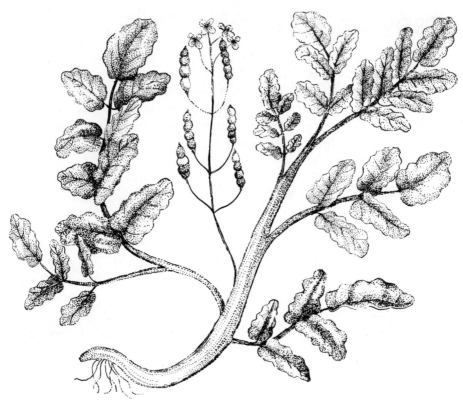

Watercress

produce, once you make it available in steady supply. The catch is that the harvesting, cleaning, and packaging is almost entirely hand labor, both slow and tedious. But the same type of gardener who doesn't mind picking and selling raspberries could be a successful cress grower, too.

Watercress is rich in minerals if the spring water it grows in is similarly rich. It contains fair amounts of vitamins A, B$_1$, C, and D. Herbalists say it is a good blood cleanser, whatever that means.

Growing Watercress Commercially Watercress likes a
cool climate, but preferably one in which winters are mild. It can die if the water it is growing in freezes *completely*, which, fortunately, spring water rarely does. Outdoor commercial production is most developed in the hilly limestone regions of Virginia, West

Virginia, Maryland, and Pennsylvania. It is not what you would call in any way a big business. Even twenty years ago, at its peak, watercress acreage totaled only a few hundred acres.

Since watercress derives its nitrogen from the water, economic production depends upon the amount of nitrate in the spring water. It can be as low as 2 parts per million in a large flow of water, says the Virginia Agricultural Experiment Station, but smaller springs should contain considerably more than that—up to 15 to 20 ppm—for profitable production. You can have your water tested by a laboratory, but the best way to judge is whether wild watercress is growing vigorously in the spring water you intend to use.

Commercial growers usually grow their watercress on artificial beds surrounded by low dikes with bypasses and water gates to control the level of water in the bed, and to allow complete drainage when necessary. Slope of the beds is kept at about 2 inches per 100 feet so water will flow on through the beds, but not too fast.

Since it takes about thirty to forty days for a crop to mature for harvest, growers like to maintain a dozen beds, each of a size they have the facilities to harvest in two or three days. Harvesting moves from bed to bed, so that by the time the last has been cut and packed, the first is ready for a second harvest.

If you have no established patch from which to secure cuttings or transplants, you sow seed on well-worked soil as you would in the garden. The seed is very small. An ounce of it will seed, by broadcasting, about 70 square yards, and should produce about seventy thousand seedlings for transplanting. Seed needs to be only barely covered. Moisten soil after seeding. As the plants come up, gradually flood the bed.

Seedlings (or cuttings or plants from an established bed) are transplanted in summer. Cuttings should be about a foot long and planted 6 inches deep. Set plants in the bed about 6 inches apart in both directions to get a good, quick, thick stand. After the cuttings start to grow, clip the tips to induce stouter-stemmed plants. Water level should be raised as plants grow, always leaving several inches of growth above water.

When new growth is 6 to 8 inches long, harvesting can begin. After harvest, raise water level and/or clip stubs of cut plants so that entire remaining stems are just under the water. Plants should be clipped as evenly as possible. As they regrow, keep raising the water level so that only several inches of growth are above water.

After the late spring harvest and before the fall harvest, many growers lower the water level to 3 or 4 inches, clean out weeds, and replant any empty spaces in the bed. A dense stand of cress is thus maintained, and that's the best way to keep out weeds.

Yields average about twenty-five hundred bunches—a bunch is a nice handful—per 1,000 square feet per cutting. A bed will last indefinitely if well cared for, though weeds and insect damage may necessitate an occasional renewal of a bed.

Watercress is cut with a long butcher knife, arranged in bunches, trimmed to about 4 inches long, tied near the tops, and packed in plastic bags. The bunches should be kept in cold water and/or packed in ice on the way to market.

The watercress sowbug is a sometimes serious pest of watercress. Muskrats don't endanger watercress so much by eating, but they can be most bothersome by digging holes in the dikes. Crayfish don't harm watercress and snails rarely do, but, of course, if such kinds of water bugs and creatures show up in your packaged product, you probably will find it hard to sell the next time.

MULTIPLYING A SPRING'S USEFULNESS

In natural springs of deeper water, watercress can be combined with trout raising. The cress grows along the shallower shorelines, the trout in the deep (at least 12 inches with pools twice that deep) channels. In the Minnesota River Valley, where I was fortunate enough to have ready access to a large network of springs years ago, this combination worked very well, at least on a noncommercial level. Rainbow trout, originally stocked in the running springs, had naturalized, increased, and multiplied. It was no problem hooking three-quarter pounders or larger, sometimes from remarkably tiny streamlets within the network of springs. The watercress naturalized too, spreading up and down the shallower stretches of water. We prized it especially in the Minnesota climate, since it provided us with a fresh salad green into December, even in below-zero weather, because the water never froze.

This amazing set of springs could have been an aquaculturist's paradise, but the only commercial use made of it, as far as I know, was the establishment of a health sanatorium back in the early

1900s to take advantage of the real or supposed therapeutic value of the spring water. Among the homesteader uses we found for the springs, a couple that may have wider application for other springs bear mentioning here. About half a mile from where our springs rose, they gathered into one fairly large stream and emptied into the Minnesota River. In spring, when the river rose bank-high, we were treated to an unusual sight.

The muddy water from the river backed up the creek, raising its level as much as 10 feet, and blocking the downward rush of the clear spring water. The two waters would not mingle for a day or two but, in effect, formed a clearly defined wall of muddy water juxtaposed to a wall of clear water. Fish, especially carp, moving upstream with the rising waters as is their inclination, would suddenly emerge (I think bewildered) from the muddy water into the clear. It was as if some ingenious scientist had developed a large, natural aquarium for our benefit. From the water we speared and hooked scores of carp, which we smoked for eating or used for fertilizer. We even tried diving into the clear water to catch the big fish by hand. That proved unsuccessful, although the fish did not seem particularly afraid of us swimming beside them. For a person

Weir Dam

13

who had never gone skin-diving in the ocean, the experience could be only described as sensational.

Along a similar creek a mile or so from ours, another family utilized the rise and fall of water in the creek in a way similar to that which ocean aquaculturists manage the rise and fall of the tides. In this case, about 200 yards back from the river, the homesteaders built a dam-like concrete structure across the creek where the banks were particularly high and narrow. In the center of the structure they left an opening about 2 feet wide and 8 feet tall. The sides of the weir gap were notched so that a water gate could be slid in from above, effectively closing and sealing the gap. (It leaked a little but not enough to be of concern.) The water gate was raised and lowered by means of a press screw exactly like the arrangement on a traditional cider press. With the gate raised, the creek flowed normally. Lowered in summer during times of normal water flow, the gate blocked the water and formed a swimming pool of clear and lovely water, in hardly more than an hour's time. Swimming time ended, the gate could be raised slowly, and soon the creek was back to normal.

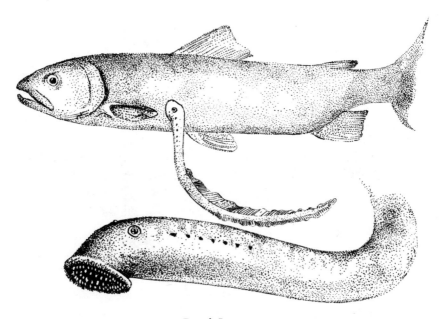

Brook Lamprey

During periods of high water in the river, the water gate served other purposes. Water backing up from the swollen river not only filled the creek but pushed on back into the drainage ditches that led into the creek from cultivated fields. By lowering the gate, water could be effectively blocked from flooding the lower parts of such fields.

In early spring, when the river usually went on a rampage, the entire valley flooded, at least next to the river, and the water gate was of no use in stopping the flood. In this case, the gate was only lowered after the water began to subside, trapping many fish in the pool behind it.

I don't need to tell you that trapping fish that way may be illegal in your area today, and that almost any kind of weir dam on public waters means serious consultation with wildlife authorities beforehand. However, if your intention is to catch carp, which are decidedly overpopulating most rivers (but which are great sources of nitrogen and protein), you might not only get approval, but lots of help from wildlife personnel. In the example described here, the water gate could also be used to block the early summer run upstream of parasitical lamprey and that reason alone might justify it in the eyes of the powers that be.

IRRIGATION FROM SPRINGS

The same water gate that prevents flooding of lowland fields, as in the example above, could also be used to flood those fields periodically. Just drop the gate and back the water up the drainage ditches. No cheaper irrigation water could be provided by any other system.

Most springs, however, don't run strongly enough to provide steady or heavy irrigation. Their value is in providing *some* water during dry periods. A landscape nurseryman I know makes excellent use of a small running spring for this purpose. He grows perhaps 4 acres of trees and ornamentals along the lower part of a gentle slope. Above the plantings, he scooped out a small pond site with a bulldozer. Into it, he put a plastic pipe with a valve on it. At the other end, the pipe intercepts a running spring at the edge of his property. It takes about three days to fill the pond from the little creek, during which time water-flow downstream does not seem to diminish. Once filled, the pond becomes water storage for use at critical times between rains. Being on a higher level than the nursery, the pond water can irrigate the trees by gravity feed. A good, 3-inch application takes almost all the water, but three days later the pond is full again. Other than irrigation pipe, there is very little cost in so simple a system. And of course, fish and ducks can take advantage of the water all year-round.

MEASURING SPRING-FLOW RATES

If you plan to use a spring for a water supply—for agriculture, aquaculture, or home use—you need to determine first whether the spring is large enough to meet the uses you plan for it. Will its natural, steady flow provide enough water at all times, or will you need a storage tank to hold a day's supply?

In most cases, you'll find yourself in the second situation, but in either case you need to know about how much water you'll need every day. For aquacultural projects using recirculated water, the

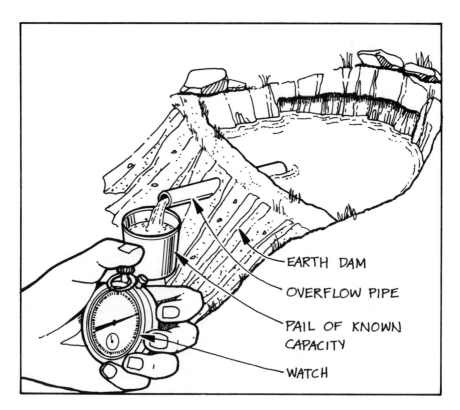

EARTH DAM

OVERFLOW PIPE

PAIL OF KNOWN CAPACITY

WATCH

question is not so critical, since little additional water is used once the system is filled. However, a spring's unique advantage to an aquacultural project is that it can provide a steady flow of oxygenated water through the tank, making recirculation and filtration unnecessary. For a small spring, this could mean a rather small number of fish, but at very low cost and few problems for the home food producer. In any case, you will need to find out how much oxygen your water contains, and relate that to the requirements of various fish as given in other parts of this book. Sometimes it is a very simple matter to allow water to tumble into a tank from a foot or two above to increase oxygen content. A certain amount of trial and error in this matter will be more valuable than general guidelines. We used to keep fish untended for years in a concrete horse trough filled with well water, which is ordinarily not high in oxygen. We didn't know about water and oxygen, and I guess the fish didn't either.

Two Ways to Measure a Spring's Flow Rate

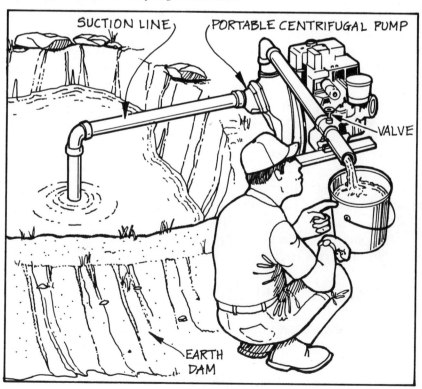

17

The rule of thumb for human use of water allows about 50 gallons per person per day, though you and I know folks who use less and folks who use a lot more. (Nearly half of that 50 gallons is allocated for flushing the conventional toilet.) At any rate, water is used in greater quantities during some parts of the day than during others, so storage must be figured on these "peak use" times. Agricultural engineers give these guidelines for livestock consumption of water: cattle, between 9 and 18 gallons per day per 1,000 pounds of live weight. (An animal will drink more warm water per day than cold.) A milk cow drinks about 8 gallons per day, plus 1/3 gallon for every pound of milk she is giving. A horse or mule needs 8 to 12 gallons per day; a hog about 1 gallon per 100 pounds of live weight. Figure sheep the same as hogs. A hundred laying hens should have about 8 gallons per day too, and a hundred turkeys between 10 and 15 gallons per day. A litter of rabbits might drink a gallon a day at the most.

To determine the flow of a spring, make a temporary dike or dam to hold back the flow, and insert a pipe through the dam. Record the time it takes to fill a container of known volume. Simple multiplication will then tell you the spring's daily flow rate. You can use a centrifugal pump to check spring flow, too. By turning the valve on the pump, you can adjust the pump to discharge the exact amount of water the spring produces, and determine the flow rate, as in the first case, by how long it takes to fill a container of known size.

If you are going to use your spring water in a commercial business serving the public—which could be the case if you are thinking aquaculture—your water system will have to meet local health regulations. If you are drinking your spring water, you'll want to have it checked anyway. But remember, the normal health department water test measures the count of *Escherichia coli* bacteria only. Tests for minerals and metals can be run by chemical labs, but are somewhat costly—around $10 each.

CAPTURING A SPRING

Small springs that come from a single, clearly visible source are called point springs. A seep spring may only show on the soil surface as a wet spot or muddy ooze. Each kind is developed differently, as the drawings show.

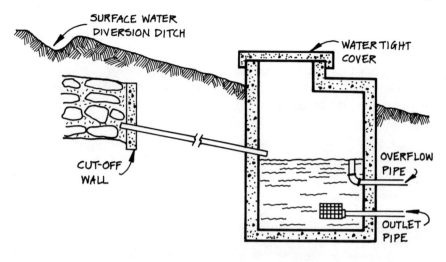

SURFACE WATER
DIVERSION DITCH

WATERTIGHT
COVER

CUT-OFF
WALL

OVERFLOW
PIPE

OUTLET
PIPE

For a point spring, dig down into the ground along the line of flow until you find a place where water is at least 3 feet below the soil surface, engineers advise. Install a cut-off wall of concrete or plastic, inserting a pipe through the wall to draw the water out into a spring box. Be sure the pipe is slanted well downgrade from the cut-off wall, so pressure doesn't build up against spring flow.

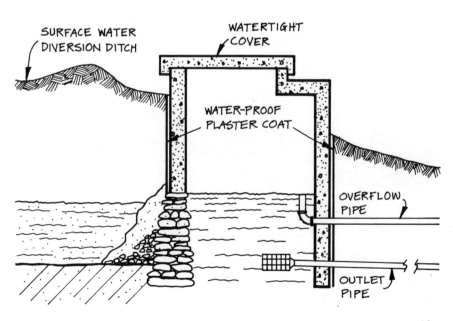

SURFACE WATER
DIVERSION DITCH

WATERTIGHT
COVER

WATER-PROOF
PLASTER COAT

OVERFLOW
PIPE

OUTLET
PIPE

Getting Food from Water

Sometimes, especially in low places, you can just dig out the spring and build a spring box over it or right adjacent to it. In one situation shown, a permeable rock wall allows the water through, while in another, perforated pipe collects the water.

That last example is similar to the arrangement used to develop a seep spring, but is shown better in still another illustra-

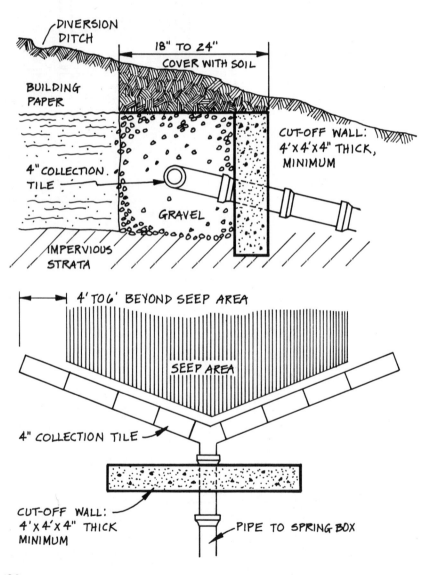

tion. You need to lay down tile about 2 feet deep along the lower edge of the seep area to collect the water. The two arms, or branches, are made of perforated plastic tile or clay tile laid with about quarter-inch spacings between tiles so the water can get in. The main pipe carrying the water to the spring box or storage tank is not perforated. A cut-off wall may be necessary to keep water from seeping past the tile collectors too fast.

Notice that in all kinds of spring collectors, there is always a ditch above the spring area to divert possibly polluted surface runoff.

The spring box, which for an aquaculturist might be a fish tank, or which certainly will lead to a fish tank like it, is best made of concrete. The box should extend at least 3 feet below and 1 foot above ground and should be at least 4 feet deep and 3 feet wide. It can be used as is that way as a cattle-watering tank too, although you will need to provide an overflow pipe to carry excess water away from the site. Otherwise, cattle will turn the ground around the tank into a quagmire.

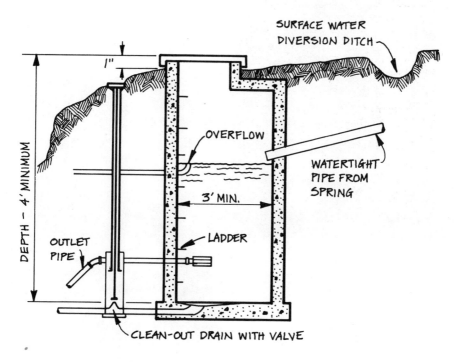

Spring Box

THE SPRINGHOUSE

It might not be thought practical to restore a springhouse or build a new one, though the structure will certainly keep dairy products and other perishables reasonably cool as they once did, at zero expense in electric energy. But for the home food producer who, in addition to being mildly interested in springhouses anyway, also contemplates raising fish, the idea begins to look more practical. Studying some existing springhouses in your area will give you some ideas you can put to use in aquaculture.

I've never seen two springhouses exactly alike, but the one thing they have in common is that they are downgrade from the spring. Water flows through them by gravity; it is not pumped

An old springhouse with an upper story for general storage.

Putting a springhouse to use.

through. Second, the springhouse is set into the ground as much as possible, sometimes into a hillside so that at least the rear half is well insulated with soil. The better insulated it is, the cooler the room will be in hot August and the less chance there is of winter freeze-up.

Remembering that water always flows downhill, seeking its own level, you can build your springhouse floor to maintain whatever water depth you desire. The best springhouses I have seen have multilevel floors: In the middle is a pit where water is nearly 2 feet deep, deep enough for a 10-gallon can of milk. Around the pit are stair-stepped "shelves," some 6 inches under water, others only 2 inches under. Dry shelves are constructed along the walls for fruit and vegetables.

More commonly, water floods the entire floor of a springhouse an inch or two deep, and the food is stored in crocks sitting in the water. Some floors slant gradually towards the center, or from one side or the other, so that part of the floor is dry and part is covered with running water. Sometimes water enters through pipes, other times the whole spring flows through the house, or through grooves and troughs formed in the concrete floor. Some houses are built right over the spring, in which case they are sort of springhouse and water storage tank combined. One springhouse I've seen is completely underground, entrance gained by stairs that descend rather steeply about 12 feet. The structure is more like a storm cellar with a trickle of water at its base. How the builder (over one hundred years ago) knew he would find water at the end of his hole, no one knows. The present owners still use the cellar for apple storage in the winter.

For aquaculture, one of the first things you want to find out is the spring's water temperature. It may be too cold for warm-water fish. Even trout, a cold-water fish, will not thrive if the water is much below 45 to 50 degrees F (7.2 to 10 degrees C)—and 55 to 60 degrees F (12.7 to 16 degrees C) is better. If the water at the spring's source is only slightly too cold, you might locate your fish tank at some distance away, so the water has a chance to warm up a bit on its way there. However, the usual problem is how to keep water warm enough in winter so fish keep eating. Obviously, if the water temperature at the spring's source is adequate, the closer you can put your fish tank, the less heat is lost on cold winter days.

Getting Food from Water

In any case, the manipulation of water in springhouses is similar to its manipulation in fish tanks—or could be in a homestead situation. The idea is to keep food and water cool, but neither freezing nor too warm, and to keep water moving without any energy other than gravity—all of which is directly applicable to raising fish in spring water. Visit some springhouses and study how they were built. There is, at least, no better place from which to view the world on a hot day in July.

THE MOUNTAIN STREAM 3

The difference between a running spring and a mountain stream is mostly speed. Mountain streams are fed mainly by melting snow rather than by springs, but it is their velocity that determines to a great extent what will live in them. There is as much difference between the life of a cold, swift stream and that of a warm farm pond as there is between the cornbelt farm and a Florida citrus grove.

Insect larvae in a cold, fast-flowing stream are usually stream-lined in shape so as to offer less resistance to the plunging water. They can hang onto rocks for dear life. For instance, most of the caddis flies (over four hundred kinds in the United States) are adapted to ponds or slow-moving streams, but the water-net caddis is at home in swift water. It builds a funnel-shaped net attached to rocks, with the wide end of the net facing upstream. At the small end, the caddis fly larva builds a silken house in which it lives unbothered by the swift current. The water rushing through the net carries smaller larvae and tiny animals, which catch in the net and are eaten by the caddis larva at its leisure.

Floating plants common in slow or standing water can't survive in mountain streams. In swift water, algae like *Cladophora* manage to attach themselves to the bottom gravel and grow, but in general, the faster the water flow, the less plant life.

Minnows and tadpoles that brave the swift water are types with strong sucking mouth parts by which the animals hang onto rocks when they need to rest—which is often. Pond fish like catfish and sunfish would be quickly swept away in a strong mountain current. Only the trout can resist the swift water, swimming tirelessly until it finds a sheltered nook. Because of all that exertion, the trout needs lots of oxygen, which it gets in a mountain stream where the churning, splashing, tumbling water mixes so much more air into itself. Take a mountain trout directly from a trout stream, and put it into a warm-water pond where comparatively little oxygen is dissolved, and the fish will quickly suffocate.

THE TROUT STREAM

For aquaculturists, trout is the most practical food to raise in cold, swift-moving waters. Many improved strains of trout are available today, but in wild waters the regular, wild breeds of trout—brook, rainbow, and brown—seem to perform as well as the

improved strains, according to recent studies in New York State. Brook trout are native to the eastern half of the nation, more or less, and rainbow trout native to the West. However, rainbow trout readily adapt to the East. Brown trout will make themselves at home in either region. Your own local fish hatcheries can advise you best on your choice.

Trout have been called the barometer of ecological conditions. Where they live, nature has been allowed to carry on its purposes unmolested by the pollution that follows in the wake of human overpopulation or greed. If you see trout in a creek, you can be sure the surrounding area is managed by men wise in the ways of ecology, or, more likely, that you are in a sparsely populated region. Trout just won't live in oxygen-deficient, turbid, dirty water.

Often though, the cause of the pollution in an otherwise adequate trout stream can be corrected rather easily. For example, back in 1969, Otter Creek, which empties into Lake McConaughey in Nebraska, would not support trout. Fish stocked in the lake would not move up the creek and spawn the way they were supposed to do. Gravel beds in the creek, necessary for trout spawning, were being covered by too much sand and silt from run-off water after heavy rains. In addition, cattle wading in the stream kept it too muddy for trout. The rancher who owned range along both sides of the creek, and who was himself a wildlife enthusiast, fenced about a mile of the stream together with a narrow strip of land on either side. The fence solved both problems. Grass and other vegetation left ungrazed soon grew thick enough to stop the sand and silt being carried into the creek by run-off water. And, of course, the cattle could not tramp in the creek either.

Results were immediate and dramatic, the rancher told me. The very next year, trout spawned in the stream. After that, the trout population stabilized in the lake and fishing improved in the creek as well.

TROUT STREAM MANAGEMENT

This and other types of watershed flood control and sane land-use practices can restore a stream for trout. Where trout already live, other measures for improving the stream can often

Black Willow

increase trout numbers considerably. Bankside vegetation is all-important. The wider the greenbelt along the stream the better; try not to narrow the corridor to less than 20 feet on either side. Plants provide not only some erosion control but shade for the trout from overhanging branches, or hiding places among roots or overhanging grasses. The shade can keep the water cooler during summer, and, where water temperature hovers near the critical point, may mean the difference between keeping trout and not keeping them. Trout like water at 50 to 60 degrees F (10 to 15.5 degrees C) but never more than 70 degrees F (21.1 degrees C)—temperatures above 80 degrees F (26.6 degrees C) can be lethal. Vegetation also harbors insect life that provides part of the fish diet. Plants also lure other animal and bird life that directly or indirectly helps keep the entire trout food chain in healthy balance.

To stop mud slides and bank erosion, and to stabilize banks, conservationists recommend several willow varieties, especially purple osier willow and common osier willow, *Salix purpurea* and *Salix viminalis*. The latter, sometimes referred to as basket willow, has done a good job of bank protection for me, but at least here in Ohio, it has a tendency to spread away from the bank and become a nuisance. Mine has marched out into one of my grain plots, and despite plowing, mowing, and cultivating, persists in sending up new shoots.

I prefer the more tree-ish forms of willow along stream banks—black willow, golden willow, weeping willow, and shining (or peach-leaf) willow. The weeping willow is best for shade. It stays where you put it, yet you can easily start new trees by sticking cuttings into the bank mud in early spring and keeping them well watered through the first summer. The trees thrive even with some of their roots right in the water.

The much smaller peach-leaf willow grows naturally across most of the northern United States down into northwestern Texas. It will establish itself and persist on sand bars and bank bends, but does not spread like a weed the way basket willow does. It grows into a small tree, or sometimes little more than a shrub. The branches and slender trunks are rather fragile and liable to break off in wind or high water. But other trunks come up to replace those that fall. The dead stubs seem to be easy pecking for woodpeckers, and in one of ours, our only bluebirds have a nest. That may be the biggest reason I'm so partial to those willows.

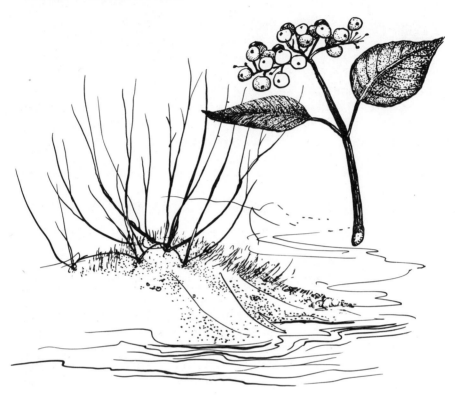

Red Osier Dogwood

Also, the warblers in spring, particularly the yellow warblers, like to fly among the branches snatching at the spring catkins and insects on the catkins. Moreover, the mob of gnarled roots the willows put down at the water's edge causes the water to swirl and churn, digging a deep pothole in the stream bed. Water life of all kinds is more abundant here than in any other stretch of the creek.

Wildlife experts also recommend silky dogwood (*Cornus amomum*) and red osier dogwood (*Cornus stolonifera*) for trout stream banks. The latter grows wild here, and I can certainly vouch for its benefits if grown in a moist place. The attractive red-stemmed bush blooms profusely in spring (the scent is a bit too cloying for me), then bears bluish white berries that the birds eat with great gusto. When the berries are gone in late fall, the bushes (at least here) sometimes become infested with a juicy white worm that the birds also gobble. The worms come so late in the year they apparently do no damage as they eat leaves about to fall off anyway. The bush is very tough, and, growing along a stream bank, will survive raging floodwaters without ill-effect.

Trout enthusiasts build wood or stone structures in their streams to preserve banks, to provide hiding places for trout, to concentrate stream flow and increase velocity, to aerate the water, and to force the water to dig out deeper pools between riffles. These structures are called V-dams, straight dams, single- and double-wing deflectors, and check dams (see illustration). None of these completely block the channel to upstream migration. In larger, swifter streams, upstream migration of most fish other than trout can be stopped by what is called a barrier dam. Fish barrier dams increase flow rates to such velocity over a comparatively long raceway that only trout can make it upstream. Such barriers demand the planning and engineering of experts. The other deflectors and dams are quite simple to build.

A trout stream should ideally be half riffles and half pools. Trout rest in the pools but find the greater proportion of their aquatic food in the riffles. A good way to increase the number of both pools and riffles is with a "digger" dam. This low (no more than a foot above normal water surface) dam impounds very little water, but as the current falls over it, the water digs out a pool on the downstream side. Sand and gravel churned out of the pool come to rest just beyond it downstream, creating riffles.

Place these dams where the stream runs straight, not at a bend, and preferably where banks are steep and the stream bed narrow. The ends of the dam should be dug back into the banks so the water does not run around the end and dig out the bank.

Deflectors are usually placed on outer bank curves to control a stream's natural bent (no pun intended) for meandering. Water hits the deflector and "bounces" toward the other, or inside, curve of the bend, curtailing the growth of looping meanders.

Double deflectors built on opposite sides of the stream narrow the channel, and so increase the velocity of the water. The rule of thumb to go by is that a 50 percent reduction in the width of the channel doubles the water velocity.

If you want to fix your trout stream more or less permanently, and not have to fiddle with it every year, use cedar or treated posts and plenty of riprap, as shown. But driftwood logs and handy boulders are far cheaper and more natural looking. Even if you have to replace them often, the cost is just your time.

Net traps on public waters are illegal for trout everywhere, I

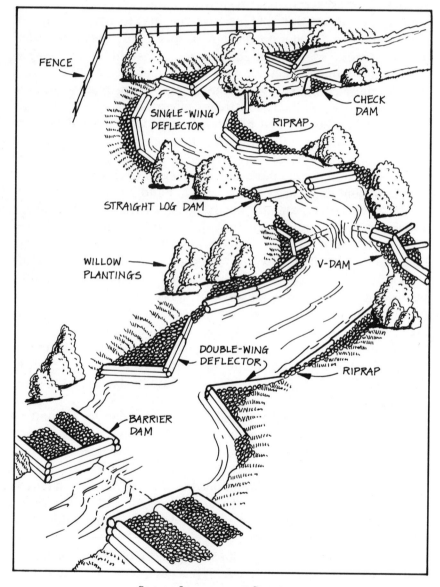

Stream Improvement Structures

believe. Where you are stocking and raising trout, you can work out arrangements with fish and game authorities to monitor the fish population and harvest the excess by seining. The whole idea of improving trout streams, however, is to improve hook-and-line fishing, certainly one of the finest of all outdoor sports.

COMMON WARM-WATER CREEKS 4

Interlacing the flat midland of America, the sluggish, mostly mud-bottomed creeks look neither aesthetically nor aquaculturally attractive. All they seem to do is carry polluted run-off water from village streets and farm fields to the larger rivers. They wind unromantically between flat cornfields, wander aimlessly across old pasturelands, duck apologetically past ramshackle barns and sawmills that no longer need them, and slip quietly through the occasional woodlot that has miraculously escaped the bulldozer farmers. The creeks are too deep to plow but too shallow to fish. When rains fall abundantly, they swell into rolling, muddy torrents of eroded soil, fertilizer, and who-knows-what-all washing off the land. When rain does not fall, they diminish to trickles reeking of pollution. Sometimes they finally dry up altogether except where septic effluent empties into their stagnant channels.

Not all the warm-water creeks are ruined yet, however. Where not all the forests have been turned into cornfields and not all the swamps drained and not all the springs dried up, the creeks maintain a steadier flow. With a little luck and not so many factories or feedlots around, the water may even be fairly unpolluted. In such waters, aquatic life can be richer than in the babbling brooks that make those pretty calendar pictures.

BUILDING A SMALL ROCK DAM

We are fortunate enough to have a good creek through our land, saved from ruination by seep springs that refuse to die completely despite every effort of hard corn farming in the area. A surprising amount of aquatic life flourishes along the creek, and by

37

Getting Food from Water

Twenty dollars' worth of rocks put some babble in our brook. It was a common, sluggish stream without much to say. But our dam has broadened the stream into a shallow, quiet pool that's good for fishing and swimming. Best of all, the stream seems to have lots to tell me when I sit on the bridge and gaze at the water gushing over the rocks. The dam gave the stream a voice.

building a small rock dam that raises the water level just 2 feet, we have increased the life of the creek noticeably.

There are so few rocks in our fields we had to buy the stones for our little dam. But what a wealth of experiences our $20 has brought us! Shortly after my wife, two children, and I finished building the dam, I found an absolutely huge blacksnake sunning itself on it. Had it lived here before, or had the increase in water lured it here? All I knew was that it was blocking my way to the water. The snake, no doubt, figured I was trespassing in its swimming hole. Out of my way, blacksnake. Go build your own dam.

The blacksnake meant no harm, but something violent and primeval in me would see it dead and gone anyhow. Its gross size, nearly 4 feet long and as thick as my wrist, only increased my revulsion. I fought the urge to kill. Why is the human instinct to fear all snakes without reason? Why is the snake instinct to fear all men with good reason? It is man who is supposed to be rational.

But the snake was not so much interested in me, so long as I remained motionless, as it was in a chipping sparrow which had alighted at the creek's edge only 15 feet away. The bird wanted a dip in the cool water too, or so it seemed. It ruffled its feathers, fluttering water droplets about it, as ecstatic with the cool wetness as a child splashing bare feet in a puddle. It stretched first one wing, then the other in grotesque fashion, as if wholly caught up in the pleasure of its water frolic. All the while, the snake watched and edged toward the bird—rather, seemed to grow at one end and shrink at the other. Inch by inch the distance between them narrowed. Did the bird sense the danger it was in?

I was not scientist enough to find out. Chipping sparrows do much more good controlling insects in my fields than do blacksnakes. I threw a stick between the two creatures, sending bird into the air and snake disappearing into some unseen crevice in the bank. I congratulated myself. I had intervened, god-like, into the affairs of nature, and caused certain events which might have happened, not to happen. I had saved a chipping sparrow, perhaps a family of them, and so a whole line of sparrows multiplying into the future. I was a good scout.

Then I read later in Edwin Way Teale's book, *A Naturalist Buys an Old Farm*, how he watched a bird perform bizarre motions in front of a blacksnake and thereby lure the snake away from the vicinity of its nest.

Perhaps my chipping sparrow had been performing such a trick. My intervention, rather than helping matters, might have only stopped it abruptly at midpoint, chasing the snake closer to the sparrow's nest. How complex is this thing called ecology. How terrifying even to try to contemplate all the ramifications of any intrusion into the world of nature.

I was reminded of this complexity again when a heavy shower raised the water level until it covered the little dam completely, plunging over the 2-foot height with swift and merry chatter. I sat on the bridge we had built across the creek just below the dam, wondering if the fast current would bowl the rocks of the dam on downstream. I worried, too, that the current might be too strong over the dam to allow the normal upstream migration of fish.

Suddenly I was startled out of my wits by a large carp, weighing perhaps 2 pounds, leaping from the swirl of water below the dam up over the falling water into the upper pool—an arc of flight measuring 5 feet. Scarcely had I recovered from that shock when a smaller chub, about 5 inches long, hurled itself clear of the lower water up into the upper pool. The little fellow did not dive over the way the carp had done, but "danced" across, head up, tail down, twisting in this vertical position until the law of gravity caught up with it, then falling clumsily back into the water, just barely above the brink of the falls.

Next, while I waited breathlessly for more leaping fish, I noticed what looked like dark streaks shooting straight up in the water going over the dam. Focusing my attention and riveting my eyes to the water, I could see that the shooting streaks were fish, some larger, some quite tiny, all swimming *vertically* up the column of water pouring over the dam. To me, it seemed like defiance of the laws of physics. If a fish could swim up a column of water like that, there was no reason one could not swim up a column of water being poured out of a bucket, into the bucket itself!

But it was the jumping fish that intrigued me most. How did they know how far to jump? If the dam were higher, could they have jumped higher? If lower, would they have put less energy into their leap? Why had they decided to jump at all when other fish were demonstrating that they could swim over with great ease? Had the fish checked out the whole length of the dam before deciding there was no way through the dam but only over it, or had they jumped out of impulse upon first meeting the obstacle? Had they perhaps jumped for the joy of jumping?

Whatever the answers to my questions, events a few days later completely overshadowed them. The marvelous cleverness I thought I had observed in the fish now appeared to be incredible stupidity. The same fish that had swum almost vertically up the waterfall, or that had leaped saucily over the dam, now, after the water level had fallen to normal, allowed the gentle current of the upper pool to carry them languidly into crevices between the rocks of the dam. There they became trapped and would have died if we had not rescued them. They had not the wit to swim away from the rocks, or if they wanted to go on downstream, to leap over them. Such a leap would have been far easier to accomplish than the leap from below into the upper pool, which they had already performed.

Had we foreseen how the dam would trap and kill fish, we could have built it to avoid the problem. All we had to do, now, was reshuffle the outer rocks of the dam on the upstream side so that the smaller stones fitted better into the cracks between the larger ones. Then only the smallest minnows could slip into the cracks, and they were able to work themselves on through the dam. Later on, I also installed a plastic liner under the outer layers of rocks—at a cost of a few dollars and a couple of hours work. However, the liner is unnecessary if you place the rocks tightly together on the upstream side of the dam.

Building the dam in the first place was a pleasant weekend job for our four family members. We ordered a dump-truck load of rocks from a quarry—the $20 was mostly for the hauling. The trucker dumped the load right at the creek bank and we carried and/or slid them, one by one, into place.

We chose a point where the creek narrowed a little between two steep banks. The gap measured about 12 feet from bank to bank. First we slid the largest boulders into the stream—they were too large to lift, but could be rolled and levered into position. We laid a double row of these rocks across the stream bed, using the biggest rocks of all at each end, against the bank. It is at the bank that a creek will wear away the dirt and wash a big leak in a dam first. The correct way to build would be to extend the stones back into the bank at least 2 feet, but we were not interested in building anything that permanent or leak-proof.

Getting Food from Water

We continued to pile rocks over the base rocks, using the biggest ones first and medium-size ones on the outside and top, with the smallest ones as chinking. As we built the dam upward, we packed clay between the upstream rocks of the dam to stop the water flow as completely as possible. We built the dam approximately 3 feet tall, which meant that the creek depth was raised to an average of about 3 feet, with the deeper holes as much as 5 to 6 feet deep, ample for a cooling dip on a hot day, and to maintain at least a few fish over winter. (I have in mind keeping fish cages in the deeper holes to raise fish for the table, but I have not yet gotten into this project.)

On the back, or downstream, side of the dam, we spread the left-over rocks on the stream bed, forming an apron as wide as the creek and about 8 feet downstream. The first reason for the apron was aesthetic. Ours is a mud-bottomed creek, and I wanted the water tumbling over the dam to ripple along on rocks at least for a bit. Second, the apron protected the creek bottom from the tumbling water which otherwise would have stirred the water to a muddy froth and then dug a hole below the dam—like a digger dam on a trout stream—into which the rocks might eventually slide.

Our dammed-up stream offers a kind of swimming experience you can't have in a chlorinated, filtered, concrete backyard pool.

High water has not destroyed our haphazard little dam. The current washes a few rocks off the top, but they can easily be retrieved from the downstream side and repositioned. The clay seal between the rocks washes out in about six months, but it takes only about two hours to pull the upstream rocks back and apply another seal. We just shovel clay from the upstream bed for sealant. An application in May to keep the water level high for June swimming and fishing, and another application in fall to insure optimum water level for muskrats and for winter skating suffices.

Raising the water level 2 feet in a small stream may not seem like much, but for so little cost and effort, the increase in water area is considerable. Our stretch of creek is a little over 500 feet long. Before the dam, its width varied from a mere trickle a foot wide to potholes as much as 6 feet wide. With the water level raised, the creek widened to 6 feet average, with potholes as much as 12 feet wide in places. I figure it increased an average of 4 feet in width which over a 500-foot length amounts to 2,000 square feet more surface area, at a cost of a penny per square foot, from our $20 worth of rocks.

NATURAL AQUACULTURAL DIVERSITY

We certainly are not going to set any aquacultural records with our little creek, but results already are interesting and point out a potential more promising than we expected. After the dam was built and the first spring floodwaters had subsided, the water in our "creek pool" cleared more than it had ever done before, no doubt because the dam slowed the current so that sediment dropped to the bottom. There had always been a few sunfish, shiners, small pike, chubs, bullheads, and dace in residence, plus carp and suckers coming up from the river in spring. Now small *schools* of bluegills were visible in the deeper water, and catfish seem to be biting much better. The two most remarkable changes in fish population, however, are among the minnows and pike. A few small pike have always lived in this creek, but in the fall after the first year of deeper water, we observed one more than a foot long. The minnow population may or may not have increased, but I think the fact that the pike can pursue them all along the creek where once the minnows could easily escape into water too shallow for the pike, may explain the increased size of the latter. Perhaps, then, the minnow population will decrease? Not likely. Late in November, while looking for muskrats at night, I shone the flashlight beam into the deepest hole in the creek. The clear water was dense with tiny dace. Never before had I seen such numbers of them here, and I could only attribute them to the increase in the entire food chain brought about by more water.

Muskrats appeared along our deepened creek almost immediately. None had lived here the previous several years. Snapping turtles, once plentiful here, had all but disappeared in recent years, but I spotted a nice-size one, hiding among the yellow water lilies. He, along with the numerous common water turtles, is probably the reason I can't seine a meal's worth of crayfish from the creek anymore. The poor crayfish must feed not only turtles and carnivorous fish, but raccoons too. But so prolific are crawdads, I expect them to increase in numbers again.

Meanwhile, the great blue heron and the little green heron visit our rejuvenated waters almost daily, and a kingfisher patrols the length of it all summer. Mink follow muskrats, on whom they prey, as night follows day, and if the population of the latter increases properly my son can trap the excess for pocket money. Already the 'rats have trimmed down the giant bulrushes that were threatening to choke the channel (the roots are good for humans to eat, too), and next year I suppose they will exact a portion of my grain crops in payment for this good deed. Muskrats are edible too, having very clean meat, grown on a strictly vegetarian diet. In the old days, after pelts were skinned off, the carcasses were often hung in the chicken coop to provide the hens with a rich source of protein.

Mallards have wheeled overhead and dropped down to try the new water, but did not stay to nest yet. I expect them to, though I doubt the wild geese honking high in the sky will find our bit of water sufficient for them.

Yellow water lilies are rare now in creeks of this region, but here they have survived because of the spring water that keeps the creek running. In the deeper water this past summer, however, they grew more luxuriantly than they had previously. Under them, small turtles and frogs, especially, find hiding places from the herons and other animals who savor the flavor of frog legs. I expect bullfrogs to migrate in, as I know they inhabit lower reaches of our creek, where the water is naturally deeper.

Fishing in the early spring.

In summary, what we are doing, out of the sheer fun of it, is setting up an ecologically rich system of subsistent aquaculture that eventually can provide us with a small amount of each of a marvelous variety of food and fiber, in addition to providing outdoor activities like bird-watching, swimming, fishing, and ice skating.

There are other benefits. The "wild" area along the creek will shelter increasing numbers of birds, animals, plants, and insects. I have planted black haw, persimmon, pawpaw, elderberry, and nut trees. Wild grape, hawthorn, osier dogwood, and blackberry already grow there. A grove of ash stands back from one bank to supply firewood in the future.

Some of my food and grain plots I have laid out adjacent to the wild area where the creek bends close by. Though the wild animals and birds will do some harm, I feel they have already proven more beneficial than destructive. Sure, the redwing blackbirds eat corn, but ornithologists have found as many as twenty-two cutworms in the stomach of one redwing. Our covey of quail keeps the Colorado potato beetle under control all summer. Mourning doves, which love to roost near water, frequent the creek by the score. As

45

many as nine thousand weed seeds have been found in the stomach of one dove.

But the deepened creek performs an even greater service for the gardens. Digging postholes back from the banks, I have discovered that below the loam soil is a layer of light clay that is always moist in the driest of times. Even before the dam, crops grown here withstood drought better than elsewhere. Water from the creek or the seep springs along the banks evidently spreads out through that clay, and is drawn up to the plants by capillary action. With 2 more feet of height, the water will reach out even further under the roots of my crops.

And, of course, in case of critical drought, I have an adequate source of water handy for drip irrigation.

It all started with a $20 pile of rocks. You probably have plenty of rocks for free.

THE MANY FACES OF FRESHWATER WETLANDS 5

Like most generic terms, "wetlands" means many things to many people, but not much of anything particular to anybody. The term mentally conjures up a mishmash of ponds and pools and swamps and bayous and sloughs and bogs and marshes and streams and lakes and rivers—or in other words just about any kind of terrain you can't drive a pickup on. The mental mishmash is not easy, or perhaps not even possible, to define clearly, because the reality is so inextricably bound together. Who is to say when a stream becomes a river, a slough a marsh, a bog a swamp? The best one can do—and what I am attempting in this chapter—is to single out manifestations of wetlands as they differ because of climate, region, or type of wildlife.

Of the kinds of wetlands, swamps and bogs deserve a special mention because they have a bad image. Too many of us see them only as dank and stagnant havens for mosquitoes. Yet where we don't pollute, water quality in swamps is usually quite high. There are "bad" mosquito swamps and there are swamps where mosquitoes aren't or need not be troublesome. Bad mosquito swamps are temporary swamps where water stands only for part of the year. Here mosquitoes can breed, hatch, and be gone before the ecological chain of predators that keep mosquitoes at an endurable level gets established. Draining such swamps is only one way of getting rid of the insects. The other way is deepening the water where practical, and stocking it with fish that prey on the mosquito larvae. Soon other predators of mosquitoes, like dragonflies, also become established. As early as 1944, the Tennessee Valley Authority demonstrated that water impoundment and malaria control were not opposed interests, but could be, in fact, mutually beneficial. Experience has shown that tidal pools that can be

49

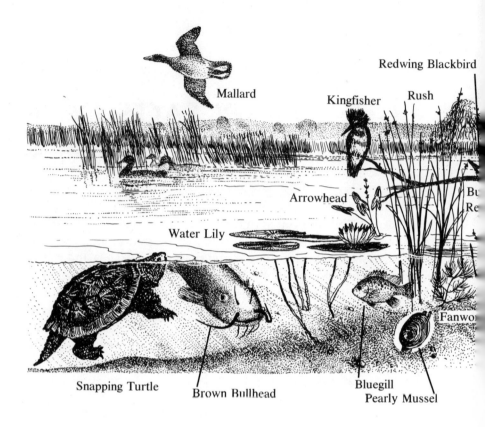

Mallard · Redwing Blackbird · Kingfisher · Rush · Arrowhead · Water Lily · Snapping Turtle · Brown Bullhead · Bluegill · Pearly Mussel · Fanwo... · Bu... · Re...

deepened so that killifish (saltwater minnows) can live in them permanently, cease to be vicious mosquito breeders. Rice growers are proving that even temporary pools like rice paddies, which are heaven to mosquitoes, can be stocked with fish to control mosquitoes as effectively as chemicals can.

Here are a few "types" of freshwater wetlands that offer special possibilities for backyard aquaculturists.

THE CRANBERRY BOG

Thanks to intensive agriculture, the cranberry bog has become extinct where it once was common. But there are still wild cranberry bogs around. A Pennsylvania agronomist tells me his state "still has some, but we don't publicize them anymore because the public would just loot them." I asked him if swampy areas in

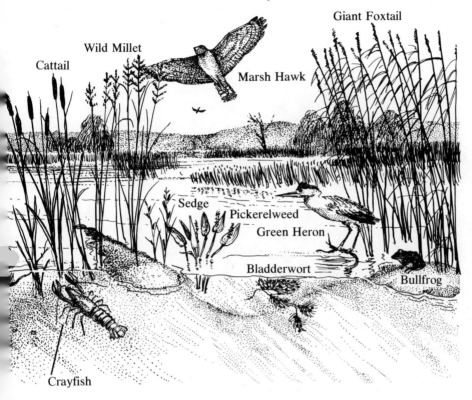

Giant Foxtail

Wild Millet

Cattail

Marsh Hawk

Sedge

Pickerelweed

Green Heron

Bladderwort

Bullfrog

Crayfish

A Freshwater Marsh

cranberry-bog country might be converted into bogs even if no cranberries were growing there presently. He thought a little bit and nodded. "Very possible."

I know where there still are cranberry bogs in Minnesota, or were, a few years ago. Wisconsin has them yet, I understand. The New Jersey Pine Barrens is, of course, full of cranberries, though most of the plantings are commercially operated. In fact, cranberries can be grown in a surprisingly wide area. Wisconsin, New Jersey, Oregon, Washington, and Massachusetts are the leading commercial producers, but growing the berry is a possibility over the whole eastern half of the nation from Minnesota to New England and south as far as North Carolina. The cranberry requires acid soil along with plenty of moisture. In the North, it needs protection by a cover of water or heavy snow to keep from freezing in severely cold weather.

Getting Food from Water

The cranberry is a fruit that likes lots of water but that can't be in water all of the time, or it will rot. The best growing medium is a bog with a sandy soil high in humus. Commercial growers, consequently, use old swamps that have been drained and cleaned up for cranberry cultivation. The cranberry cuttings are spread upon the prepared soil and, using a special tool, are pushed partway into the ground. Like strawberries, the vines will take root at any spot that touches the ground. The bog is flooded during the winter, drained in spring. In early fall, the berries are harvested.

For the self-subsistent backyard aquaculturist, the cranberry could have great significance. If other fresh fruit were suddenly unavailable in the North during the winter, a cranberry producer could get along just fine. The fruit is high in both vitamins A and C. The Indians attributed almost religious significance to what they deemed the medicinal value of the fruit. Urologists and doctors recommend it today for kidney disease and arthritis.

Moreover, cranberries are available on the homestead when there's no other fruit: November, December, and again in early spring. We used to gather "floaters," still in good condition, off the bog waters of the New Jersey Pine Barrens right after spring thaw. Under heavy snow cover, cranberries in a wild bog will last all winter long, too.

The cranberry has a waxy coating on it that helps preserve it. Early colonists shipped the berries to Europe in barrels of water. Wild-cranberry lovers in Wisconsin keep a box of the fruit on a cool porch where temperature does not fall below freezing, and the fruit keeps all winter.

You can dry cranberries, make relish, sauces, jelly, pie, juice, even bread. Indians pounded the dried fruit into meat for pemmican.

To grow cranberries, you need a level, swampy area with enough water available to protect vines and berries from late spring and early fall frosts, say the experts. Ideally, the soil should be mostly peat underlain with clay, the peat soil having a pH of between 5 and 6. On a small backyard patch, you can supply the water from a hose. (In less frosty areas, cranberries can be grown under irrigation in the garden in acid soil). Often two or three inches of sand are added to the soil surface as a kind of mulch. Henry Hall, the first man to cultivate cranberries in this country (on Cape Cod), observed that wherever the soil was covered with sand the berries grew larger. Among other things, the sand mulch keeps the vines from growing in too great a profusion; fewer, stouter vines make bigger berries.

Cuttings are thrust down through the sand into the peaty soil about a foot apart in all directions. Soon the cuttings root. Seeds can be planted, too, if the soil is acid and wet enough. Then comes a long wait. It takes between three and five years for the vines to begin producing well.

Of the more than two-hundred known varieties, the ones

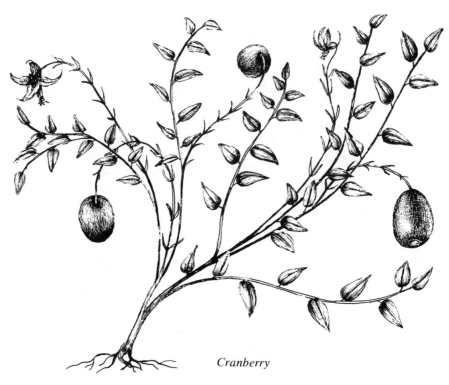

Cranberry

grown most frequently for commercial production are Early Black in Massachusetts and New Jersey; Howes, a late variety for the same areas; Searles in Wisconsin; and McFarlin in Oregon and Washington.

Plants bloom in midsummer and the main harvest is from September to December. Commercial bogs are flooded and drained several times during the year—much the same principles involved as in watercress production, only the "beds" are much larger and the water deeper. Flooding is used not only to protect against untimely freezes, but for weed and in some cases insect control.

Harvesting is all done mechanically now. The traditional wooden cranberry scoop, which in the hands of a skilled scooper can harvest a hundred pounds of cranberries an hour, is used less and less in this country.

PEAT BOGS

Any marshy area may be referred to as a bog, especially in the North, but a peat bog is a fairly special kind of marsh. The water is usually more acid than that in "regular" ponds, low in mineral content but high in organic matter. The organic matter comes from layers of sedges or mosses that grow up and fall over into the water every year, there to remain in a semirotted state that, when dried, makes peat. Peat bogs in the Far North might be called black spruce swamps, or tamarack swamps, or, in New England, red maple swamps, because these are the trees that can grow next to wet bogs. Bogs are also likely locales for valuable "insect-eating" wild plants like the pitcher plant and the sundews.

Peat is dug out of old bogs and used for fuel, for mulch, and for a plant-growing medium. Not all peat is the same, and most gardeners remain confused about the various products. (Even if you don't have a peat bog, it pays to know your peats.) Peat from sedge plants, often called sedge-peat or Michigan peat or just plain peat (the temptation to build a pun out of "just plain peat" is almost overwhelming), is used mostly (in Europe) for fuel since it burns slow and hot. It can also be used as a mulch or soil builder, especially for acid plants.

Regular *peat moss* is something different. Rather than from decomposed sedge plants, peat moss comes from various mosses, one of the more usual being hypnum moss. It has fairly good moisture-holding qualities and is used often for bedding animals. I once was able to get horse manure from a stable bedded with peat moss. It made one of the finest soil conditioners I ever put on my garden. Peat moss can also be used as a mulch, but as a growing medium it tends to cake too much when wet.

Sphagnum peat moss is a high-quality peat with much better water-retention properties than other peats. It is an excellent mulch and soil conditioner and more expensive than regular peats.

Dried sphagnum moss is something different. Rather than a dried peat that has been rotting in the bog for decades or centuries, plain sphagnum moss is the current year's dried plant crop. You can buy it simply dried, or dried and chopped to a fine texture. This moss has amazing absorption powers, twice that of cotton, and is the growing medium preferred by many horticulturists for acid-loving plants. Nelson Coon, in his book, *Using Wayside Plants*, calls sphagnum one of the most useful of wild plants. It has medicinal properties and makes a good temporary bandage. It is also in demand as packing material to ship nursery stock in. The moral of the story is, when you buy peat moss, know what you are buying or you might pay sphagnum prices for sedge quality.

Sphagnum is a long-stemmed, upright-growing plant rooting in the bottom of the bog. It grows in profusion, dies in the fall, falls over, and in time forms a deposit of decayed vegetation that may go down as deep as 20 or 30 feet, the same as other peats.

This deposit of organic matter is dug up by machine, dried, and sold. Needless to say, the homestead aquaculturist will probably not choose to mine out his sphagnum moss bed in that fashion, but will only harvest the annual crop, which commands a much higher price. Usually such a harvest is accomplished by hand, pulling or cutting masses of plants off the bog and drying them carefully in the sun. I noticed in one of the seed catalogs this year that sphagnum is selling at $9.75 for a 2-bushel bag, and higher than that in smaller volumes.

The point is that you should not discount any natural swamp as worthless. A bog is a unique piece of real estate and should be

checked out in every possible way for aquacultural uses. I was reminded of that forcefully at a botanical brain session held at the Rodale Research Center last year. Under discussion by a roomful of scientists was an aquatic fern *Azolla,* sometimes called the mosquito fern, which is known to be a good natural nitrogen-fixer that also stores relatively high amounts of the nutrient in its leaves. As a mulch, someone suggested, it could make an excellent renewable fertilizer. And, said an agronomist from Penn State, it could probably be grown in peat bogs, which are common in Pennsylvania and surrounding regions.

THE BEAVER POND

Fortunes were once made from beaver pelts, and man's pursuit of the glossy-backed rodent hastened considerably the

Beaver Pond

settlement of the northern United States and Canada by Europeans. But the best prices were paid for skins that had been worn by Indians, the longer worn the better. These hides were exceedingly soft and pliable and much desired by the rich French folk who ultimately wore them after the fur was cleaned up. They never suspected, says history, but the knowledge must have warmed the hearts of trappers and other poorer blokes like us who can never afford to buy the very best.

The beaver population declined in all but very inaccessible areas, but has been on the comeback ever since wearing beaver hats has not been so fashionable. In recent years, especially in some areas of the South, the beaver has become an exasperating pest to many farmers. Its dams flood arable land or back water up into land-drainage systems. The beaver cuts some trees valuable for lumber, like the sweet gum. The animal has, on occasion, taken a fancy to fruit trees in Appalachian orchards.

But there is no doubt the beaver is extremely valuable from an environmental point of view. The dams alleviate flood threats, and the water held back is released slowly during periods of drought. The water, in addition, supports amazing numbers of fish, ducks, and other wildlife. In Maine a few old beaver ponds preserve the only known habitat of the very rare blueback trout. And when beavers cut down trees, the cutover areas grow back first to shrubs that provide good browsing for deer and food for birds.

In spite of their valuable pelts and many benefits, you can try to exterminate the beavers as some farmers have. But you will find them worthy adversaries. They do not frequent places human beings frequent, and require extensive brush and forest growth around them, so you won't find them in any typical farm-pond situation. But they are difficult to trap or shoot out of existence where the environment is suitable to their life-style. The beaver can build dams faster than you can tear them down. Nor is the price of furs always high enough to motivate professional trappers to the kind of greed necessary to exterminate a colony.

Smarter, more farsighted landowners (and certainly home-steaders) know that maintaining the beaver for sustained yields is usually a wiser course than extermination. Beaver can make you money. Fur buyers have been interested only in northern beaver but are now looking southward. "They didn't know we had a beaver problem down here," says Skip Shelton, extension wildlife spe-

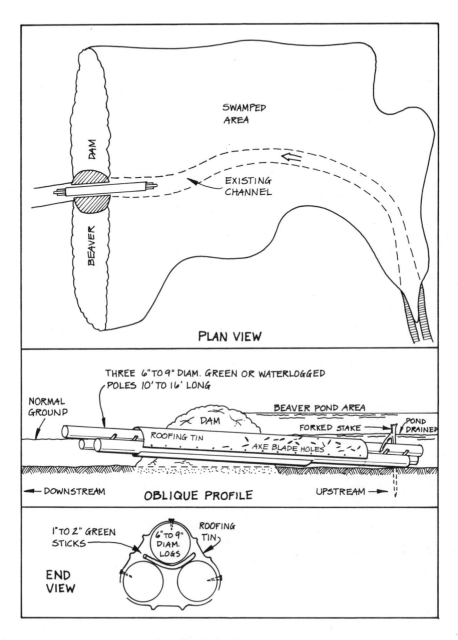

Log Drain for Beaver Pond

cialist at Mississippi State University. "We've started a drive to interest them in southern beaver pelts and the overseas market for them seems to be picking up. At $5 to $8 a pelt, the usual price in the past, trapping doesn't pay. We need a price of $12 to $15 and then beaver becomes a definite asset."

But beaver are a definite financial asset in another way. Properly managed, a beaver pond can be "rented out" quite profitably for fee-fishing and hunting. "A friend of mine recently caught 55 pounds of largemouth bass from a well-managed beaver pond in one afternoon," Shelton told me.

To increase the duck population dramatically, another form of beaver-pond management has been found effective. Dr. Dale Arner at Mississippi State (Mississippi has about twenty-four thousand acres of beaver ponds) developed a way to drain beaver ponds in summer, sow millet in them, then reflood them when the millet seeds mature, that is, in about forty-five days. The grain heads stick above the water and provide ducks with both food and hiding places, with enough seed falling into the water to provide a crop the next year. Only one seeding every three years is necessary. Wildlife specialists say a 1-acre beaver pond with millet will provide food for fifty ducks over winter.

For seeding beaver ponds to millet, you must first have at least 3 acres of shallow water, 2 to 30 inches deep. In that pond area, the majority of the trees still standing should be dead. With these two conditions met, proceed as follows:

Break the dam at the existing channel of the original waterway sometime between mid-June and the end of July. The break should be in the form of a narrow V. When the flow slackens, you can begin to build the drain that will outwit the beavers. Refer to the illustration as you read these directions:

Fasten three logs together with nails and short pieces of wood as indicated. The logs should be approximately 6 to 9 inches in diameter and 12 to 16 feet long. Place a piece of tin approximately 2½ feet wide and 6 to 8 feet long in the break in the dam. Then place the three-log drain on the top of this tin with the upstream logs completely covered by water on the intake side and at least one foot lower than the outlet end. Peg down the logs on the upstream side with a forked stick. Now place a piece of tin over the top of the logs and pile some mud and sticks on top.

When all the water has drained out that is going to drain out,

Japanese Millet

broadcast Japanese millet on the exposed mud flats at the rate of 20 pounds per acre. No other millet will work. Browntop or Starr will not grow under beaver-pond conditions. It is important that the ground be moist. Best conditions seem to be when the soil is ankle-deep in mud. No further land preparation is needed and no fertilizer has been found necessary for at least the first two years.

When the grain has matured, in forty-five to fifty days, remove the drains and let the pond fill up. In the meantime, check the drains about once a week to make sure they haven't become blocked.

While you enjoy your ducks and your beaver, you can harvest a little of that millet seed yourself. It makes a delicious and nutritional meal.

CATTAIL MARSHES

Cattails are a characteristic plant of wetlands. The tall stalks grow along the edges of lakes, in ponds, in roadside ditches where water stands at least part of the year, and even in salt marshes. Cattails rarely grow in water with a pronounced current or in water over 2 to 3 feet deep.

Crayfish farmers consider cattails a major pest since, if left unchecked, the plant will take over the shallow crayfish ponds. Many farm-pond owners consider cattails undesirable too, though this need not be the case, as we shall see.

Where cattails really aren't wanted, they can be difficult, if not impossible, to eradicate. In some types of marshes, wildlife advisors sometimes recommend burning off old stands of stalks. I have helped burn off acres of cattails in early spring and have never seen any advantage to it. The cattails grew back better than ever.

All parts of the cattail are useful—a potential food source of more than dilettante interest. The root rhizomes are a very practical food and the young shoots, young stalks, and the pollen are also edible. The long, tough summer leaves can be dried and used for chair caning and plaiting baskets. As a homestead food, the most significant fact about cattail is that it can provide a fresh vegetable in fall and through winter, when little else fresh is available from the homestead garden.

I'm not wild about wild food, but the cooked flesh of cattail rhizomes is tasty and filling. There are some stringy fibers toward

Cattail

the outside of the cooked rhizomes, but these can be easily separated as you eat.

The rhizomes are, however, better used as a source of flour. Instead of cooking, cut them into sections about 6 inches long (you should do that when you cook them, too) and dry. They can be sun- and air-dried, or in a solar heater, or over a stove or whatever. When they will snap in two rather crisply, and the whitish powder falls out, they're dry enough. That powder is the flour you're after. It contains more protein than corn or rice and more fat and minerals than corn, rice, or wheat. "On land shaped and leveed so

A cattail swamp.

you could flood it or drain it at will, cattails could be a practical farm crop," says Dr. Leland Marsh of State University of New York at Oswego, who has been studying the cattail for years. "It will produce 30 tons of flour per acre dry weight," he says, "and enough rhizomes will be left in the soil for the next year's crop." Thirty tons per acre is many times the amount any crop of grain can yield. The highest wheat yield ever recorded is less than 3 tons per acre, and half that is considered a good crop.

Mechanical harvesting can be done with conventional farm tools, says Marsh. The land would have to be drained sometime before harvest so the soil could dry enough for machinery. The rhizomes can be disked and harrowed to the surface, says Marsh, air-dried or picked up and dried artifically, then ground and processed into flour. I would think that some of the methods proven practical for harvesting and drying sugar beets might be applied to cattail rhizomes, too.

For the homesteader, the flour is only one practical food from the cattail. On rhizomes dug up in the fall, you will find yellow green shoots growing up to 6 inches long. These sprouts will make next year's plants. They will also make good eating right now, fixed just like asparagus. *These shoots are available all winter and early spring*, unless the marsh freezes solid, which is not generally the case.

In the spring when the sprouts grow up out of the mud and water, they are still fairly tasty until about 2 feet tall and before the flowers appear. Eat them raw, boiled, or creamed.

In May and June the flowers develop on the stalk, the female flower below the male. It is the female blossom that makes the fuzzy, brown seed head from which cattail gets its name. When the male flower is just emerging from its (his?) sheath and beginning to turn from green to yellow, it can be cut off and cooked. Strip away the husk and boil as you would sweet corn.

A little later, the male flower produces fine golden pollen, which can be used as a substitute for flour in pancake batter. Bend a flower over and shake it into a paper bag to collect the pollen. It's slow going, but about thirty heads should give you enough for a batch of pancakes. Mix batter as, you would ordinarily.

Digging up the rhizomes by hand is not easy in my experience. There is always a rhizome connecting one plant to the next, so you should be able to locate some between the plants without any problem. I generally just reach down into the muck and feel around until I find one, pull it loose from the base of one plant and then pull steadily until it breaks loose altogether. You can pry rhizomes loose with a shovel, too.

At least you can assure yourself that it would be pretty hard to starve to death in the eastern United States. Drainage ditches along the sides of our superhighways are filled with cattails for miles and miles as you drive along. The water drains away from these stands by summer, and I'm sure a potato digger or sugar beet harvester or some sort of machine could be modified to dig them up. They could be loaded on trucks, hauled away, and processed into food, if we needed it. The highway department could quit wringing its hands and demanding a herbicide powerful enough to kill cattails—which would have to be so powerful that it would kill just about everything else, too. And the wordy worriers over world food shortages could stop wringing their hands, too, for awhile, and help harvest the stuff.

Meanwhile, interest in cattails has sprung up in Minnesota for another reason. Scientists believe they could be an efficient source of fuel. The University of Minnesota has been allotted a large sum of money by the state to study the harvesting, drying, and conversion of cattails into fuel.

Various types of edible bulrushes grow in wetlands not suitable for cattails. The giant bulrush, *Scirpus valudis*, rates special mention. Its roots make flour, its pollen can also be used like cattail pollen, and the lower stems of younger plants, which look like green onions, are also edible. The bulrush will grow in a current; it persists in our creek where cattails won't grow and provides the muskrats with a food source.

Arrowhead, another ubiquitous marsh plant, develops small tubers on its roots, which can be cooked like potatoes. If you are really hungry, the seeds of bur reed and of wampee, both marsh plants, can be ground into meal.

Any good wild food guide will tell you of many more marsh plants that are edible, and also those, like skunk cabbage and water hemlock, that can be dangerously poisonous. Few of them have any present commercial value for the homestead aquaculturist, but you can never tell what the future will bring.

Bulrush

Arrowhead

THE PRAIRIE POTHOLE

Prairie potholes dot the north and central Great Plains—a characteristic part of the landscape of western Iowa, Minnesota, and the Dakotas. The pools resemble large farm ponds, usually varying in size from about 2 to 10 acres of surface water. They act as natural water catchments on the Plains when water is plentiful and release moisture slowly in dry weather. Some are only temporary; most of the ones remaining hold water year-round. In 1955 there were still some 1,210,000 potholes in the upper Plains covering 4,450,000 acres. Already many had been drained, and since then, many more have been destroyed by the bulldozer farmers and the Bureau of Reclamation, which should be renamed the Bureau of Aggrandizement. Since the soils where potholes abound are good chestnut, chernozem, and prairie types, greedy *Homo sapiens* is not about to leave 4,450,000 acres of it for the ducks. So millions of acres have been "drained" and you know

Prairie potholes dot the farmlands of Minnesota, Nebraska, and the Dakotas.

what? Now the Bureau of Reclamation is building huge canals for irrigation through this land.

I don't believe that a farmer will destroy a pothole just to make an extra dollar. I think it's a habit. After all, in a country where farms often are thousands of acres in size, draining a little 2-acre pothole every 500 acres or so represents very little "profit," and some years, none at all. But there is, in today's tractor farmer, a persistent desire to erase *any* "aberration" on the land that detracts from the crop he wants to grow there. Having been a modern tractor farmer, I recognize this propensity in myself. Perfection somehow comes to mean "nothing in the way"; to plow and to plant in straight rows that go on forever. Super neatness. I see this inclination—I consider it an almost lethal gene in men— displayed all over the country. In the East and Midwest it goads a farmer until he finally moves in with bulldozers and erases the last little woodlot on his fields, the last lone tree in the fencerow, the last lone fencerow on the landscape. He might run into the tree and bash up his $50,000 machine, he rationalizes. Even if he doesn't, he has to *worry* about running into it. The lethal gene that, if left unchecked, would reduce the earth to one large square cornfield with troughs around the edges for people to eat at, and no other living thing on the landscape, is not characteristic only of the tractor farmer. It affects the superneat suburbanite on his lawnmower too. Somehow, the riding lawnmower breeds vast lawns of grass *only*. That clean sward becomes beauty in the eye of the beholder. A brushy area in a corner of the lawn? God forbid. A patch of vegetables? Zone them out. Finally, even trees and pretty bushes have to go, because it is just too much trouble to mow around them.

With nothing left but a vast carpet of lawn, you would think that a human being would prefer a little variety at least in the kind of plants that compose his lawn. But not for today's psychotically insecure homeowner. No, by heaven. It must be bluegrass, or something that looks exactly like bluegrass, and nothing else. No other plant is allowed. So millions of units of unnecessary energy are consumed in "grooming" the lawn. And why? Because we have the machines to do the work easily—to erase woodlands and potholes overnight—to change the whole suburban world into a golf green. It's not the machine's fault. It's the fault of the people who own them.

Fortunately many Plains farmers are not so driven, and have recognized not only that the potholes are part of the whole ecological food chain (three-quarters of the nation's ducks used to nest along the potholes), but that these wondrous ponds can be much more profitable than the grain plots that would replace them.

The pothole owner never wants for roast duck. If he follows wildlife and soil conservation recommendations, he can change the pothole into a veritable garden of Eden—a wildlife haven that can afford the owner priceless hours of recreation and consistently reliable sources of all kinds of aquatic food.

THE OXBOW

An oxbow is a bend of a creek or river cut off from the main channel. Oxbows form naturally from the meandering action of running water. As a stream meanders, the force of the water always erodes the outer bends more intensely because the water runs faster there. The bend, therefore, keeps moving in an ever-more-

A classic oxbow lake.

acute loop. Finally, the two ends of the loop converge, and the water cuts a new channel, severing the loop into an oxbow lake. The name derives from its shape—just like the wooden bow around the ox's neck that holds the ox yoke in place.

Like every pool of water, oxbows age and eventually die completely (in a century or so). Where man steps in, an oxbow can die much quicker than that. When young, an oxbow is a teeming center for fish and wildlife, easier to care for and manage than a river or stream itself. Oxbows are naturally stocked with fish during high water. On our creek there is physical evidence of an oxbow that now holds water only in winter and early spring. But sixty years ago, say the old-timers, much larger fish were caught in that oxbow than in the stream itself.

Oxbows are nature's way of straightening a creek. Compare nature's way, which produces more life as it straightens, with the Corps of Engineers' way of channelization.

The best description of the oxbow's possibilities for homestead aquaculture was given by Ed Bry, noted conservationist and writer in this touching lament he wrote in *Audubon* magazine, May 1969.

> It was a lovely, wooded watercourse then, twenty-five years ago. . . .
>
> It was called the Horseshoe, an oxbow a bit longer than a mile, once the route of a nearby river but severed from the main channel years ago, refreshed by high water each spring. It was clear and cool all summer, a shady place for a swim on a scorching prairie day.
>
> The high ground beyond was the familiar, almost treeless North Dakota plain. But near the oxbow the land turned lush and green with native trees and shrubs—oak and elm and basswood and ash, hackberry and chokecherry and wild plum and wild rose. It was a place for picking berries or for exciting exploration by the youngsters from the village nearby.
>
> Lessons in the ways of the wild were free for anyone who took the time to walk its banks. How clearly I remember a great horned owl snatching up and making off with a pheasant from almost under my nose as I was checking my spring trapline. I caught my first mink just around this bend under the roots of a massive elm.

Memories are strong. But I don't believe I could mark those spots within fifty yards. And neither owl nor pheasant nor mink could survive here now.

At first the changes were gradual. The land on the oxbow's perimeter was cleared of trees. Inside the narrow woodland, a few cattle grazed—but not enough to destroy the wildness. Then the place changed ownership.

The new owners did not have cattle. They were young and vigorous with only grain and sugar beets on their minds. And, like most Dakota farmers nowadays, they had the heavy equipment necessary to change the landscape to suit their desires.

The easy areas, the level ground some distance from the water's edge, were bared first. But eventually, with idle time and idle machinery, the job was finished. For a few more feet of farmable soil (can that really have been the reason in this fertile, successful Red River Valley, with its crop surpluses?) the last trees were hideously crushed, the earth stripped, the final remnants of beauty, the ancient oaks and elms, pushed into the water, mere playthings for a mighty bulldozer.

. . . Does anyone care what has been lost? Is anyone aware that with such mindless destruction, small of scale and unimportant though it may seem, North Dakota . . . can become as barren of such beauty as the concrete jungle of the largest city?

I know and I care and I am sad.

DUCK PONDS AND FROG PONDS

Ducks and frogs will use any body of water deep enough to float a yardstick in, so I'm not being at all scientific when I refer to the more or less permanent, more or less common neighborhood ponds as duck ponds or frog ponds. The nomenclature is colloquial. What these ponds should be called are "kid ponds" because that is the wild creature who inhabits them most of the time. Lucky the child who can, because such ponds are classrooms of nature and the youngsters who play beside them or in them get a first-class, basic course in subsistence aquaculture. I would bet that 75 percent of our farm ponds are built by men who first got their feet wet in aquaculture as boys in a neighborhood frog pond.

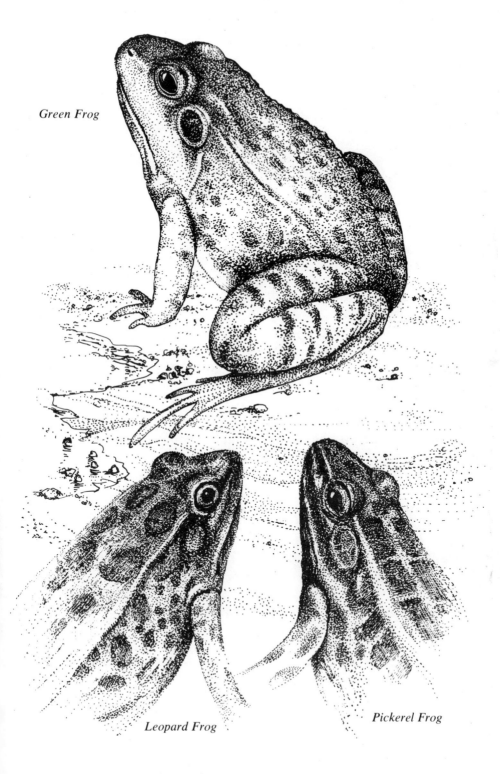

Green Frog

Leopard Frog

Pickerel Frog

Getting Food from Water

The frogs most often seen (or heard) on the banks of ponds and creeks are leopard frogs, pickerel frogs, and green frogs. As you walk along, they jump—green streaks of lightning—into the water. There are many other kinds of small frogs you might encounter; revere them all. They provide food for larger water animals while spending most of their time eating insects that would otherwise be bothering you. You can eat the legs of small frogs like the leopard and the green, but each one is hardly a bite and not really worth the effort. However, green and leopard frogs are sometimes salable as bait, or if you are in the right place to find the market, for laboratory specimens.

The bullfrog is the only frog in America really practical for food production. Most ponds of long standing and many creeks will have bullfrogs in them, though they are often hunted too hard and so become scarce. Bullfrogs ought to be caught only where, by law or by ownership, one can control the harvest well enough to sustain the population.

The bullfrog is dark brown to olive green. Sitting on the bank with its legs folded under it, the frog looks larger than a softball and almost that round. But when it jumps, its body lithely stretches out to a foot or more in length. Over half of that length is taken up by the back legs, which are what you eat. The front legs are also delicious, and though much smaller, should not be wasted.

Some fishermen buy bullfrog tadpoles for bait. The skins of the mature frog are used to make expensive gloves and shoes.

Bullfrogs grow faster in the South than in the North, which explains why commercial frog-raising ventures for marketing the meat are mostly in the southern states. But bullfrog breeding stock is sold by many northern fish hatcheries. Some fishermen like to stock bullfrogs in their ponds as they believe bass grow larger with the frogs around. This is probably true because the frogs will eat some bass minnows when they can catch them, allowing other minnows access to more food and so to faster growth.

Tadpoles eat mostly benthic algae in the pond or any soft vegetable or even animal matter. At the University of Michigan, zoologist George W. Nace raises frogs indoors, and feeds tadpoles romaine lettuce two times a day and cubes of raw and boiled liver three times a week. Adult frogs are more carnivorous and sometimes cannibalistic, though experimenters say *well-fed* bullfrogs are not cannibalistic. Whatever they eat, bullfrogs like it to be

Bullfrog, showing the stages of its development from a tadpole.

moving: insects, minnows, young crayfish, small fish, tadpoles, fiddler crabs, mosquito fish, sailfin mollies. The Japanese feed silkworm pupae to frogs, but put the pupae in oscillating trays so the movement is enough to attract the frogs.

In the wild pond, all you have to do for bullfrogs is maintain as full a variety of plants and animals as possible to achieve ecological health, if not balance. The bullfrogs will come or can be stocked. You'll know their presence by the sound: a deep basso harrumph! not unlike the groaning of a bull. If you see a bullfrog at all, what you usually see is just a bit of its head and eyes protruding from the water, looking to the casual eye like nothing more than a bit of flotsam on the surface. The best way to catch the frogs is with a spear or net at night with the aid of a boat and a flashlight. But check the laws where you live before you try gigging or you may end up paying out in fines much more than the cost of a couple of good restaurant meals of frog legs.

There isn't much work to raising frogs, at least if you just want a few pounds to eat. Every adult frog needs about 8 feet of shoreline to call its own, and the more shoreline you have, everything else being equal, the more frogs you can raise. That's why ponds with small islands and uneven bank edges produce the most frogs.

If you want to get a little more serious about bullfrogs, you can build pens for them: board or metal fences, 4 to 6 feet tall around the pond. Frogs can jump a fence 3 feet tall. Ideally the whole pond should be fenced if you are going to control the frogs, so only small ponds can be economically fenced. There should be as much land in the pen as there is water. If you *really* get serious, you should, say the experts, have at least two ponds: one for tadpoles and one for adults.

Should your frog population build up beyond the level of the natural food, frogs will migrate to greener pastures. If you have them penned, or if you want more than a usual number around, you will have to feed them extra. The same bug lights (see page 276) used to attract insects for fish feeding will help for frogs, too. Or you can burn a fire at night (a kerosene smudge pot, for instance) on the bank. Insects drawn to the fire will get their wings singed and many will drop into the water. At any rate, allow plenty of tall grass and weeds to grow on frog-pond banks to attract grasshoppers and other insects. Tadpoles can be fed lettuce leaves, cottonseed meal, a little ground liver.

To skin a frog, make an incision down the back, then peel the skin down the legs with a pair of pliers. Keep the frog wet beforehand and it will skin easier. Also, if the frog dries out, the meat tends to lose flavor in a hurry. A good way to prepare frog legs is to powder them with flour, dip in egg batter, dust lightly with cracker meal, and place in vegetable oil preheated to 400 degrees F (204.4 degrees C) until the legs begin to brown. Then fry the legs at a reduced heat of 375 degrees F (190.5 degrees C) as you would chicken.

In the South, a bullfrog can mature in six months or less. In the North, figure on two years. In an enclosed system where some form of artificial heating is used, the northern frog might be forced to grow as fast as the southern, but at a rather high cost.

A few frogs could be raised even in a garden pool if you surrounded it with a fence, at least 4 feet high, of a small-enough mesh so the frogs could not escape. The water needs to be only 6 inches deep. In such a situation, the frogs would probably eat some of their own tadpoles unless you separated them. However, this kind of cannibalism might be an effective way to provide the frogs with extra food since the small garden pool can support only a very few frogs, anyway. A light bulb hung above the pool would attract night-flying insects for the frogs as well.

One of the nurseries that sells bullfrogs, Zetts Fish Farm & Hatchery of Drifting, Pennsylvania, publishes an interesting and often delightfully irreverent booklet full of pond-management information. Andrew Zetts advises buying tadpoles to stock farm ponds, especially if you aren't serious enough about raising frogs intensively to fence the pond. Adult frogs have a homing instinct, and purchased specimens might try to migrate back to where they came from. Zetts gives another reason for tall bank growth: herons, owls, and hawks savor bullfrogs too, and the tall growth helps the frogs hide.

Zetts passes on a slick way to harvest frogs in winter. Dig a hole in the pond 2 to 3 feet deep in the shallower water, with about a foot of oozy mud in the bottom. Frogs will tend to hibernate there. Then in winter, cut a hole in the ice directly above the hibernating hole and scoop out the frogs.

Toads Usually toads will use shallow, temporary ponds formed by overflow from a stream, but any shallow-edged pond will do. The toad lays eggs in long strings of a jelly-like substance early in spring, the mating and egg laying accompanied by their song—the first true sound of spring, which many people mistakenly attribute to frogs. Once the tadpoles develop into miniature toads, the amphibians leave the pond, not to return until the following spring. Each one will eat over ten thousand insects over summer, then burrow deep into the earth below the frost line to wait for spring.

Gardeners can hardly get too many toads in the garden, and hardly ever do they get enough. But toads are one more reason a pond is a wise investment. Two of the toad's favorite dishes are cut-

Fowler's Toad

worms and slugs. Slugs and toads like the same kind of weather, warm and moist. In some cases where slugs are too numerous, man has not provided enough natural habitat for toads. One bad effect of mowing all lawns to a carpet-like sheen is to chase away the toad and the garter snake, both excellent slug demolishers.

Turtles

Frog, duck, or kid ponds, almost always shelter turtles of one kind or another. Several are excellent eating, but because turtles grow so slowly, they have seldom been raised commercially—at least not freshwater turtles. For the same reason, turtles, like the snapping turtle, that are easy to catch with a hook baited with fresh meat, are soon diminished to a danger point when an area is too steadily hunted. The increase in artificial ponds has been the salvation of the common snapping turtle in the Midwest, providing a sustaining, if limited, source of meat to fanciers locally.

Besides the snapping turtle and its larger cousin, the South's alligator snapper, several other wild turtles are good table fare: the saw-toothed slider in the South, the false map turtle, the soft-shelled turtle with its sharp beak, and others. But before you take any turtle, better check the game laws in your area.

Commercial production of freshwater turtles is not commonly practiced, but at least snapping turtles can be raised easily in captivity. My son has had one in an aquarium in his room for three years. He feeds it hamburger and fish worms, but its rate of growth has been very slow. In our creek, there have almost always been 8- to 12-pounders available in limited quantity—three to four per mile—nearly every year, until recently. Now after several years of not catching them, I again have a sizable pair in my stretch of creek. In flood time, however, we can sit on our bridge and watch a considerable number of very young snapping turtles float helplessly by on the wings of the high water. We catch them when we can, and return them to the creek after spring flood time passes. This would also be an excellent way to catch a supply for stocking a pond.

Larger snappers we have caught by poking a steel rod systematically along the stream bottom, especially where brush and junk lie on the water surface. After a little experience, the sound

Snapping Turtle

and feel of it will tell you when the rod has hit a turtle back. Then you step on the turtle with your boot, slide your hand down to the shell, then gingerly locate the edge. The shell of the snapper has a few jagged points on the back sides, and there is a hollow under the edge of the shell at the back legs. These signs guide your hand to the turtle's tail and not his head. A snapping turtle requires considerable caution. I've not heard of one biting a hand under water, but once you pull the nasty-tempered creature out of the water, hold it as far away from you as you can, and get it into a sack as soon as possible. A snapper can take your finger off or maul it badly, but one usually gets bitten by allowing the head to swing too close to the leg while carrying the turtle by the tail. A snapper's neck stretches out several inches more than you think it can.

We never make turtle soup, considering fried turtle meat much

80

more scrumptious. Cut the heads off and hang the turtles by the tail, so the blood drains out well. Turtles often have leeches affixed to them and may otherwise reek with the smell of the stagnant water from which they've been pulled. For the faint-hearted, that smell may mark the end of interest in turtle eating. But the meat is remarkably clean and delicious.

There are six main pieces: the tail, the four legs, and the large neck piece of white meat. With the dead and decapitated turtle lying upside down on its shell, cut around the undershell, or plastron, and lift it out. Next, peel off the skin with a pair of pliers. Then cut out the six pieces. There is another strip of meat on the underside of the top shell, faced over with a ladder of little bones. These bones must be broken to get out the meat, which we always called "tenderloin." Because it is difficult to remove and not very large at that, some butchers don't bother.

We soak the meat overnight in saltwater, though I have heard other turtle fanciers say the brine soaking is unnecessary. In the morning, the cook browns the meat after rolling it in cornmeal, then fries it as you would in preparing southern fried chicken.

Because snappers can dig (in fact they live in holes dug into the bank just at or below the water line), trying to enclose them in a natural area would be quite difficult. But any ecologically managed pond will support enough turtles to give you a meal you won't forget every year.

Large snappers can pull a baby duck under water as it swims by, and drown it. I personally think that's a good use for a duck, but if you have any prize ducklings or goslings, you might pause a little before putting them on a pond known to contain large snappers. The turtles will not harm swimmers in farm ponds—at least I've never heard of that happening. But the shark-fear psychosis engendered by recent inane movies unfortunately has induced some farm-pond owners to get rid of their snapping turtles.

Wild Ducks Some of the ducks that frequent "duck ponds" or "kid ponds" have special interest for subsistence aquaculture. Mallards are common on ponds, are, in fact, so common that their beauty is rarely appreciated. The yellow bill, green head, and white neck ring, along with a persistence of blue

Wood Duck

Mallard

and green among the brown body feathers, easily identify the mallard drake. Mallards are most adaptable ducks and will interbreed with other species, particularly their close relative, the black duck. Both mallards and blacks are good eating. What's more, mallards can be tamed fairly easily. They will then waddle around the barnyard all summer, forsaking you—if you don't clip their wings or pen the birds—only at fall migration, when, like the wild goose, the mallard may follow the call of the wild.

Mallards nest on dry ground, but occasionally in a tree. Like other ducks, they eat arrowhead tubers (duck potato) and seeds, knotweed seed, widgeon grass, pondweed seed, wild celery or eelgrass, wild rice, bulrush seeds and stems, spikerush seeds and tubers, wild millet, and, of course, any grains you feel inclined to make available.

Pintails are perhaps the third most popular and plentiful duck species that frequent ponds, after mallards and blacks. Canvasback duck is better eating than any of those three, but is more a coastal duck than a pond duck.

The wood duck is of special interest to subsistence aquaculture because it readily adapts to man-made nests. In fact, the nests will often lure a wood duck to a pond. Wood ducks, as the name implies, prefer to nest in tree hollows, which are no longer common in areas of intensive farming or development. If a pond is fairly remote from human activity, a nest built according to the design shown will meet the approval of wood ducks. (See next page.)

Raccoons, snakes, and opossums eat wood duck eggs. Starlings, woodpeckers, and squirrels crack them. Raccoons will kill the females on the nest if they can. Appropriate shielding of artificial nests is necessary. Where a nest is not molested, the same wood duck will return year after year.

The wood duck makes a striking ornament for any pond with its gaudy red, green, blue, and yellow colors. Hardly any other bird equals its beauty. I wouldn't think of shooting one, even where hunting it is allowed. But the fact remains that, because we can increase wood duck production (it was once in danger of extinction), there is a clear possibility of maintaining a sustained yield with a surplus for the table.

Wood ducks savor pondweed seed above all if they can't get wild rice; they also like acorns and dogwood berries.

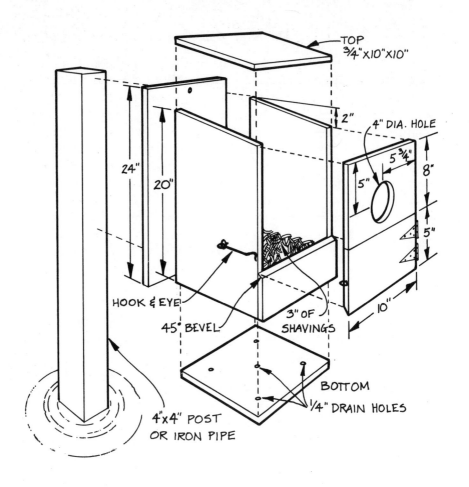

TOP
¾"x10"x10"

24"

20"

2"

4" DIA. HOLE

5 ¾"

5"

8"

5"

HOOK & EYE

45° BEVEL

3" OF
SHAVINGS

10"

BOTTOM

¼" DRAIN HOLES

4"x4" POST
OR IRON PIPE

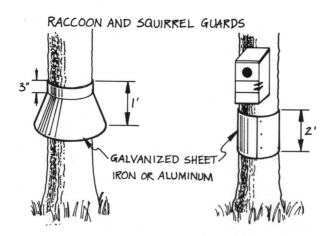

RACCOON AND SQUIRREL GUARDS

3"

1'

2'

GALVANIZED SHEET
IRON OR ALUMINUM

Nesting Box for Wood Ducks

Snow Goose

Wild Geese The Canadian goose deserves the homesteader's attention because it, too, can be semidomesticated. With bold aplomb, it struts along ponds and creeks in the Philadelphia area where we used to live. Whole flocks settled in the area. You could never walk right up and touch one but they wouldn't quite fly away, either. During nesting season, the hens found secluded places to hatch their eggs and did not appreciate intrusion. I saw a mother goose rise off her nest one day and charge a horse and rider fearlessly. The horse broke and ran away in panic. My image of quaint old Mother Goose was shattered forever.

Spreading grain on the ground or leaving some in the fields will attract Canadian geese. Talk to the game warden before you set out grain. It is, in some times and places, illegal to bait shooting grounds with grain.

85

WILD RICE LAKES

In northern Minnesota, and less commonly in Wisconsin and Canada, lie rather large, rather shallow lakes where wild rice grows in abundance enough to have supplied for centuries the principal source of carbohydrates and protein for Indians and waterfowl. The label "wild rice lake" is somewhat misleading, since wild rice grows equally well in streams and along river banks of the same region. Nor do these waters appear to be unique for wild rice except, perhaps, in the sense that they are more removed from civilization than other lakes that could, or perhaps did, produce wild rice. Historical records and place names show that at one time considerable wild rice grew in Wisconsin and northern Michigan where it no longer is an important commodity. In fact, wild rice once grew rather widely over the whole eastern half of the country, and several strains that are poorer yielders of smaller grains, still do grow wild along the East Coast. Another similar subspecies grows in a small area of Texas, and yet another, quite different from American wild rice, is found in the Orient.

Zizania aquatica, the common kind of wild rice, will grow far beyond the upper Minnesota region where it is now naturally confined. Anson Elliott, the plant breeder at the University of Minnesota working on improved varieties, says that it appears wild rice can grow in other parts of the country. "It has produced seed in the states of Missouri, Louisiana, Texas, California, Colorado, Minnesota, and Wisconsin. The types native to Minnesota mature earlier in warmer climates and must be planted earlier to avoid the extremely hot weather, or they flower so early that they produce very little seed," he wrote me. If you should get a chance to try growing wild rice, directions are simple. Don't plant it in water over 2 or 3 feet deep, and not where current is swift. The seed must be kept stored in cool water over winter. In early spring, take the seeds out of refrigeration and roll them into mud balls, says Elliott, and toss them into your pond.

In the nineteenth and early twentieth centuries, homesteaders as well as Indians practically lived on wild rice in the northern Minnesota–Wisconsin region. As one early writer put it, before population increases came along with white settlement, the Indians who controlled the wild rice lakes had seemingly found a way

Wild Rice

around the natural law that says that he who will not work shall not eat. There was no work, except harvesting in raising a crop of wild rice. Of course, some years it didn't produce very well, either.

In the fall, ripened seeds fall into the water (more shatter than are harvested, usually) where they lay at freezing or near-freezing temperatures till spring. Seeds begin to germinate when the sun warms the lake bottom above 40 degrees F (4 degrees C). The "floating leaf" stage occurs in May or early June, then sturdy stems emerge above the water's surface. The plants may grow as much as 8 feet tall, though height varies considerably. The best depth of water is from 6 inches to 2 feet, but wild rice will grow in as much as 4 feet of water if other growing conditions are favorable.

The seed ripens in early August and the harvest begins in late August. Harvest on wild stands of wild rice must, by law, be done in the traditional Indian manner. Two people in a boat glide through the stand. One rows, the other uses a stick to gather heads of the grain over the gunwhale, and beats the grains with another stick so they fall into the boat. The seeds shatter out easily, and plenty get away for waterfowl to eat and to seed next year's crop.

Even with this primitive method of harvesting, two people could, in years past, earn good money, since the gourmet grain commands such a high price. So many people flock to the wild rice stands that many laws have been made to safeguard the crop from the wild greed of the harvesters. Much of the wild rice stands

Canadian geese.

are on Indian reservations where the Indians are supposed to have sole harvesting rights. I've read that the Indians themselves eat less and less of the very nutritious grain, the more to sell to the whites. I wonder if they buy sugar-coated crinkle cruds from the breakfast food companies of America with the money they get.

From an aquacultural point of view, one of the most interesting aspects of wild rice is the rapidity with which it is being domesticated and brought into commercial production. Improved varieties planted in man-made paddies and harvested like any other grain now provide more wild rice in the marketplace than all that harvested from wild stands. We are supposed to look upon this energetic progress with grateful wonder and appreciation, but pardon me for not being impressed. All it indicates to me is the tremendous tenacity of man, especially when he possesses the seemingly unlimited power of bulldozer and dragline.

Twenty years ago thousands of acres of land in north central Minnesota seemed to be a permanent haven for wildlife and for people who enjoyed living humbly with wildlife. Certainly this kind of wilderness could never be destroyed for the aggrandizement of men, we thought. Wrong. Now this land is being carved up into rice paddies. The cost in fossil energy is enormous. The huge amount of water the paddies demand already has the rice growers at odds with water authorities. Disease and insect problems plague the crop, requiring huge amounts of chemicals. And all for what? So we can pretend we are rich once or twice a year and buy some wild rice.

The only good coming out of the development, in my opinion, is varietal improvement. If improved varieties could be grown casually in farm ponds across the nation, then man will have advanced not only the well-being of his own diet, but of the whole environment. But I doubt that the rice growers who are pushing for more wild rice research are at all interested in a development that might pull the rug out from under their enterprise.

But even from the most hard-line environmental view, the domestication of wild rice is not all bad by far. Most of the present production is confined to within one hundred miles of Grand Rapids, Minnesota, and will probably not spread much. Wild rice, barring some monumental breakthrough, will always be a specialty crop. The new paddies may take some of the pressure off the wild grain, leaving more of the latter for waterfowl.

Cost of paddy development is very high. The price of the land is climbing above $150 an acre—up from almost nothing in 1960. Building the paddies will cost twice that amount per acre nowadays, and special equipment for thinning, tilling, and harvesting will run well over $200 per acre. The experts figure an investment of over $200,000 is necessary before economic return is possible. And then you have to gamble that blackbirds, the wild rice worm, leaf blight, shattering, and bad weather don't ruin the crop. I have to believe that the Indians were smarter.

The University of Minnesota Extension Service at St. Paul is probably the best place to go for the latest information on wild rice. The Northern Research Laboratory at Peoria, Illinois, is another headquarters for wild rice research. The University of Minnesota branch at Duluth is also involved. New varieties are not yet commercially available, and if you don't live in wild rice country, you will have a difficult time getting any seed that will grow, since it should be kept cool and moist if not actually in water. Grand Rapids, Minnesota, is (if any place is) the center of wild rice production, and the North Central Experiment Station of the University of Minnesota located there would be a good place to visit, if wild rice intrigues you. The Minnesota Historical Society in St. Paul maintains a bibliography on wild rice. The Northprint Company in Grand Rapids sells an informative little booklet, too.

RIVERS

Because of the public nature of larger streams and rivers, chances for managed aquacultural production in or along them are limited. Here the aquaculturist can practice only an intelligent form of hunting and gathering, with the harvest hopefully regulated for sustained yield by state and federal laws. Hopefully. Laws or no laws, large rivers have suffered sad despoliation by man. Or perhaps the depredation just shows more plainly than it does on smaller bodies of water. Big begets big. Where streams converge into large rivers, wildlife converges also in teeming numbers, and there the carnage of man can reach its most insane heights. The *St. Louis Dispatch* in 1902, as quoted by *Field and Stream* of the same year, carried a rather triumphant story about three men who had shot and killed 1,372 ducks in a 48-hour period. The men said they did not know how many more they had only wounded.

An unspoiled stretch of river.

Some species of fish are characteristic of large rivers for the simple reason they are, or rather were, too large for anything but deep water. From the standpoint of aquacultural food production, the most promising of these, the sturgeon, the paddlefish, and the blue catfish are now quite rare, victims of pollution and hydroelectric dams.

Any budding aquaculturist interested in the potential of a big-river fish for food production or in the sad history of their demise, should read "Native Fish in Troubled Waters" by George Reiger in the January 1977 issue of *Audubon*. Smoked sturgeon, points out Reiger, was almost a food staple in the latter half of the nineteenth century in the Midwest. In 1885, five million pounds of it were shipped out of Sandusky, Ohio, along with three thousand pounds of isinglass and one thousand kegs of caviar. The isinglass was a by-product of sturgeon cartilage and air bladder, used in the clarification of wine and for other purposes. Today the American Fisheries Society puts a value of about $50 a pound on sturgeon. In 1885, sturgeons that weighed more than half a ton were still being caught in our rivers.

While biologists have been unable to hatch and raise sturgeon

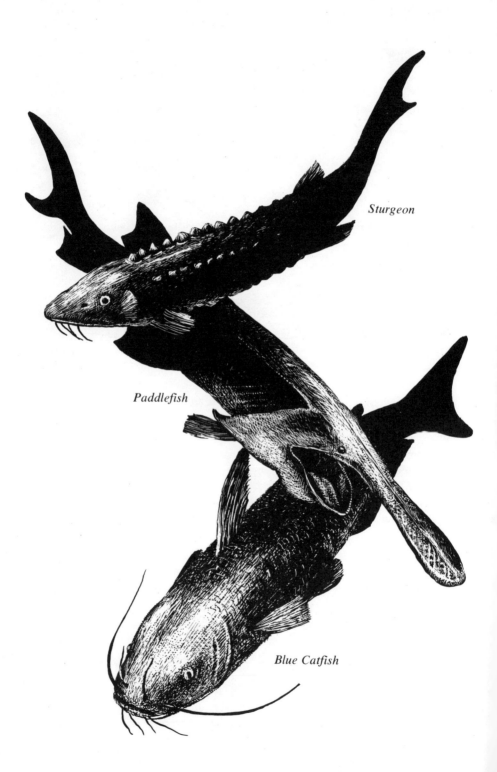

Sturgeon

Paddlefish

Blue Catfish

in an artificial environment, they have more hope for another large—and doomed—river fish, the paddlefish. A century ago, paddlefish regularly caught in the Mississippi basin weighed 200 pounds. Today 30-pounders are considered big, and some twenty thousand fishermen jam a small length of the Osage River every year, lusting to catch one. If the Army Corps of Engineers has its way, even this last refuge of the paddlefish will be dammed into oblivion.

But the large and tasty fish may not become extinct. Aquaculturists have propagated it successfully in captivity. Russian biologists in particular are interested in paddlefish. Because it is a zooplankton eater, the paddlefish can be used in a polyculture arrangement with other fish that don't eat zooplankton, the scientists believe.

The Missouri Conservation Commission first successfully propagated paddlefish artificially in 1960. The Commission now hatches large numbers of the fish at its Painted Pony Hatchery, near Marshall, Missouri. Interest will probably continue, not only among sportsmen but fish farmers too, because the paddlefish utilize a wide range of phytoplankton in their diet, giving them access to much more food than more carnivorous fish.

Another fish at home only in large rivers is the blue catfish. Blues that weighed 200 pounds used to be caught regularly. That's the same size as a market hog, only a catfish of that size would dress out more meat than the hog and, incidentally, the meat would be far more healthful for humans. If we had managed our large rivers all these years with an eye toward food production rather than managing them as open sewers fit only to float barges on, we could harvest enough blues every year to take the place of who-knows-how-many million hogs. All the soil washed off all the cornfields, which were planted with all that fossil energy to feed all those hogs, would be intact, growing renewable timber and grass for fuel and low-cost protein.

The freshwater mussel is another example of river life interesting to aquaculturists, at least the backyard food-provider kind. Though not unique to rivers (freshwater mussels come in many varieties, some found commonly in creeks and ponds) the one species that aquaculturists have had the most success propagating is a river species, *Lampsilis luteola*, otherwise known as the Lake Pepin mucket. *L. luteola* once lived in enormous beds

Pearly Mussel

along the Mississippi, the Wabash, and other interior rivers where it is still not uncommon. It and other river mussels were the chief source for buttons and a thriving "pearl" button business flourished along many midwestern rivers. Zippers, plastic, and a decline in the mussel beds brought an end to the industry, though you can still buy shell buttons today. Or make your own.

Freshwater mussels sometimes contained pearls, too, just like oysters. Pearl buyers made their rounds of the mussel fisheries regularly and button manufacturers could make a profit on this by-product of their trade. The Lake Pepin mucket was the best pearl producer, a fact that only enhances its ability to respond to aquacultural propagation.

Freshwater mussel culture for the production of pearls has been perfected in China and Japan, where it is now practiced successfully in ponds, lakes, and reservoirs. The species usually used are *Anodonta woodiana* and *Hyriopsis cumingi*. The Chinese are able to induce pearl formation in mussels in two years. A mussel may produce twenty to forty pearls by special implantation of the nucleic material from which the pearl forms. So impressed were the members of an FAO Fisheries Mission to China in 1976 that they are urging the introduction of the culture of freshwater pearls in other countries as a productive sideline occupation for small farmers and aquaculturists. A small pond is adequate and no expensive or sophisticated equipment is required. The hitch is that a special skill must be learned: implanting the mussels. In addition, more work needs to be done to improve the shape of the pearls to make them more marketable for jewelry. In China, the pearls are used for medicinal purposes, and shape is not important.

Freshwater mussels are edible and tasty when prepared correctly. Fresh from a river or creek, especially a modern river loaded with topsoil sediment, the meat tastes muddy. We midwestern boys have all tried to eat them once and never again. But University of Georgia aquaculturist Dr. E. Evan Brown tells me that all you have to do is throw the mussels into a tub of clean water for a week. The mussels will clean themselves and, prepared the same as clams, taste fine.

The mussels (which we persist in calling clams in the Midwest, far from the ocean shores where people know the difference) live most of their not-too-exciting lives on river or stream beds where the current is slow, but not so slow that the finer silt particles in the water settle on the mussel bed of fine gravel and sand. The mussel does not like to have a lot of dirt dumped on it, any more than you or I would. Even in small, mud-bottomed creeks like mine, the mussels will invariably be found on a sandy spot. The mussel either lodges half-buried in the sand, or moves very slowly along on a fleshy foot it can extend at will. The shell is kept slightly open when the mussel is "eating." Water flows through, and oxygen is exchanged with carbon dioxide in the gills, just as in all fish. Hairy cilia brush any food particles from the water as it is expelled out the back of the shell.

Though you may consider them literally "stick-in-the-muds," mussels actually have an astonishing life-style. Females, sometimes fertilized with the help of fish that transfer sperm from male to female, lay millions of eggs, most of which perish as larvae. Larvae attach to the gills of fish where they live until they reach the beginning of adulthood. Still very small, they then drop off, hopefully coming to rest in a favorable environment, where there are other mussels with which they can eventually mate. The whole cycle is a very hit-or-miss affair, and only a very small portion of the young ever reach adult egg-laying age.

But that percentage can be improved with aquacultural methods. Back in the early 1920s, when pearl buttons were still in demand but mussel beds declining, biologists successfully raised mussels in floating crates on the Mississippi, and reported that the method was economically feasible. The report, by Arthur Day Howard, is contained (entombed) in volume 38 of the *Bulletin of U.S. Bureau of Fisheries*, 1921–22, pp. 63-89. These bulletins are treasure troves for aquacultural experimenters, especially of the offbeat kind, and backyard aquaculturists should get familiar with them.) The mussels were raised in cypress-framed crates covered outside with metal screen and inside with copper cloth so the very tiny mussels could not escape. The crates were lashed to floating barrels, the whole forming long, narrow rafts next to which workmen could position their boats for easy access to the crates. The mussels derived food from the water in adequate supply and were, of course, protected from their myriad predators. The crates could not be overwintered on the river, however, but were placed in more protected water from November to spring. By the end of the second summer the mussels were large enough for buttons, but the researchers felt that in most years, better profits might be made if the mussels were kept a third year.

Lampsilis luteola was the only species of mussel to do well in the crates, though some minor success was attained with the yellow sand shell, *L. anodontoides*.

Researchers tried raising mussels in ponds, too. In cement-bottomed ponds, zilch. But in earthen ponds, production compared favorably with river crates. Crappie, sunfish, and black bass were utilized as carriers of the immature mussels, known in learned circles as glochidia.

And finally, Howard noted, a commercial fisherman at Lake City, Minnesota, sunk in Lake Pepin, a box measuring 10 by 10 feet, 8 inches high, covered with a fine-mesh chicken wire. The box contained fish infested with glochidia. By the end of the year, he counted eleven thousand healthy, growing mussels in his cage.

LAKES

The public nature of larger lakes makes them, like rivers, something less than adequate for managed aquacultural production. But a lake is a bit more controllable than a river, since by definition, its waters do not flow in and out of a particular place with a marked current. (Actually, many lakes really are parts of river systems and the water really does move through them, though

A small lake can offer more than recreation to the aquaculturally oriented homesteader.

very slowly. Even the Great Lakes are a river system, though it may take years and even centuries for a particular drop of water flowing into Lake Superior to pass on into the Atlantic Ocean.) If a person controls the shoreline of a lake, he can control to some extent what goes into and out of its water. From an aquacultural point of view, a large lake might be defined as one with public access to it and a small lake one that is privately owned—regardless of actual size.

The point is relevant because of the surprising number of small lakes that are privately controlled. Not for nothing is Minnesota called the land of ten thousand lakes. In the fifties when I was a frequent visitor to a few of them, it was not unusual to find a small gem of a lake entirely within the holding of a lucky dairy farmer, or perhaps two or three very closely related dairy farmers. I understand that since then many of these lakeside properties have been developed into suburbs for motorboat and water ski enthusiasts. I know that the solitary lake where we used to skinny-dip blissfully with the cows and the dogs is now ringed with houses. Even so, the people who live there, as well as owners of yet unspoiled lakes, may, by and by, look for ways to use the water for greater food production. So, too, with small lakes in other parts of the country—from the ponds of the Northeast to the "tanks" of the Southwest.

Another kind of small lake is increasing in number: the city,

97

town, and village water reservoirs. Sooner or later, especially if man insists on breeding himself into extinction, these reservoirs will be utilized for some kind of aquacultural food production since it would be plain stupid not to. These reservoirs are more or less privately owned by municipalities or utility companies that have the means to enforce strict regulations as to how the public uses them. The public accepts these regulations, understanding that the water is ultimately their drinking water. The stage is thus set for the possibility of managed aquacultural production should that become desirable.

Many of these lakes become as lovely as natural lakes—more so, in my estimation, since only a minimum amount of recreation is allowed on them. Since all one can do on most reservoirs is fish from motorless boats and watch birds, the raucous nature consumers with their beer, tents, guns, motors, and garbage are not attracted, leaving the scene to true nature lovers and fishermen. If you want to see a fine example of what I'm talking about, spend an afternoon on the Green Lane Reservoir north of Philadelphia. When we lived in the area, we spent many peaceful days rowing along the shoreline, sometimes catching fish, always seeing birds, deer, and wild flowers.

Highway construction has brought into existence another type of lake. Big superhighways need lots of dirt to build a roadbed, and where engineers dig out the dirt along the right-of-way, small lakes are formed. Some are quite large, others, simply large farm ponds. Farmers who own the land are the usual beneficiaries and many such landowners have developed the little lakes for fee-fishing and recreation.

Many of these lakes, especially in hilly country, are lovely— marred only by the unending bestial roar of heavy trucks on the nearby highway. Eventually, even the trucking industry will become civilized enough to want to spend another $200 per truck to muffle them adequately. Then these wayside highway lakes will become enchanting places for man and wild beast and will be situated nicely for aquacultural production. With the highway nearby, aquatic food could be handily loaded onto (quiet) trucks and whisked directly to city food centers.

Knowledge of how water reacts to temperature change in lakes is essential to any backyard aquaculturist, even if he is thinking only in terms of a small pond. Unlike streams and rivers, water in a

Winter   Summer

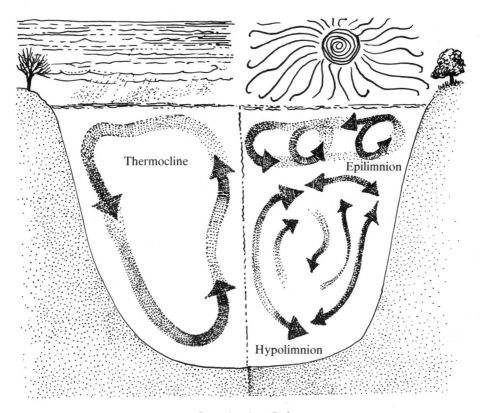

Layering in a Lake

lake without current stratifies according to temperature, which affects water density. Fresh water is densest at about 39 degrees F (3.8 degrees C), not at freezing. Therefore, in winter the coldest water lies right under the ice and the warmer water sinks to the bottom. A lake that is deep enough doesn't freeze solid. With the insulating protection of ice in addition, the water seldom freezes more than a foot thick here in northern Ohio, even in 1977, the coldest winter ever.

However, the lack of wind action whipping the water surface under the ice means that oxygen is not readily replenished. If there is a large number of fish in the water they could use up the available oxygen in the bottom zone and die. Even for a normal number of fish in a pond, water should be at least 8 feet deep in the North.

Getting Food from Water

In summer, the top layers of water warm up fast, while the bottom layer remains at about 40 degrees F (4.4 degrees C). With wind action, the lighter, warmer water above is recharged with oxygen. But where water depth is around 20 feet or more, the coolest water remains undisturbed on the bottom, sealed off by a zone of warmer water called the thermocline. Oxygen cannot get down to the bottom layer. Bottom-feeding fish will be forced to spend most of their time up in the thermocline zone, and, as a result, will not eat as much as they otherwise might.

You can begin to see why aerators become important to intensive aquacultural production.

In the fall, the bottom layer of a deep lake will naturally be recharged with oxygen. At that time, water on the surface begins to cool. At some point, surface-water temperature becomes the same as bottom-water temperature, and, for a brief time, the water loses its stratification. There is a complete turnover of bottom water and surface water, replenishing the oxygen supply at the lake bottom, hopefully enough to last through the winter.

TIDAL WETLANDS 6

Visiting the coast of Maine, I have little trouble reaching quick empathy with the fishermen. Their philosophy, their problems, their purposes are so like those of the small farmers in my home neighborhood. Instead of tractors, they drive boats. Their livestock are fish and shellfish; the weather, as with farmers, is their victory or defeat. And like small farmers, the independent fishermen work long and hard knowing they will not get rich, but they are willing to maintain a tough and menial work schedule for the privilege of minding their own say-so. They may be in bondage to nature, but not to any man. "You can never starve a Maine-iac out," my friend Forry Wall, a Maine farmer, likes to say. "He can always go dig himself a bucketful of clams."

Not surprisingly, it is a farm magazine, the *American Agriculturist*, which publicized the way small, independent baymen of Great South Bay, Long Island, organized a cooperative to help them compete with the big dredging companies in the harvesting and marketing of clams. The Great South Bay Farmers' Cooperative is a replay of the classic small farmer/big agribusiness struggle. The larger operations can afford to lease tracts of 20,000 acres of bay bottom from which to dredge up clams, while the small bayman in his little boat works by hand to make a living digging clams on his own. Working independently, he can only bring his bags of clams to market every afternoon and take what the buyers offer him. With the co-op, he may get a better price, since the co-op can hold his clams with those of other independent baymen for better market muscle.

The backyard aquaculturist or homesteader with access to the seashore has the same choices open to him as the gardener/ homesteader has in agriculture. If he can get together the money

103

The independent fisherman, like this lobsterman, is the ocean's small farmer.

and the necessary skill, he can start his own "aqua-business" by leasing clam bottoms or oyster beds. Or lease shoreline and turn it into a "farm" for mussels or algae or salmon or whatever. Second, he can become an independent, small commercial fisherman taking his chances alone or with a cooperative like the one described above. Or third, he can procure a noncommercial home license (much cheaper than the commercial license the first two methods require), and use the shore merely to replenish his own family's stock of food.

Most backyard aquaculturists will fall into the third category. The ideal model might be the small Maine farmer with fields running right down to the shore of a tidal pool or estuarine pond, or the landholder on the edge of the New Jersey piney woods with acres of marsh between him and open sea, or an islander off the coast of North Carolina, or a Creole fisherman/farmer just inland of the Gulf Coast, or an artichoke farmer on the cold, wind-swept bluffs overlooking the Pacific Ocean in California.

The beachcombing homesteader, knowledgeable about tidal

wetlands, views their various manifestations as distinct from one another, just as he distinguishes his orchard from his grain fields, and his garden from his woodlot. There is a place he might gather mussels, another he might dig for clams, and still farther out in the water a spot he might set a lobster pot. In the marsh, he knows where he can gather salt hay and where he can gather only eelgrass. Each crop has its time and place, and the shore dwellers orchestrate all into a harmonious song of harvest.

TIDAL PLANTS

Where does the sea stop and the land begin? The sea's influence on the land is in direct proportion to the amount of salt in the water, an amount that diminishes as it mixes with fresh water farther inland. As far as the tides carry the salt, the sea is master.

From the open sea, one meets first the outer islands, then outer beaches, shoals, and bars. Where the land is hillier, you might sail a skiff from the open bay straight up a rocky-shored cove and at high tide on up a narrowing "pond" to firm pastureland sloping down from a barnyard. Or where the land tends to flatness,

Garden mulch just waiting to be harvested.

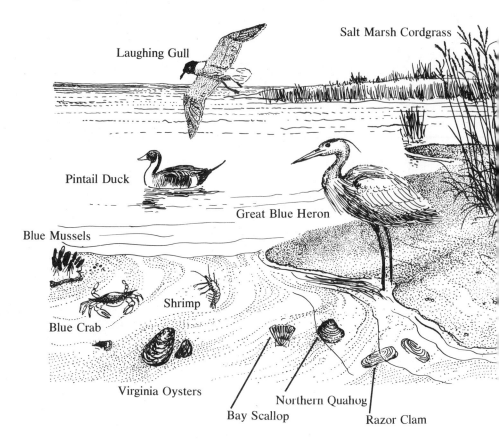

Laughing Gull

Salt Marsh Cordgrass

Pintail Duck

Great Blue Heron

Blue Mussels

Shrimp

Blue Crab

Virginia Oysters

Bay Scallop

Northern Quahog

Razor Clam

you might find the low intertidal marsh behind the outer beach, and beyond that, to landward, the higher marsh or salt-hay meadows. Beyond that lie the freshwater marshes interlaced with streams in which the salt content of the water disappears.

The freshwater marshes resemble inland swamps. Cattails, marshmallow, some kinds of cordgrass, and phragmites are typical plants. Muskrat and mink are at home here, along with most common wild animals of the interior.

The high marsh or salt meadows produce the salt hay upon which, in an earlier era, the coastal farmer relied for stock feed. The marshes were usually diked to keep tidewater out except at certain seasons when sluice gates were opened and the meadows flooded to insure the continual growth of *Spartina patens* and *Spartina alterniflora*, the grasses that make the best hay. Some is still cut and sold, more now for garden mulch than feed. It is

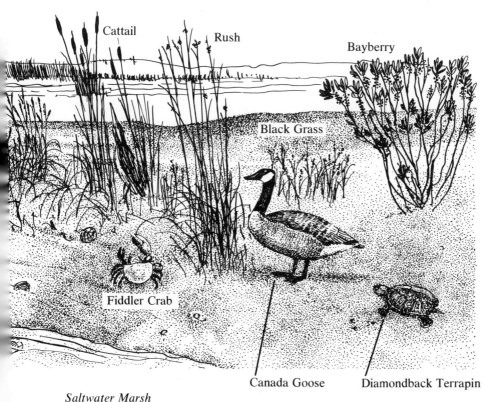

American Bittern

Cattail

Rush

Bayberry

Black Grass

Fiddler Crab

Canada Goose

Diamondback Terrapin

Saltwater Marsh

excellent for both purposes, containing no dryland weed seed and being rich in minerals.

Other grasses, like spike grass and cordgrass, may compete with the salt hay, the governing factor always being the amount of tolerance a given plant has for saltwater. The more tolerant grow closer to the sea, the less tolerant, farther away. Also on the high marsh you will find chairmakers rush, black grass, groundsel bush, marsh elder, and sea lavender, all with valuable roles in the tidewater wetland food chain. Where tides reach only occasionally, grows glasswort, or samphire, a fine salad green.

In the intertidal marshes, constantly awash with seawater, saltwort and salt marsh cordgrass are predominant plants. Here, too, the shellfish begin to occur. On the shoals, widgeon grass and eelgrass grow for the ducks. On the beaches, seaweed washes up to provide gardeners and farmers with excellent mulch and fertilizer.

Getting Food from Water

Rockweed clings to shoreline rocks; it's good to eat steamed. Near low-water lines, on rocks and pilings, laver grows, its fronds a purplish hue. It is good in soup or cooked like cabbage. Reddish dulse is another seaweed that is edible. It is dried, cured, and used like an herb for flavoring. The dark, greenish black moss carpet of tidal pools is Irish moss which can be boiled and eaten if you're hungry enough. Giant kelp, too, is edible, but is perhaps more practical as fertilizer and mulch.

In the water and among the grasses and plants of the varying shoreline, the homestead beachcomber learns to live with a variety of animal life that, in an earlier era, easily could have fed his family with little recourse to the livestock in his barn. And which could feed him again if wise game laws were enforced and aquacultural management perfected. There is the secretive diamondback terrapin, once almost extinct, now slowly coming back to the inner reaches of the tidal marshes and streams. There are the shorebirds and waterfowl that depend wholly or partly on the estuarine systems of the tidal wetlands for survival. Many of these birds were almost gunned to extinction in the early years of this century. Now, somewhat protected by game laws, they face danger from a different kind of gunner—the drainer of the tidal wetlands and the developer of shoreline vacation cottages, motels, parking lots, and the idiocy of boardwalk amusement parks.

There are several ways to "cultivate" or harvest tidal wetlands for homestead food and fiber without injury to the ecosystem. The first and simplest is as a source of garden fertilizers and mulch. Seaside gardeners learn to become adept scroungers, spading into their sandy soil in the fall the "wastes" of the sea: potassium and trace-element-rich seaweed flung up on the beach; phosphorus-rich seashells; nitrogen-rich fish scraps discarded by fishermen at public landing points (if you can beat the gulls to them); marsh hay and eelgrass bunched by wind and water in piles on protected shores.

Salt hay can be cut, dried, and barned like any hay once the flats where it grows are diked or partially drained so that at haying time the ground is firm enough to hold machinery or horses. Or, as in the earliest time, you can scythe it by hand in wet marsh and dry it partially on racks or stakes and boat it up nearby streams to firm ground for curing.

Various forms of seaweed algae are staple foods in some

108

oceanside countries. Algae are rich in protein, fat, and carbohydrates and can be dried, powdered, and mixed with other foods. Nori and laver are big business in Japan—the red algae being the single most commercially valuable marine product in the country. Growing it on racks in protected waters and processing it into the dried sheets sold in food markets, is an extremely complex procedure perfected only after centuries of practice. Dulse is another red alga widely eaten in Canada and Europe. A few small beginnings have been made on American shores, too—at least one enterprising homestead family in Maine gathers, dries, and markets algae.

Seaweed's apparent fertilizer value has made it a marketable commodity as a soil conditioner, too. Many organic farmers and gardeners use it under a variety of brand names. Research at Clemson University and the University of Maryland supports many of the merits organic growers have claimed for seaweed fertility.

Algae are also being used increasingly as a principal food for larval fish and shellfish raised in artificial confinement. Aquacultural experiment stations like the National Marine Fisheries Service's Gulf Coastal Fisheries Center in Galveston are developing special algal culture tanks to raise food for shrimp, fish, and other marine animals. Tanks like these may have special interest for homestead food producers in the future.

SHELLFISH

There are three general ways shellfish can be managed aquaculturally. The first requires very little management at all, and consists of merely holding lobsters and crabs of marketable size in ponds or tanks, or the similar holding of market-size clams and oysters in tanks or inshore beds. The purpose is usually one of storage until the shellfish can be marketed and/or eaten fresh. Sometimes the holding has the further purpose of fattening or finishing the shellfish. Oysters, for example, are kept in small marsh ponds or claires in Brittany for "greening" prior to marketing. Commercial clam diggers also maintain holding ponds to keep a day's catch or more until it can be sold. This practice can supply the homestead situation very well, where harvesting shellfish may be only a weekend task. Keeping marine animals this way temporarily can be a first step in learning more complex methods of artificial culture.

A second kind of management is the cultivation of the shellfish in natural waters. Oysters provide a good example. They are collected from the wild, or purchased, then seeded onto a growing bed or rafts. The resulting clusters of oysters are then separated and either harvested or transferred to other growing beds for further growth.

In this second kind of management, shrimp, for example, can be cultivated by trapping young ones in tidal ponds as the tide rises and waiting for them to grow up, either with or without supplemental feeding. This kind of aquaculture occasionally can be practical in the homestead situation where one has access to a tidal pond or off-shore bed.

A third form is the totally confined production method in artificial surroundings: shellfish larvae and crustacean larvae and juveniles are hatchery-produced in treated or recirculated seawater, followed possibly by growth to market size in artificial tanks or ponds. This method for shellfish has at present few possibilities for backyard aquaculturists. Artificial rearing of shellfish is far from being a perfected science—or art. Progress is being made, however, and a day may come when a homeowner can raise even his own lobster in the backyard.

Lobsters Egg-bearing females are being taken to laboratories, the eggs hatched, and the young returned to the sea, but so far there is little evidence that seeding is actually raising the population of this dwindling resource. Marine biologists believe that lobsters can be raised profitably in the warm effluent water from power plants located on coastlines. But that's not much help for a do-it-yourselfer. If you want your own lobsters, you will have to trap them like the lobstermen do. (Inlanders will have to be satisfied with crayfish, see page 243.) A "home" license, entitling you to set up to ten lobster traps, costs around $20 (commercial licenses are much higher, of course) and what you catch probably will not be worth the effort. To keep, a lobster must measure 3⅛ inches long from eye socket to the aft end of the carapace. If a lobster is carrying eggs—a berried female, as she's called—the

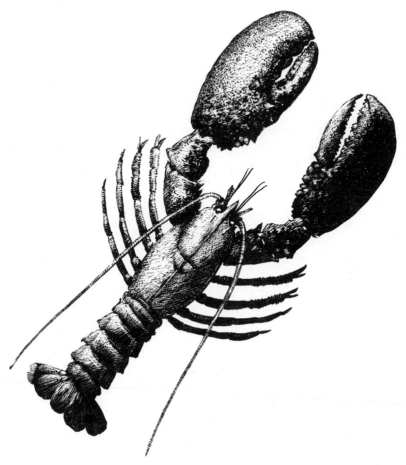

Lobster

law says throw her back. If you don't, I hope you get caught and fined plenty.

Don't try to keep a live lobster in a bucket of water. It will soon die from lack of oxygen. Air (temporarily) keeps lobsters alive better than water, especially in a cool ice chest or similar enclosure. Boats often have a compartment through which water circulates and provides enough oxygen for the lobsters. Back home, you can keep your catch in floating cages alongside a wharf for awhile. My favorite restaurant in Maine keeps a stock of live seafood right outside the kitchen in this manner. In a holding tank, you'd have to circulate the water. Lobsters need lots of oxygen.

Crabs The Jonah crab and the rock crab in the North, the blue crab in the mid-Atlantic region, the stone crab and the lady crab in the South, and the dungeness crab on the West Coast are all harvested commercially and as leisure sport. Crabs get into lobster pots and you can catch them in special crab pots, though use of these is generally limited to local residents. The easy way to catch crabs is with a dip net if you have good eyes and quick wrists. You can also tie a bit of fish scrap to a line, lower it into the backwater of a tidal flat, and wait patiently. The crab will grab on and you can pull him out—the way we inlanders catch crawdads. A small net in the other hand helps, in case the crab lets go before you land him.

Can crabs be domesticated? Yes. At the Institute of Marine and Atmospheric Sciences at the University of Miami, W. T. Young raised crabs to marketable size in 1969. Work continues also at Duke University under J. D. Costlow. The outlook is good, say the experts, though as yet crab raising seems to be too expensive to be practical commercially.

Clams Clamming is a favorite pastime of shore dwellers. Most shore communities require special permits or licenses. Permits are easy to get for family consumption, not so easy for commercial fishermen. Clammers hardly think of their food-gathering labors as gardening ventures, yet as they bend over digging with a clam hoe or dragging the bottom with a quahog rake, the parallel is undeniable. The Japanese, who wrote the book on clam culture, actually harrow their closely managed clam beds for better production.

Crabs like clams as much as humans do, and keeping them off the clam beds is a major problem. Experiments show that crushed oyster shell, crushed stone, or pea gravel spread over the surface of the beds discourages the crabs from preying on the clams to some extent.

Clams can now be hatched in laboratories and the "seed" distributed back on the beds. Another step toward domestication of clams is hybridization: the northern quahog has been successfully

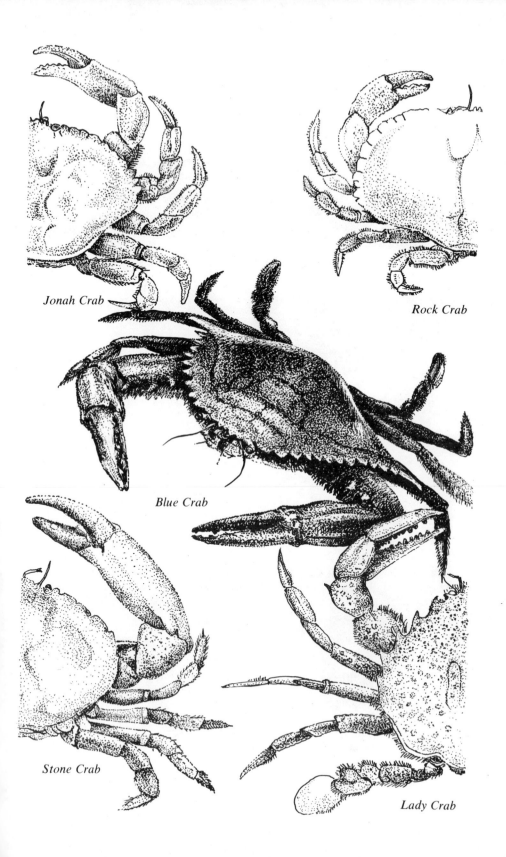

Jonah Crab

Rock Crab

Blue Crab

Stone Crab

Lady Crab

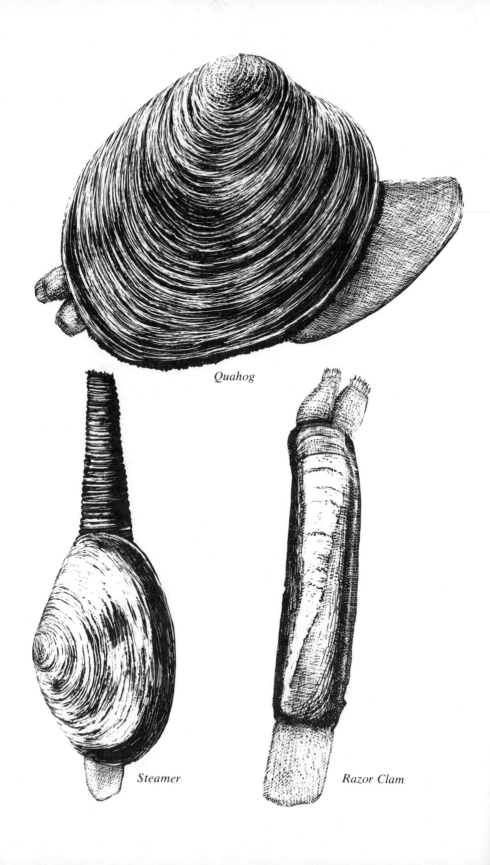

Quahog

Steamer

Razor Clam

crossed with the southern quahog to produce a more vigorous strain.

The quahog (cherrystone, littleneck) and the steamer or soft-shell clam are the two important food clams. Steamers are dug from the sand in shallow water on shoal beaches, the quahogs out a little farther in deeper water. With experience, you can feel the clams under the sand with your toes. Steamers leave breathing holes in the sand at the spot where they burrow 6 inches to a foot into the sand. (Quahogs are usually right under the surface.) The hole gives away the steamer's presence. If you jump up and down on the sand, water will often squirt out of the hole from the steamer's siphon. The stamping makes the clam retract its shell suddenly, forcing out the stream of water.

Razor clams are longish and narrow, about the size of a pocket comb, and usually lie under the surface sand. They are dug with clam hook or hoe.

Scrub clams before cooking them; a wire brush will take off the black "beards." Then steam them in a kettle for about twenty minutes.

Mussels The blue mussel is edible, but has not been as popular in the United States as it is in other countries. Pacific mussels can't be eaten from May to October because of a poisonous

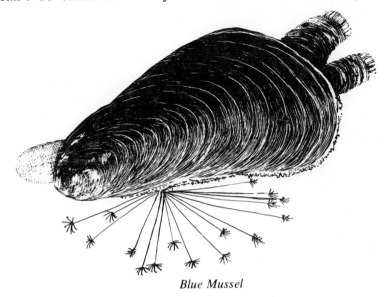

Blue Mussel

microorganism present in certain plant plankton the mussel eats at that time.

Mussels can be gathered by picking them off rocks and pilings where they affix themselves by webs of strong black threads. These threads, or beards, like those on clams, should be removed from the shells before steaming the mussels. After twenty minutes of steaming, the shells will open like other hard-shell clams. Don't harvest any not firmly attached to something. Never keep a dead or injured one—of *any* kind of shellfish.

In Europe, long poles are stuck in shore waters, to which the mussels attach and grow to maturity. The bottom portions of the poles are sheathed in smooth plastic that keeps the crabs from climbing up and eating the crop.

The first small-scale commercial mussel-raising project on the East Coast has been started: Abandoned Farms in Walpole, Maine. Its owner, Ed Myers, cautions at this writing that the operation is still pretty much experimental. If you have access to a saltwater mooring, and you'd like to grow some of your meals in a backyard marine garden, saltwater mussels may be a good place to start. Start-up equipment needed is inexpensive: all it takes is old tires, filled with urethane or Styrofoam for buoyancy, with ropes dangling down in the water from them, says Myers. Free-floating larval mussels then settle on the ropes in April to form shells and mature. Unlike raft-cultured oysters, mussels will do well in the open ocean with the tires attached to buoys.

The key to growing mussels fast and large is not allowing too many to cluster on the rope or other mooring. In the wild, a mussel takes seven years to mature, but Myers can produce mature mussels in only fifteen months. The ropes are lifted from the water at regular intervals and their contents are washed and sized. One-inch mussels are transferred to plastic trays and resubmerged until they reach marketable size—about 2½ inches long.

To avoid predators and keep the mussels clean, the ropes must not be allowed to touch bottom. Starfish and crabs—major mussel predators—can't reach mussels on a suspended rope.

Maintenance demands of mussel culture are minimal—Myers says you can get by checking them only four times a year. The more you thin the mussels and prune the seaweed, the faster they grow.

Oyster

Oysters Oysters are nearly as much a domesticated animal as chickens and sheep, especially in Japan and elsewhere where they have been cultured for centuries. Oyster raising can be practical for anyone with access to a protected body of moving saltwater or brackish water because you can buy seed oysters, or even larger yearlings to feed to maturity.

For Ingram Richardson on the southern coast of Maine, raising oysters on 2-by-4-foot wooden trays with hardware cloth bottoms is an interesting hobby. The first few months the seed oysters keep him busy, as they must be changed to larger trays as they grow. Getting a good flow of plankton-rich water around the oysters is important for maximum growth, so the larger the mesh the better. Beginners are advised to start small, with three hundred yearling oysters and a few trays to raise them in, which by 1977 prices will cost about $20, say Steve Smyser and Tom Gettings in *Organic Gardening and Farming* ® magazine. Then suspend the trays 4 to

117

Ingram Richardson raises oysters on trays suspended in water off the coast of Maine.

5 feet below a mooring, out of sunlight to discourage the growth of seaweed. In a year or two, the oysters will be ready for shucking.

Most commercial oysters, at least in the U.S., are grown on beds rather than on stakes, trays, or ropes. Production has been declining for a number of reasons, not the least of which is pollution. To combat the decline, marine biologists are constantly seeding new, natural beds or renewing old ones. Seed oysters are planted on hard beds at the rate of about two hundred bushels per hectare in shallow water. As these oysters grow, they are picked up and redistributed over larger areas. By redistributing oysters five times in the first year, the original two hundred bushels will (hopefully) increase to two thousand bushels and, by the end of three years, to four thousand bushels.

Farming the oysters entails little other work. Silt settling on the oysters may smother some or prevent them from feeding properly. The redistribution helps to alleviate that problem. The predators of oysters, the oyster drill and the starfish, become troublesome but they can be controlled—at least so far in experiments—by burying them with an underwater implement that looks very much like an offset disk.

Oyster farming in Brittany is very much a family, homestead operation, or at least it has been in the past. Production is reminiscent of cattle feeding. Oyster farmers "herd" the oysters about on the shallow beds or "parcs," as they are called, so that each has room to grow and proper space to maintain a food supply. The moving also keeps silt from covering them. At a certain age, the oysters are moved out to deeper water for two years, then back to the parcs where they are fattened especially for the half-shell market. The process may take 4½ years and may end with a short stay in special small marsh ponds for finishing—a process called "greening."

Shrimp
Shrimp farming in artificial pools is progressing faster than other forms of crustacean aquaculture. Totally closed systems of shrimp culture are commercially practical in Japan where shrimp prices are astronomically high. Some commercial success has been achieved in the United States. Problems are many and complex but are so indicative of what the aquaculturist (even the hobby variety) faces in raising marine animals in a totally artificial environment, that the processes deserve more than passing attention from seaside homesteaders.

In natural bodies of water, shrimp have been corralled and raised to maturity in tidal ponds for generations—even centuries in some countries. Malaysian production methods are typical. Malaysians build earthen dikes around tidal ponds, with screened sluice gates to control water level and prevent trapped shrimp from escaping. In most such pools, the shrimp eat only what natural food is carried in with the seawater, but additional feeding can also be practiced to speed growth. Shrimp eat clam meat and various algaes.

If you have access to such a tidal pool (or could even make a very small, screened holding pen) but no shrimp, you might be able

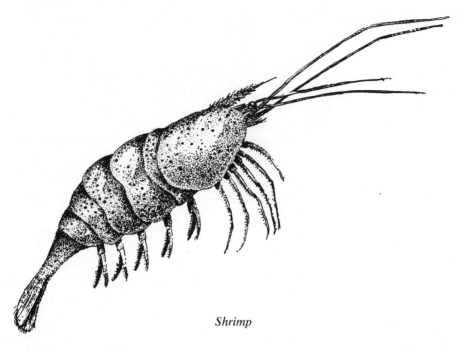

Shrimp

to purchase gravid females from commercial fishermen and let the shrimp spawn in your pool. Juvenile shrimp may also be purchased from southern fisheries.

Scallops

The scallop has been called a prime cash crop in New England coastal shallows, but it might more appropriately be called a prime source of sideline income and gourmet sustenance for seaside families. The season begins in mid-autumn and is keenly anticipated by those who know good food. A home license allows you to harvest a bushel a week and the hunting is closely watched by special wardens who make sure little cheating occurs.

A scallop hunter uses a scallop dredge to collect the tasty morsels. The dredge is sort of a rake with a little basket on top of the tines. You can use a dip net or a quahog rake, too. Stick a knife just in front of the shell hinge to pry it open. Only the abductor muscle is eaten, but the shell and entrails make good fertilizer. A bushel of shells yields about a gallon, or 9 pounds, of meat.

Atlantic Bay Scallop

THE DIAMONDBACK TERRAPIN

The diamondback straddles the fence between being a marine animal and a freshwater animal. Its natural home is along the inner estuaries of the tidal wetlands where the salty water and the fresh mingle. Sometimes it has been spotted even farther upstream, but

Diamondback Terrapin

121

nevertheless, it is a decidedly coastal turtle and a decidedly eastern-coast native at that.

The diamondback so delighted the palates of nineteenth- and twentieth-century Americans that it was hunted nearly to extinction, and is only now making a slow comeback. The reason the turtle is of interest to backyard aquaculture is that in the heyday of its popularity in restaurants, extensive and somewhat successful turtle farms were established by the Bureau of Fisheries and at least several businessmen. Data concerning these ventures was published by the Bureau of Fisheries (Department of Commerce) in government bulletins and circulars, particularly during the 1920s, and it is from this source that I glean the following information.

There are (or at least were) five varieties of the diamondback: The Carolina terrapin (*Malaclemys centrata*) with a range extending from central North Carolina to Florida; the Chesapeake terrapin (*M. centrata concentrica*), which occurs in the Chesapeake Bay and southward to the North Carolina Sounds; the Florida terrapin (*M. pileata macrosopilota*), along the Gulf Coast; the Louisiana terrapin (*M. pileata pileata*), which inhabits the coast from the mouth of the Mississippi to Florida; and the Texas terrapin (*M. pileata littoralis*), along the coasts of Texas and outlying islands. The Carolina terrapin—and when it was gone, the Chesapeake terrapin—were the two turtles best known to gourmets, but only the Carolina and the Texas were used in the aquacultural experiments carried on at Beaufort, North Carolina. "However," wrote Samuel F. Hildebrand and Charles Hatsel in 1926, "it is believed that results would have been essentially the same with other varieties, and we know of no reason why terrapins could not be bred in many localities along the Atlantic and Gulf coasts of the United States."

Starting in 1902, the Bureau of Fisheries began to build what it called "turtle pounds" to rear the diamondbacks in captivity, since it was already apparent that the animal was doomed to near-extinction. By 1926, thousands of turtles had been raised to maturity, but as years passed, high costs, high labor, and a general lack of interest on the part of consumers to pay the high prices that had prevailed earlier, led to a decline until finally turtles were held only as a precaution in order to reseed wild stocks in case total extinction became a genuine possibility.

A coastal homesteader would find the design and methods of

the turtle pounds most interesting indeed. If and when breeding stock becomes available again, there is little doubt that a casual, backyard operation would be most successful, since most of the problems incurred in raising diamondbacks (as is true of most aquacultural ventures) come from the necessity of intensifying production by crowding the animals in much denser populations than nature intended, in order to make a profit.

For commercial production of terrapins, you need a suitable enclosure to hold and feed adults, including a safe place for females to lay their eggs. Second, you need another growing pen for young terrapins. Third, you need a building that can be heated during the winter months, if you want the turtles to grow faster than they would in nature. Most of the disease problems experienced by commercial terrapin producers occurred as a result of this warm-weather environment in winter, so the homesteader would probably be wise to dispense with it in favor of a longer feeding-out period. Once you have the system producing annually, you'd have turtles to eat every year anyway. All you lose is a year during the start-up period.

The ideal turtle pen, or pound, is built on a well-protected, gentle sloping shore of sand or mixed sand and clay, where tidewater brings in an abundant supply of unpolluted saltwater or brackish water. Ideal situations, however, rarely exist, so you will have to make use of the location that best approaches that ideal. (See the plan for the enclosure and the construction details.)

The pen's enclosure must be built so that tidewater covers the floor of the pen at least at high tide *except* for that part of the sand bed reserved for egg-laying. At low tide there should be water over only part of the floor space. What you are after is some dry land part of the day, but some water all the time. This arrangement forces the females to seek the higher sand bed to lay eggs in, and provides both sunning and swimming and a winter hibernation bed.

Locate the outside or seaward wall of the pound slightly above mean low water so that some water is retained in the pen at all times. Put a pipe through the wall at the low water mark so that the pen can be drained completely once a year for thorough cleaning. If not cleaned this way every year, warned the Bureau of Fisheries, the pen becomes unsanitary. The pipe, of course, is plugged between drain-outs. To clean, rake the sediment and turtle wastes to the low end and shovel out. Makes excellent fertilizer.

CROSS SECTION

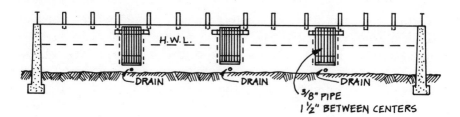

H.W.L.

DRAIN   DRAIN   DRAIN

3/8" PIPE
1 1/2" BETWEEN CENTERS

LONGITUDINAL SECTION

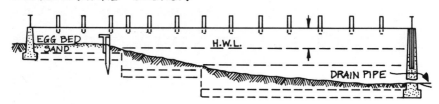

EGG BED
SAND

H.W.L.

DRAIN PIPE

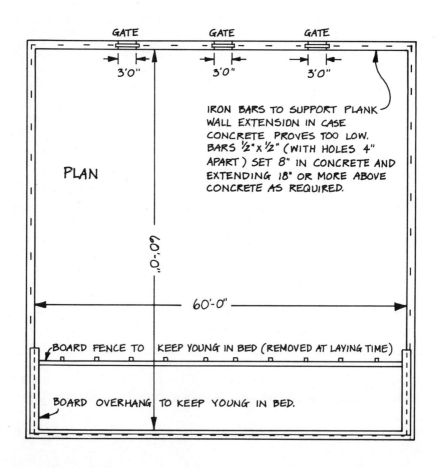

GATE   GATE   GATE

3'0"   3'0"   3'0"

IRON BARS TO SUPPORT PLANK
WALL EXTENSION IN CASE
CONCRETE PROVES TOO LOW.
BARS 1/2" x 1/2" (WITH HOLES 4"
APART) SET 8" IN CONCRETE AND
EXTENDING 18" OR MORE ABOVE
CONCRETE AS REQUIRED.

PLAN

60'-0"

60'-0"

BOARD FENCE TO KEEP YOUNG IN BED (REMOVED AT LAYING TIME)

BOARD OVERHANG TO KEEP YOUNG IN BED.

Plan for Terrapin Pound

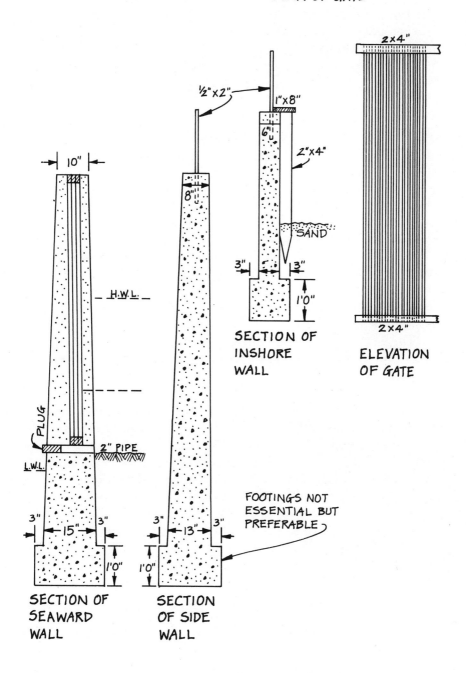

3'-0"

PLAN OF GATE

½"x2"

1"x8"

6"

2"x4"

8"

SAND

3"   3"

1'0"

SECTION OF
INSHORE
WALL

2x4"

2x4"

ELEVATION
OF GATE

10"

H.W.L.

PLUG

2" PIPE

L.W.L.

3"   15"   3"

1'0"

SECTION OF
SEAWARD
WALL

3"   13"   3"

1'0"

SECTION
OF SIDE
WALL

FOOTINGS NOT
ESSENTIAL BUT
PREFERABLE

For commercial production, the Beaufort researchers allowed approximately 5 square feet for each adult terrapin and about half a square foot for each young one. If parallel experience with farm livestock is any indication (and I think it is), the homesteader should double (at least) that space requirement if he wants to avoid health problems cheaply. If a pen 60 feet square will comfortably accommodate 720 adult turtles and several times as many young ones, as the Beaufort researchers said, then you'd be best advised to keep less than half that many in the same space. That's still more turtles than a homesteader is going to have time to tend. Indeed, the happy ending to the story I'd hope for, is that the homesteader would set free at least half of the young ones for restocking the wild. That's the only way I could justify eating any of our slow-growing but marvelously desirable turtle species.

On the other hand, you can't afford to let a hole develop in your pen or you will lose turtles in a hurry, as any boy knows who has tried to keep one for a pet. Best to build walls of concrete or masonry, as wood rots or is attacked by shipworms and soon must be replaced. Inside walls, however, can be made of wood, as, for example, divider walls between adults and juveniles. There's advantage in being able to move dividers depending on relative populations of adults to juveniles. All walls must be high enough to overtop the highest tides by at least 3 feet and strong enough to resist any waves.

The seaward wall, if built of concrete, should be about 15 inches at the base, tapering to 10 inches at the top, and sunk into the ground deep enough to reach a fairly solid bottom. The side walls need to be about 13 inches thick at the base and 8 inches at the top. The inshore wall can be a straight wall, no more than 6 inches thick and just tall enough so the turtles can't get over it.

A pound with a seaward wall 60 feet long needs about three water gates, each about 3 feet wide (see illustration) and just high enough in the solid wall to allow for inflow and outflow of water without draining all the water out at low tide. At Beaufort, it was found difficult to determine exactly how high to build the wall under the gates in order to retain that desired amount of water at low tide. Researchers advised not making the wall too high in the beginning, then adding to it if necessary after the rest of the pound is completed.

The gates are built of iron bars. At Beaufort, a 2-by-4-inch board of the proper length was set upright in the concrete on each side of the gate with the broad sides exposed. Two 2-by-4-inch crossbars are placed at some convenient distance (12 to 18 inches) from the top and bottom of the gate. Holes, spaced 1½ inches apart, to accommodate ⅜-inch galvanized iron pipes are bored through the 2-by-4s, then pipes of the proper length are slipped into the holes in the crossbars. (See illustration.) The pipes of such a gate are not close together enough to prevent the escape of very small terrapins, and if such animals are to be held in the pound, the gates must be covered on the inward side with wire screen.

The interior of the pen should be divided into two or preferably three parts, a large area for the adults and two smaller ones for the young. The very young do better if separated from the larger young.

The egg bed in the adult enclosure goes on the shoreward or uphill side. Allow about 1 square foot of clean sand, leveled off and well packed down for each female, the surface about 1 foot above extreme high tide. The bed should slope downward gradually so the turtles have no trouble crawling up on it.

Enclosures for young turtles should be supplied with some water. The wall around them should have a metal sheet or wooden board on top of it, projecting inward 3 or 4 inches like a shelf to keep the turtles from crawling over the wall. Young turtles—to about age three—are very good climbers.

Some fresh water should be supplied to the turtles for drinking.

The Beaufort reseachers believed that natural saltwater ponds could be utilized as pounds at less cost where such ponds existed, though they mention no experiments using natural ponds. All that would be necessary, they said, was to surround the pond with a suitable fence and a screen at the inlet. However, they thought locations on high ground without tidal flow to be entirely unsuited for terrapins.

No covering is required over the pens. Rats killed many turtles at Beaufort and had to be kept out at all costs. Crows killed some turtles, too, and muskrats tried to burrow under the walls, thereby making an escape hole for the turtles.

The cheapest adequate food available at Beaufort for the turtles was fish, chopped into bite-sized chunks. Diamondbacks have relatively weak jaws and can't tear up whole fish very easily.

Blue crabs, fiddlers, and oysters are also good turtle food, but, of course, rather expensive. Records at Beaufort show that 300 pounds of fish were enough food for 100 adult terrapins for a feeding season.

The turtles stop eating at the beginning of colder weather and soon hibernate until spring, though they may emerge temporarily on an uncommonly warm winter day. In the pounds, a large pile of eelgrass was placed in the deepest water, and the turtles crawled under it to hibernate. (Be sure to remove the grass in the spring, or it will foul the water.)

The female lays her eggs in a sort of nest she scoops out of the sand with her hind feet. The hole is about 5 inches deep. After laying the eggs, she covers them with sand, packs it down, and leaves. If the sand becomes too dry, the females may not use it, but just drop their eggs carelessly wherever they happen to be. The laying season is from May through July.

Don't walk on the egg bed. Handling eggs or removing them for hatching elsewhere is very risky and almost always results in decrease in the hatch. If the bed has been made properly, rainwater will drain away and cause no excessive moisture problems. If an unusually high tide covers the eggs for several days, the hatch can be severely reduced.

As soon as possible after the egg-laying season ends, pen the turtles off the bed. A 10- or 12-inch plank set on edge in front of the bed will do the trick. In about nine weeks, eggs will begin to hatch. Young females recently captured may produce only fifteen eggs. Older ones, acclimated to pen life, may lay eighty-five to ninety. The newly hatched turtles are very agile, and if the walls are not enclosed as described above, they will climb over. At corners, they can even climb cement walls. Best to keep them in a small, secure pen away from adults. In a natural environment, they eat very little at this time, if at all, and soon hibernate, emerging in spring in a very weak condition. In the pound they are protected from natural enemies and can be fed adequately when they emerge from hibernation, thus insuring a far greater survival rate than would be the case in the wild.

At the end of the hatching period and before the first hibernation (about the middle of September), the turtle producer must dig over the entire bed and remove all the young that have burrowed into the sand. Digging must be done by hand as tools would injure the little turtles. Dig over every part of the bed to a depth of 6 to 8 inches.

The young are then put into a hibernating box, a bottomless rectangular box with sides 8 to 10 inches high. This frame is sunk into loose sand, usually a bed previously dug over, to a depth of about 6 inches and filled with seaweed. The little terrapins are placed in the frame, and they burrow under the seaweed. Loose boards are laid over the frame with a bit of space between them to allow rainwater to trickle through. You can put fifteen hundred terrapins in a box 4 by 6 feet, according to the Beaufort researchers.

In spring when warm weather arrives, the turtles are taken from the box and put in a special pen and fed. Don't allow excess food to accumulate.

It can take five years or more to grow diamondbacks to butchering size, at which time carapace length should be 5 to 6 inches. It is almost certain that if terrapins were selectively bred over a period of years or centuries the way chickens and hogs have been, that turtles larger than that could be achieved in half that time. But it is the long waiting period before income is possible that has been the principal reason little interest remains today in the diamondback, commercially.

To grow turtles quicker, Beaufort researchers kept them in hothouses over winter and fed them instead of allowing them to hibernate. This tactic produced the same growth in six months as would normally take place in a year. The cost of winter hothouse feeding can be justified only when high demand for turtle meat brings high prices and when feed and heat costs are low, which, of course, is not the case presently.

Only females grow to the larger size; males usually remain smaller and rarely marketable. However, males are in the minority; the sex ratio at Beaufort stayed at around one male for every seven or more females. A rate of one male to twelve to fifteen females in the pound was found to give good fertility.

Terrapins in captivity live a long time and will survive mistreatment amazingly well, said the Beaufort experimenters. Few diseases are troublesome, and those mostly become apparent in the hothouse growing situation. The researchers concluded: "The care of adult terrapins presents very little difficulty, and in suitable localities the cost of feeding is very small. If supplies are reasonably close at hand and the pen well arranged, one man should be able to care for fifty thousand animals easily.''

Feeding young turtles out to butchering age, especially with winter hothouse feeding, was not so easily handled, however, and some disease problems occurred. But from the purely homestead

The Pacific Northwest's salmon ranchers are engaged in a very speculative kind of aquaculture. At Oregon Aqua Foods, where these photos were taken, salmon eggs are hatched, and the week-old smolts are placed in saltwater pools for two to three weeks before being released into the ocean. Salmon always return to their birthplace to spawn, and the Aqua Foods' fish return, are harvested, their eggs extracted, and their bodies sent off to market. Out of every 100 salmon hatched, only two to four survive to become part of the harvest.

point of view, raising turtles for family food and perhaps a little sideline income seems worth a try.

SALTWATER FISH

Commercial marine fish farming endeavors are varied and numerous worldwide, but I will mention here—and only briefly— just a few ideas that seem applicable to the seaside homestead.

In nature, salmon spawn in freshwater, return to the sea to grow to adulthood, then go back to the place of their birth to start another generation. The mature salmon are then mostly too spent and discolored to be marketable. Fish "ranchers" have found, however, that they can take fingerlings from freshwater spawning grounds, and hold them in saltwater ponds or "corrals" along the coast for two or three weeks, and the salmon's homing instinct will reassert itself in favor of its corral. Let loose to "graze" the ocean nearby, the salmon return to the holding pond still in marketable shape. Their eggs are extracted for hatching and the fish sold. But it's still a tough life for salmon, and ranchers figure on no more than two to four mature fish returning per hundred fingerlings let out to the sea.

Marine fish farmers distinguish six types of rearing pens for fish: three enclosure systems and three cage systems. As you can see in the illustration, the main differences between them are their relative positions in the water.

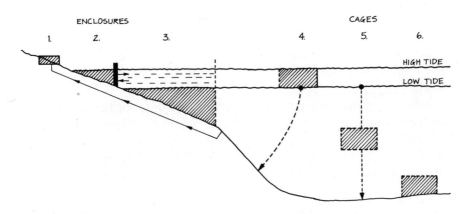

The six possible zones for marine fish farming are: 1. shore, 2. intertidal, 3. sublittoral, 4. surface floating, 5. mid-water, 6. seabed.

131

The Japanese use enclosures, generally sublittoral types made of wire and mesh curtains attached to poles driven into the seabed. The enclosures hold yellowtail fish while they are growing to market size. Fingerling yellowtail are easily caught in the ocean where they move in very large and dense schools.

English and Scottish aquaculturists raise sole and plaice in intertidal enclosures, behind seawalls which close off sea lochs or inlets from the ocean, but with screened sluice gates to let water in and out. James Shelbourne, in a research paper he gave at the aquacultural symposium at Oregon State University in 1970 (the papers from that symposium are printed in *Marine Aquiculture*, by William J. McNeil and published by Oregon State University at Corvallis in 1970), reported the problems of one such enclosure and how the problems were solved. No matter what kind of fish you might try to raise in a coastal enclosure, Shelbourne's report could be pertinent.

High fish mortality followed the first stocking of fish in this British coastal loch, said Shelbourne. There were three principal reasons: (1) decay of intertidal organisms, which had died because the change in the water level in the enclosure robbed fish of needed oxygen; (2) inadequate diversion of freshwater inflow aggravated the shortage of oxygenation by restricting the vertical circulation of deeper and more saline waters; and (3) shore crabs killed too many hatching fish.

To solve these problems, experimenters drained the pond and removed the decaying plant life. The shore crabs were destroyed. The pond bottom was plowed to make it sandier. An aeration system was installed to safeguard against oxygen depletion. And finally, new diversion channels routed fresh water more effectively around the enclosure. Fish were again introduced with minimal fish mortality.

Several kinds of cages have proven adequate for rearing fish in the sea. Those that appear below are recent developments being utilized in Norway as reported by D. Møller of the Institute of Marine Research, Bergen, Norway, at the FAO Technical Conference on Aquaculture held at Kyoto, Japan, in 1976. There are many other designs, but these should give the seaside homesteader some familiarity with the engineering involved and perhaps an idea or two on building his own.

The Floating Net Cage is of most interest to homestead

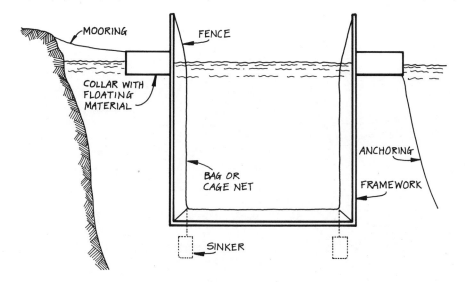

Floating Net Cage

aquaculturists because it is adaptable to the smallest hobby pen as well as to a large commercial project. Units can be any size, and commonly consist of a framework for the net and some kind of flotation unit. Empty barrels, Styrofoam, plastic and metal pontoons all can be used for flotation. These can be built into a framework large enough to bear a man's weight or can amount to no more than moored buoys with an unattached net bag tied to them. Galvanized metal, aluminum, wood impregnated with preservative, or bamboo hold up well in seawater for framework material. Nylon and weldmesh are both used for netting.

The Octagonal Cage developed by fishery adviser Ingar Holberg in Norway is a popular cage in that country and has proven its worth after years of use in raising trout and Atlantic salmon. The collar of the cage is octagonal in shape, composed of eight units each 16.4 feet long. Depth of the net is about 13 feet. Volume is 17,500 cubic feet.

The bearing frame is constructed of 2-by-6-inch preservative-treated planks with blocks of Styrofoam for flotation. One-by-3-inch boards nailed to the top and bottom of the frame keep the Styrofoam blocks in place. The top crossbars are about 1⅛ inches longer than the bottom side crossbars, extending outside the

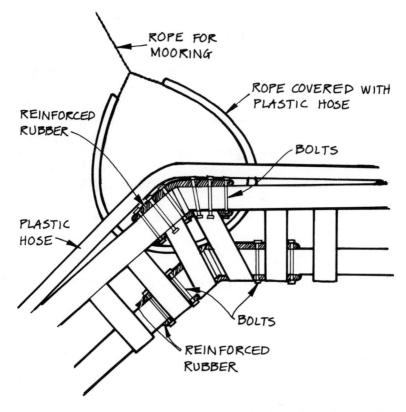

ROPE FOR
MOORING

ROPE COVERED WITH
PLASTIC HOSE

REINFORCED
RUBBER

BOLTS

PLASTIC
HOSE

BOLTS

REINFORCED
RUBBER

outermost edge of the frame so as to hold a 2-by-2-inch board used
to fasten the net.

The units are held together by reinforced rubber (pieces of
conveyor belt or tires will work, says Møller). Look at the
drawings. "Four pieces of rubber are used in each corner,"
reported Møller, "fastened to the planks with ¾-by-3½-inch galvanized bolts. The collar is also reinforced by a wire inside a 2-inch
plastic hose nailed around the lower part of the outer side. The
plastic hose prevents net wear. For mooring, loops of nylon rope
inside a 2-inch plastic hose are threaded through holes in the planks
of adjoining units. The nylon net bag which is made to fit the collar
is laced to the lath around the rim and stretched vertically by
sinkers. Inside the collar, four 2-by-2-inch boards each about 4 feet
long are nailed to each of the eight units. Nylon net is stretched
between the laths to act as a barrier against leaping fish. The net
should be slack in the corners to allow movements of the collar."

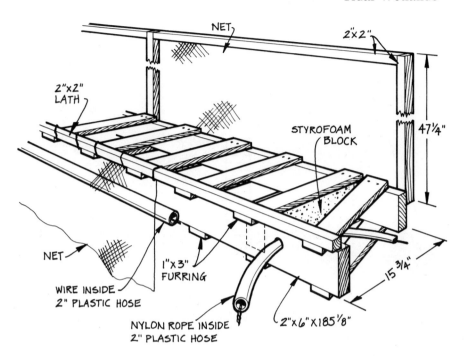

NET

2"x2"

2"x2" LATH

STYROFOAM BLOCK

47¼"

NET

1"x3" FURRING

WIRE INSIDE 2" PLASTIC HOSE

15¾"

NYLON ROPE INSIDE 2" PLASTIC HOSE

2"x6"x185⅛"

Octagonal Cage

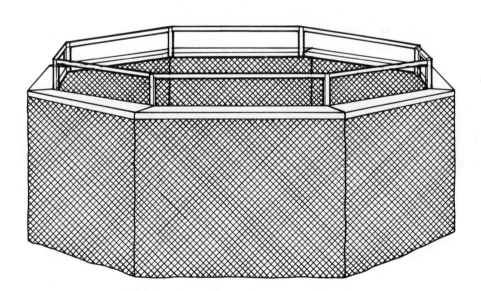

135

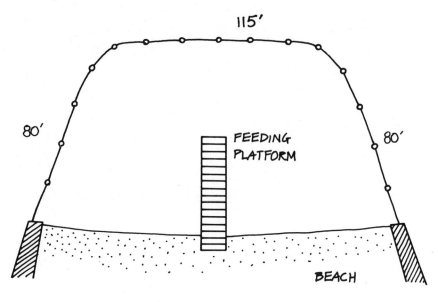

TOP VIEW

The *Osland Enclosure* developed by fish farmer Erling Osland in Norway needs a sloping shore. The water ought to be about 32 feet deep about 80 feet from the shoreline, Møller reported. Concrete or timber dock piles are driven into the seabed forming a square or horseshoe shape of about 80 by 115 feet (see illustration). The piles must rise above the water level at spring tide. A concrete wall at the shoreline moors the net.

"Two nets are stretched along the piles, one on the inside to hold reared fish in and one on the outside to ward off driftwood and keep away predatory fish," Møller explained. "Nets are reinforced by a headline, a midline, and a leadline. The headline is connected to the pile with a crossbar and the midline to the bottom end of the pile. The net between the midline and the leadline lies on the bottom stretched out without any additional hold. In this way, the inside and outside nets are attached on each side of the piles. making a barrier for confined fish.

"The nets are controlled or exchanged with the help of hauling ropes which also protect the nets against wear by providing clearance between piles and nets (see illustration). When the enclosure is in use, the connection between the midline and the

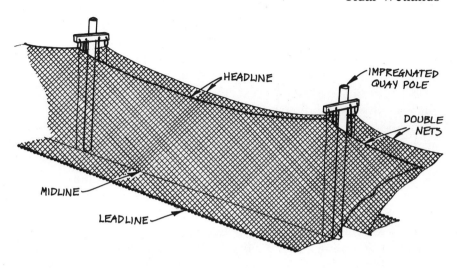

Osland Enclosure

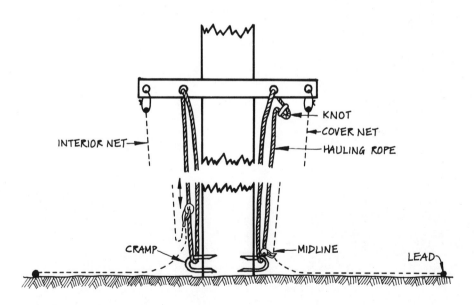

hauling rope is in low position to the cramp and the hauling rope is knotted to secure that position. By loosening the knot and hauling the rope, the midline with the net can be inspected at the surface," Møller concluded.

Getting Food from Water

A complete, commercial fish farm in coastal seawater is a complex affair, construction of which demands extensive knowledge of both engineering and aquaculture. In selecting a site, a fish farmer gives consideration to favorable ground elevation, soil types, type and density of vegetation, stability of shore banks, vulnerability to flooding, physical obstructions, and weather, not to mention social and economic factors. A complete farm consists of ponds of various kinds and purposes, such as a nursing pond, rearing ponds, and temporary holding ponds. Water-control structures must be built, including embankments, canals, and sluices, along with roads, bridges, culverts, workshop, and farmhouse. All of which is somewhat beyond the scope of this book. For homesteaders wanting an idea or two about fish farm layout, look up a copy of "Planning, Design and Construction of a Coastal Fish Farm," by Y. A. Tang, Department of Fisheries, FAO, Rome, Italy, a report given at the FAO technical conference on aquaculture in Kyoto, Japan, in 1976. It will impress upon anyone the need for professional know-how in designing and building advanced aquacultural structures.

ENJOYING A FARM POND 7

Last winter the ice on our farm pond froze crystal clear, rather than opaque as it usually does. Walking on it seemed magical, even miraculous, like walking on water. On the whole upper half of the pond—the water level was unusually low at the time—we could peer down through the ice and enjoy an unobstructed view of frogs, turtles, and fish, all of them languid with the coming of cold weather, not quite sure what to make of the two-legged creatures they were unaccustomed to seeing directly above them. Children squealed in delight, scarcely believing what they saw a mere two feet from their noses pressed against the ice. It could well be something they will not experience again in their lives.

I think of that crystal-clear ice now as I try to sum up the reasons that make a farm pond such a wonderful place to experience and learn about life. The "common, everyday" occurrences around a pond are so changing and varied as to absorb the curious intellect. But on top of that, every pond watcher is rewarded with the unexpected, the never-repeated, the accidental happenings no book can teach you to anticipate. There was a time, for instance, when my brother-in-law stood quietly on the bank of our pond, watching the sun go down. Suddenly, out of the twilight, a great blue heron glided lower, lower, until it folded its wings and settled softly down right on top of brother-in-law's head! Brother-in-law does not look *exactly* like a pier post, but perhaps the bird had poor eyesight. Ever so slowly, brother-in-law reached up, grabbed the bird by the legs as one would a chicken off the roost, and brought it triumphantly home for all to see. (Incidentally, should this happen to you, I would think twice before handling the bird, if I were you. A great blue heron can use its beak lethally and lightning-fast to stab a man through the eye and into the brain—so say the experts, anyway.)

THE POND AS A RECREATION CENTER

My father built our pond over thirty years ago. It was the center of our family activity as I grew up—and remains so today, when we kids are all grown and have families of our own. "The Pond" is the hub. Summer and winter, it lures us to its side: fishing, swimming, ice skating, trapping, gigging, and, most of all, daydreaming and simply watching. If the water itself loses momentarily its fascination, we become engrossed with the shore—picnics, football, softball, bird-watching, bug collecting, tree planting, berry harvesting, camping, camp fire singing. More than one marriage proposal has been made and accepted on those banks, more than one quarrel forgotten, more than one sorrow consoled.

The food the pond has produced has been incidental to our enjoyment—something that just happens rather than something specifically planned for. Even so, that production is not insignificant, and one can only marvel at the potentialities that exist if any of us would farm the pond the way we manage our gardens.

There have been times when we have pulled over ninety bass from the water in one day—but many days when fishing yielded nothing. There are wild ducks and perhaps a goose now and then to grace our tables, but no one will shoot them in season or out. We all fancy snapping turtle, but when the boys occasionally catch one now, it usually is freed again along the creek or at some other pond. Turtles grow so slowly and until there is sign of an increase in numbers in the wild, we just don't have the heart to eat many of them. Bullfrogs manage to increase enough in population in the pond to provide a meal every other year or so. The carcasses of muskrats trapped in the winter would make fine eating, but we don't eat them. Ditto the roots of the cattails. However, the roots have not spread and become a nuisance since the muskrats (which would be a problem if they were not trapped) eat them for us. From time to time, someone keeps a domestic duck on the pond, but there has been no concerted effort in that direction, either. I have, on occasion, used the algae for mulch in the garden, and, though it works wonderfully well, that, too, has been a hit-or-miss affair. I

The farm pond serves the year-round, offering boating and swimming in summer, skating in winter, and fishing every day of the year.

143

often think that if we would again plant the pasture below the dam to a truck patch, as we did when I was a child before the pond was built, we could irrigate it easily—and mulch some of it—from the pond. Pond water is rich in fertilizer value from the wastes of fish and pondweeds settling on the bottom.

THE POND AS A NATURE CENTER

But so far, we have been content to use the pond for play and the observation of nature. Certainly there are few better ways to grasp the complexities of ecology than by living beside a pond with your eyes open. I think it was baseball's Yogi Berra, who, in commenting on success as a manager, said: "You can observe an awful lot just by watching." So too, in managing a pond.

The first thing you observe is that a pond is not an entity isolated from the land around it. The life of the one receives the life of the other. The two are bound in a marriage that can be fertile or barren, depending entirely on whether nature is allowed to establish an environment there, conducive to life.

You learn, if you work with pond water very long, that it is not all that different from working with soil. Soil has its range of pH—acidity and alkalinity—in which plants grow well. So does water, though its pH influences not only plant growth but that of fish and other water animals as well. Pond water can be fertile or sterile, can be improved for better fish and water-plant growth with fertilizer just as soil can. The water can be treated with chemicals like the soil, with similar results. The only difference is that evidence of poisoning in water will show up much more quickly and more graphically than poison in the soil.

As you watch your pond and the fringe of land surrounding it, there should evolve in your inner vision a scene of seething, roiling, dynamic food production. The pond is an endless, entwined, labyrinthine dining table, at which sits the eating being eaten. That's a barbaric vision, and yet it's the clearest view of what nature means, a view without which ecology remains only a word. To manage a pond wisely (or a garden, or a field, or a community that lives off of the food of that field) you must see that life is not so much a progression from birth to death but a circle of eating and being eaten, the chemicals of one body passing on to form another. Production and consumption are simultaneous, parallel, inextricably joined, and continuous. There is a sense in which a frog can become a charming prince or vice versa, not by a kiss but by the magic of the encircling dining tables of the biological chain of life. And until we can *see* that reality is not beginning and end but eating and being eaten, the cry of the ecological prophets in the desert will not be heeded.

Sit on the bank of your pond and watch. Watch a water lily. A muskrat feeds on its rhizomes. If it eats all the rhizomes there will be none for the next year's muskrats. The muskrat feeds with one eye over its shoulder watching for the mink that would feed on it. A young snapping turtle eats the water lily's leaves. If it makes a mistake and eats too many leaves, the heron will see where it is hiding under the lily and eat the turtle. Sunfish hide among the lilies, too—hiding from the bass—but while they hide, they eat snails that are there eating the algae that is competing with the lily for the nutrients in the wastes dropped by the turtle and muskrat and heron. A frog sits on a lily pad, half-hidden by its camouflage colors and half by other lily pads. The frog doesn't know that the lily pads protect it; it is sitting there waiting to eat the bugs that fly by, attracted by the flowers of the lily.

Watch any organism around the pond and you will see chains of eating and being eaten linking forms of life in all directions. Even those organisms that die a "natural" death (the most unnatural death of all) do not escape the role of victim at a feast, for even in death they become food for hosts of other organisms.

Attached to the pondweed, often in symbiotic relationship to it, are diatoms and blue green algae being eaten by insects, worms, and snails. Ducks and other insects eat the pondweed.

In another area grow filamentous algae. Pupal insects and frog tadpoles eat them. Bass eat the tadpoles. If there are no osprey above, or bears, or men to catch them, the bass may be the climax organisms in the pond. But will that mean too many bass? Seldom. Bass are cannibalistic.

A dragonfly sits on a weed at the edge of the pond. It waits to eat a mosquito. Its larvae in the pond wait to eat mosquito larvae. Fish wait to eat both dragonfly and mosquito larvae.

Bacteria eat decaying organic matter on the pond bottom, and produce ammonia. Other bacteria eat the ammonia and turn it into nitrites. Still other bacteria eat the nitrites and turn them into nitrates. The algae and plankton eat the nitrates and turn them into

A pond's food chain is fueled by the sun. Green plants, which capture and store the sun's energy, are food for a variety of animals that are, in turn, food for larger fish. The fish are eaten by animals, birds, and, yes, aquaculturists. Enough plants and animals die off and decompose on the pond bottom to help generate new turns of the cycle.

plant protein. Minute animals eat the plant proteins; small fish eat the minute animals; large fish, birds, snakes, and raccoons eat the small fish.

The birds overhead derive their protein from the fish and bugs, many of which spent larval stages in the water. The swallow skims the surface of the water, the sparrow flits in the bushes at the shore edge, the redwing sits on a low branch over the water, a waxwing flutters above it, a wood duck floats on it, a flycatcher darts out over it, and a kingfisher dives into it.

You could spend a lifetime just studying the plants in your

pond. Each has its characteristic place in the pond: cattails and bulrushes in the shallowest water; hornwort and stonewort completely under water; floating leaf plants, like the emergent water lilies, on the surface of the water.

Scientists divide a pond into zones defined by water depth. The *littoral* zone encompasses the area where sunlight penetrates to the bottom in sufficient intensity to permit vegetative growth; the *limnetic* zone is the middle range of water between the littoral and the *profundal,* the deep, dark center water. Most farm ponds have only littoral and limnetic. Each zone has its characteristic animals as well as plants. The large fish lurk most of the time in the deepest waters, minnows dart in the shallows. Clams walk the bottom of the pond. Some insect larvae only drift in the water. Water striders run on the surface. Grasshoppers jump in, by mistake, and often pay for the error with their lives.

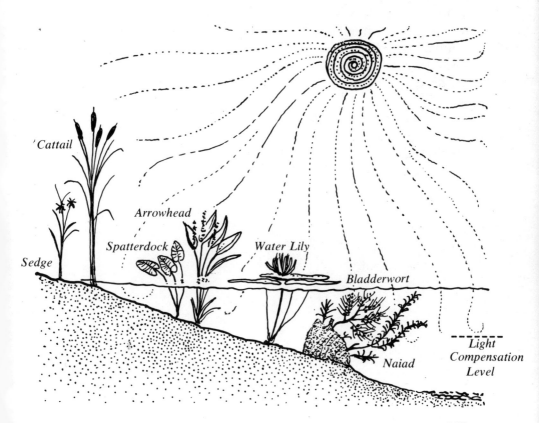

Cattail

Sedge

Arrowhead

Spatterdock

Water Lily

Bladderwort

Naiad

Light Compensation Level

No two ponds are alike. No two years at the same pond are alike. One year you notice a population imbalance of one organism, which no sooner rights itself than another pops up the next year. Weather, disease, the intervention of man keep worrying the stability nature seeks. And the pond ages, like any living organism.

The pond can be seen as a microcosm of nature, but it must be seen also as an integral piece of the larger hydrologic pattern. The pond helps stabilize the hydrological cycle; if *enough* ponds were built, they could become the savior of the hydrologic cycle, and we might achieve something at least close to a geological paradise. The pond is, first of all, a storer of water. When rainwater is prevented from running off the land immediately after a rain, that water is saved for use later on. It slows the process by which humid regions become arid regions. Whether water sinks into the ground directly, whether it is held in ponds to sink more slowly into the ground or to be evaporated back up into the sky to fall again, more water has a chance of doing what it is supposed to do *where it falls*, which is to preserve the humid conditions for life. Just as important, by not running wastefully away, it also is not carrying billions of tons of topsoil wastefully away with it. And furthermore, the more ponds in the upper parts of a watershed, the less flood damage lower down.

There are two kinds of monuments *you* can build to your memory and the richest king can do no better: one is a pond and the other is a forest grove. Build the one and plant the other around it. Make your own little garden of Eden.

BUILDING A POND 8

I have worked for the Soil Conservation Service—the government agency charged with the responsibility of helping landowners design and build ponds correctly—and I have worked for private contractors who do the actual pond building. Some of them are very good and some are only fair to middlin' and all of them can make mistakes. But unless you have built ponds yourself, you are safer even with the fair to middlin' than striking out alone. Seek the counsel of as many people as you can. Whose advice to follow is a decision you have to make yourself. Success at that is, of course, the secret of life.

The whole question may be academic in your area because some states require a permit of some sort from a certified agency before you can build a pond. As a starting point, the safest route to follow is to contact your local Soil Conservation Service office. SCS advice is free if you agree to follow a conservation plan on your land, which any good homesteader will be doing anyway. Of course, advice and planning by a building contractor is usually "free" too—he adds his time in consulting and planning to his earth-moving bill. What usually happens is that the SCS personnel and the builder get into a few good arguments, if they are worth their salt. You may have to weigh both sides and settle the question, or pray that the best man wins. But generally, SCS planners and designers have worked with the pond builders before, and each knows what the other wants to achieve, and things work out for the best. At any rate, your local SCS office has plenty of reading material on pond construction that you should look at *before* you build.

CONSIDER YOUR CLIMATE AND GEOLOGY

Deciding how—or even if—to build a pond depends mostly on the geology and weather of your region. Soil must be of the right admixture of clay, sand, and silt to hold water, and you must have enough water available from rain runoff, springs, or other sources to keep the pond adequately filled.

Clay and silty clay soil are usually best for holding water with a minimum of seepage, says the Soil Conservation Service. (All man-made ponds seep a little.) Sandy clay is usually suitable too. Sand and gravel are not suitable, though some sandy soils can be sealed with a topping of clay or with commercial materials. Sealing a leaky pond can be expensive and may not be worthwhile. Here's where a soil technician can help you, especially one who has no financial interest in your pond. He may tell you to forget the whole idea, which, in gravelly locations, is exactly the right thing to do. Also, where there are sinkholes or crevices in bedrock, a pond may suddenly drain as fast as a bathtub when you pull the plug.

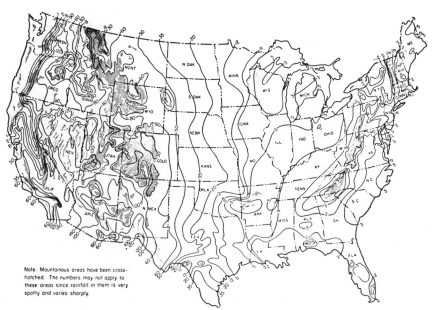

Note. Mountainous areas have been cross-hatched. The numbers may not apply to these areas since rainfall in them is very spotty and varies sharply.

Approximate acreage required in the drainage area for each acre-foot of water stored in an embankment or excavated pond.

Assuming the soil will hold water well enough to make a pond practical, your next question is: Where will the water come from? If from rain, then you must be sure that the run-off area feeding your pond is large enough to supply sufficient water, but not too large. Recommended acreage in a watershed varies with the amount of annual rainfall. SCS also has a sophisticated way to figure what the twenty-five- to fifty-year peak storm runoff will be for every area—a figure you need to know to make sure your emergency spillway is designed large enough to handle the heaviest rain. If the water source is a spring or other groundwater aquifer, spring-flow can be measured (see chapter 2) to find out if more water comes in than goes out from seepage and evaporation. If the water is to be used for irrigation, home supply, or stock water, these uses will have to be figured into the final design determination. Most farm ponds are not very practical for spray irrigation, since they are not big enough to supply much water, and have their lowest water level during the driest time of the year, when irrigation may be necessary. However, with drip irrigation methods, which use a smaller volume of water, even a small farm pond can supply sufficient amounts to an orchard, or berry or vegetable garden of several acres.

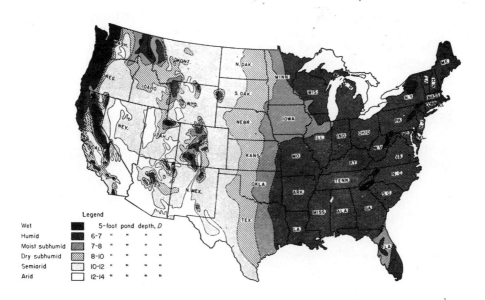

Recommended minimum depth of water for ponds in the United States.

153

Small ponds (quarter-acre) not fed by runoff or springs can be pumped full of water from wells and kept full by falling rain, and perhaps an occasional pumping, if seepage is minimal. I know one very small pond that stays adequately filled from water off the roof of a nearby barn.

Weather dictates another design feature of your pond. If you intend to keep fish in it permanently, your pond should be at least 8 feet deep in the deepest part to provide sufficient water during bad droughts and deep freezes. For a dependable water supply, pond depths depend on the amount of precipitation; the more humid the region, the shallower the pond needs to be, to a minimum of 5 feet. Ponds can be shallower in the humid South, but where trout are kept in spring-fed ponds, deeper water than that usually recommended may be necessary to insure the trout of enough cool (50 to 60 degrees F, 10 to 15.5 degrees C) water for good growth.

One more design criterion may be more a matter of your geological situation than choice, and that is whether to build an embankment pond or an excavated pond. An embankment pond is one formed by an artificial dam constructed between two hills across a more or less narrow ravine or draw, blocking surface water running off after rain. An excavated pond is a hole in the ground, usually dug out with a dragline. Where there are no convenient hills and small valleys for a good site, a dug or excavated pond is the only kind you can build. This type is usually found in regions of level or nearly level terrain. Water source may be either from runoff or from ground aquifers or a combination of both. An embankment pond may be, and usually is, partially excavated too, so that the pond edges and the upper end of the pond are deep enough to limit weed growth.

When choosing a pond site, pay particular attention to the fields that drain into your pond. Ideally, this area will be in grass and/or woodland. If intensely cultivated, the soil will wash into your pond and pollute it with sediment and agricultural chemicals.

Where run-off surface water is polluted, an excavated pond can be built in such a way that embankments keep such water out of the pond. Some ponds—where terrain slopes enough to get the proper fall—are filled only by water from field-drainage tiles. Since such water has filtered down through the soil into the tile before coming to the pond, it is cleaner than surface water.

CONSIDER YOUR PURPOSE

So now you have determined that you have the right soil and the right kind of pond design for your terrain and weather. Your next question—which was really the one you asked and answered when you first decided to build a pond—is this: What is the purpose of the pond? Why do I want a pond? Almost always, I'm sure, you have a number of reasons in mind, and you want your pond to serve them all. But list your reasons anyway, in order of priority.

Some folks build a pond because they want a swimming pool. They try to turn the pond into a swimming pool, which costs more money than building an in-ground concrete pool in the first place. Not that you can't have many hours of safe and pleasurable swimming in a farm pond. You can, but it is not going to measure up to the seashore or the municipal pool. A farm pond will have turtles and frogs and spiders and leeches and all manner of creepy-crawly things to send the Beverly Hills bikini types screaming to the bathhouse never more to roam from their patio pools.

A farm pond has mud on the bottom. Trying to cover that mud with gravel and sand, turning the pond into Miami Beach, is the pond-owner's version of the Impossible Dream. I know one such owner who tried—*really* tried, because he owned a stone quarry and a fleet of trucks. Ton upon ton of sand he dumped upon his farm-pond "beach." It oozed and washed he knows not where in hardly a year of heavy rains. Not to be outdone, he dug out the muddy earth of the shoreline and replaced it with pea gravel and sand, and poured more of the same into the water so one might wade out to the deepest part without sinking into mud. Still, the water did not sparkle. Then he got his back up. American technology would not be denied. Truckload upon truckload of crushed stone he dumped into the pond and onto the shore. To keep water weeds and algae and other living things out, he also poured on the chemicals. Now he has something that looks a little bit like a swimming pool and a little bit like a pond but not a whole lot like either. In early summer the water is beautifully clear—as it is in most healthy farm ponds anyway. In late summer the water is not so clear—as it is not in less sterilized ponds. And the owner admits the money might have been better spent going to Acapulco.

155

But the idea may make a practical swimming pool if you think small enough. A very small pond might be beached, or at least stoned, if you don't expect more service from the beach than from a glorified child's sandbox. We *cemented* a very small section of shore on our pond so the toddlers could play in the water without sinking to their ears in mud. The sand piled above that concrete section is just that—a sandbox for the kids.

If your purpose is raising fish, you may want to design a pond for commercial production purposes. If you intend to go into the fee-fishing business, you will design parking lots and other facilities into the plan. If irrigation is your main purpose, size of the pond could be very important. If you want a pool just for the fun of being part of its ecology and to raise lots of food for your family, I would urge you to build a smaller rather than a larger pond. An acre is plenty, and in many cases a quarter- to a half-acre, or even smaller, is better. The reason is that the smaller the pond, the easier you can control weed, fish, and other populations without chemicals— which, as we will see, are no more satisfactory in the pond than in the garden.

My own criterion for pond size is simple: It has to be large enough to play hockey on. And at my age that doesn't necessarily mean a standard-size rink.

Even if the main purpose of your pond is water for livestock, you will hardly ever want cattle, and certainly not hogs, to have direct access to the water. They will ruin the shoreline and muddy the water. A pipe carrying water by gravity, as shown, to a watering trough below the dam is a better way. Incidentally, that same kind of gravity-feed system could feed a drip irrigation system if a garden or orchard were established below the pond.

CONSIDER THE DESIGN

The illustration gives you an excellent schematic view of what the perfect embankment pond should look like. There is an engineering reason for everything you see there except maybe the boat. The embankment, or dam itself, has a core fill and a cut-off trench that together keep water from seeping too much under or through the dam. If you just heaped up a dirt pile, water would find its way through and the dam would leak excessively and fail eventually. When you hear pond designers or builders use the term

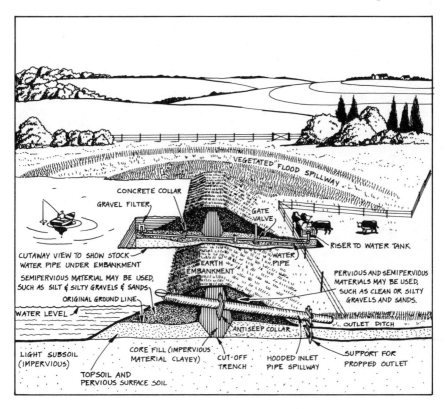

CONCRETE COLLAR
GRAVEL FILTER
GATE VALVE
VEGETATED FLOOD SPILLWAY
RISER TO WATER TANK
CUTAWAY VIEW TO SHOW STOCK-WATER PIPE UNDER EMBANKMENT
WATER PIPE
EARTH EMBANKMENT
SEMIPERVIOUS MATERIAL MAY BE USED, SUCH AS SILT & SILTY GRAVELS & SANDS
PERVIOUS AND SEMIPERVIOUS MATERIALS MAY BE USED, SUCH AS CLEAN OR SILTY GRAVELS AND SANDS.
ORIGINAL GROUND LINE
WATER LEVEL
OUTLET DITCH
LIGHT SUBSOIL (IMPERVIOUS)
CORE FILL (IMPERVIOUS MATERIAL CLAYEY)
CUT-OFF TRENCH
ANTISEEP COLLAR
HOODED INLET PIPE SPILLWAY
SUPPORT FOR PROPPED OUTLET
TOPSOIL AND PERVIOUS SURFACE SOIL

"dam failure," they mean the dam washes away. If not built right and, say, a muskrat digs a hole through the dam, the water will quickly follow and enlarge the hole, turn the hole into a gaping gully and, in less time than it takes to say "minimum design criteria," the pond is empty.

Make the dam large enough to drive over with tractor and mower. If the height of the dam is 10 feet or less, top width should be 8 feet minimum. If the height is 11 to 15 feet, top width should be 10 feet minimum. If height is 15 to 20 feet, make the top width 12 feet.

Builders know all about core fills and how the clay has to be moist or it won't pack right. If they don't, you're in trouble.

Back slope of the dam should be gradual enough so you can mow without upsetting—a 2-to-1 slope at most on clay soils and 3- or 4-to-1 on sandy soils more inclined to slide or wash. The bank on the pond side should be sloped 3-to-1.

CROSS SECTION OF DAM

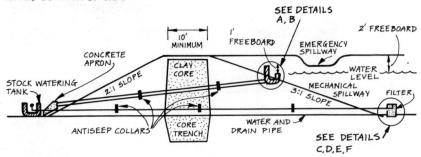

SEE DETAILS A, B

2' FREEBOARD

EMERGENCY SPILLWAY

1' FREEBOARD

10' MINIMUM

CONCRETE APRON

CLAY CORE

WATER LEVEL

STOCK WATERING TANK

2:1 SLOPE

MECHANICAL SPILLWAY

FILTER

3:1 SLOPE

ANTISEEP COLLARS

CORE TRENCH

WATER AND DRAIN PIPE

SEE DETAILS C, D, E, F

TOP VIEW OF DAM

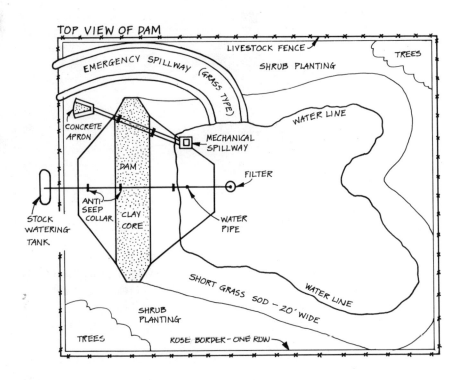

LIVESTOCK FENCE

TREES

SHRUB PLANTING

EMERGENCY SPILLWAY (GRASS TYPE)

WATER LINE

CONCRETE APRON

MECHANICAL SPILLWAY

FILTER

DAM

ANTI-SEEP COLLAR

CLAY CORE

WATER PIPE

STOCK WATERING TANK

SHORT GRASS SOD - 20' WIDE

WATER LINE

SHRUB PLANTING

TREES

ROSE BORDER - ONE ROW

DETAIL A

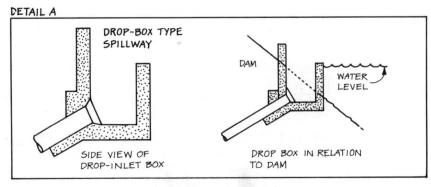

DROP-BOX TYPE SPILLWAY

DAM

WATER LEVEL

SIDE VIEW OF DROP-INLET BOX

DROP BOX IN RELATION TO DAM

DETAIL B

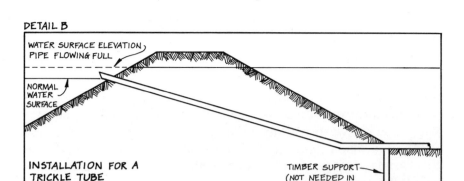

WATER SURFACE ELEVATION
PIPE FLOWING FULL

NORMAL
WATER
SURFACE

INSTALLATION FOR A
TRICKLE TUBE

TIMBER SUPPORT
(NOT NEEDED IN
STABLE SOIL)

DETAIL C

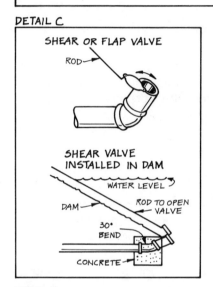

SHEAR OR FLAP VALVE

ROD

SHEAR VALVE
INSTALLED IN DAM

WATER LEVEL

DAM

ROD TO OPEN
VALVE

30° BEND

CONCRETE

DETAIL D

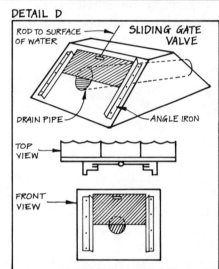

ROD TO SURFACE
OF WATER

SLIDING GATE
VALVE

DRAIN PIPE

ANGLE IRON

TOP
VIEW

FRONT
VIEW

DETAIL E

STAND
PIPE

CAN ACT AS
TRICKLE TUBE
OR SPILLWAY

STAND PIPE DRAIN
TO DRAIN, UNSCREW STAND
PIPE OR TURN PIPE DOWN

DAM

ANTISEEP
COLLAR

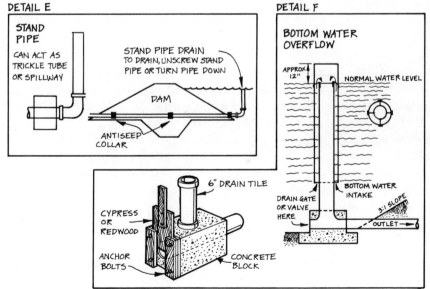

6" DRAIN TILE

CYPRESS
OR
REDWOOD

ANCHOR
BOLTS

CONCRETE
BLOCK

DETAIL F

BOTTOM WATER
OVERFLOW

APPROX
12"

NORMAL WATER LEVEL

BOTTOM WATER
INTAKE

DRAIN GATE
OR VALVE
HERE

3:1 SLOPE

OUTLET

The next most important part of the picture on page 157 is the flood spillway at the upper end of the dam. This is also called an emergency spillway. Its role is to keep excess water, in times of heavy runoff, from going over the dam. Water going over the dam would quickly wash it away. The spillway is kept sodded and is built with a much more gentle grade than the dam, so water can flow harmlessly down it. Sometimes spillways wash out a little and have to be repaired.

Usually on small ponds, a spillway 10 feet wide will be adequate, with a crest 3 feet lower than the top of the dam. But you need an engineer or the data from SCS on peak storm runoff to know for sure.

At the near end of the dam in the picture you see what is called a hooded inlet pipe spillway. This pipe takes normal amounts of excess water from the pond, thereby maintaining a specific level of water in the pond. It is also called a trickle tube. Another kind of trickle tube is called a drop-inlet pipe rather than a hooded inlet. The difference is that the drop-inlet pipe is L-shaped, going from the surface of the water straight down to the floor of the pond, then straight out through the dam, while the hooded inlet type slants from water surface through the dam and out. Drop-inlet pipes are more expensive, but a drain with a valve can be added at the elbow of the L on the floor of the pond. I'll say right now (I'll say it more than once) that, even if laws in your state do not require the pond to be built so it can be drained, by all means *do* build a drain into your pond. In most, if not all, cases, there will be times when you will want to drain the pond.

Pipe spillways are sometimes built large enough to handle some of the water that would, in flood times, go over the emergency spillway. An emergency spillway, on the other hand, might be the only spillway on a pond with a very small watershed. At least we have no pipe spillway in our pond and, though engineers shake their heads, we really haven't needed one. Only about 8 acres drain to our pond, almost all of it woodland.

Emergency spillways should be designed wide enough so that peak overflow will seldom, if ever, run more than 6 inches deep. If water gets much deeper than that for very long, larger fish may swim out of the pond. You can hardly put a screen across the spillway unless you are going to be there to keep trash from building up and blocking the flow of water. You may lose many, even thousands, of very tiny fish in the overflow, but the experts say that normal reproduction in the pond will replace them.

Special structural spillways sometimes must be built instead of earthen grassed spillways where soils tend to wash badly. They can be made of concrete or treated wood. You really do need an engineer to design one of these, if you have a pond of any size. Again I have to point out that necessity is the mother of invention, and when our earthen spillway began to wash a little, I paved the eroding areas with some old bricks. This worked—again—only because our watershed is so small. Only rarely is there any overflow at all, and then hardly more than a trickle. In fact, when my father built our pond (without professional help, he being as knotheadedly independent as I am), bets were taken that the pond would not fill up at all, or only after a long time. On almost every pond I've worked, in fact, farmers invariably estimate the time it will take a pond to fill way wrong. They have little concept of the amount of water that can run off a 15-acre field in a hard rain, or from a winter-snow melt and spring drizzle. An inch of water over an acre of land represents 27,154 gallons of water. In a normal March in this part of Ohio, 4 inches of rain are very likely to run off the land, or 108,616 gallons per acre. On 15 acres, that's 1,629,240 gallons in just one month. A pond of half-acre size, 9 feet deep at the dam, holds approximately 1.8 acre-feet of water. One acre-foot equals 325,851 gallons. The half-acre pond then holds about 586,531 gallons and, with just a 5-acre watershed, will be overflowing before March is over. Incidentally, the way to figure your pond capacity in acre-feet is to compute the surface area of the finished, filled pond. If that is half an acre (.5 acre), then multiply that by .4 of the maximum depth at the dam. If depth is 9 feet, then .4 times 9 equals 3.6 times .5 equals 1.8 acre-feet.

All of which is another way of trying to convince you to think small when you build a pond. If the map on page 152 says in your area you need only 5 acres of drainage per acre-foot of water, believe it. In fact, better a watershed on the minimum side than maximum. The water level in your pond may drop substantially in drought seasons, but if everything else is right, it won't dry up before rains come again. Of course, if you get drought like California was going through in 1977, that's another story. But then a larger watershed wouldn't do you much good anyway. Zero times 10 or times 100 both come out more zero.

CONSTRUCTION

To begin construction, remove all trees from the area that will be covered by water, and from the dam site. Most pond designers advise clearing all trees from a 30-foot strip around the perimeter of the pond too, for easier fishing and bank maintenance. However, a pond mostly for a wildlife habitat might well have a tree, or several, bending over the water. Your choice—just keep trees off the earthen dam, since water can follow roots and perhaps start a hole through the embankment. I do know of some old ponds with very wide embankments where shallow-rooted brushy trees grow on the dam, but that's risky.

A good rule of thumb is to shape the pond sides to a 3-to-1 slope. The less shallow water along the shore, the less weed growth. If you happen to be a lover of water weeds, you'll still get all you want and more.

Topsoil removed from the pond area should be saved to put on the dam or banks. As soon as construction is finished, the dam and emergency spillway should be seeded or sodded. Seeding is, of

course, much cheaper. Spread straw or some other suitable mulch over the seeded areas to hold the soil and provide moisture protection for the germinating seed. If the dam is not too large, laying fence wire over the surface until the grass gets going will hold the mulch in place. The spillway, the mouth of the spillway, and the bottom where it feathers out at the toe of the dam are all critical erosion spots. Sodding at least these areas can be worth the money. But if not sodded, mulch and tie down the mulch in and around the spillway very assiduously.

Construction of an embankment pond involves heavy earth-moving equipment. The first step is to clear the pond area of vegetation and strip the topsoil. Then the core trench is excavated, to be filled, as the embankment is heaped up, with impervious clay. Any pipes passing through the core of the dam are placed and fitted with antiseep collars. Eventually the embankment grading is completed, and the pond starts to accumulate water.

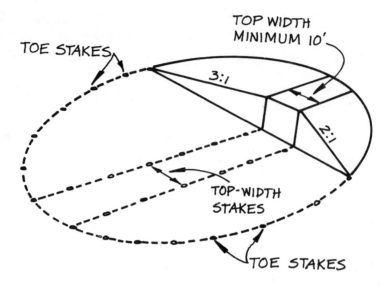

Staking Out a Dam Embankment

EXCAVATED PONDS

When a pond is built by digging a hole in the ground rather than throwing up an embankment, construction is much simpler. However, since size directly depends on the amount of dirt dug out, excavated ponds are usually smaller. Digging out a couple of acres to a 10-foot depth is a big job for a homesteader's resources. A quarter-acre dug pond is within reason, especially if the dirt can be used (or some of it) to build up the pond on the lower end, which is often the case. Then the pond is more properly a dug *and* dammed pond.

The main advantage of dug ponds (other than the fact that you don't have to worry about a dam giving way) is that you can control, to some extent, the amount and kind of water going into it. If fed by run-off water, the pond banks can be built to accept water from only part of the drainage area, especially where the whole area is much too large for the pond. I know of dug ponds installed right next to fair-size creeks and filled by diverting water through a pipe from creek to pond. (Ponds built along streams may be inundated in flood times, and often have gravelly bottoms that will not hold water very well. But banks can be built up to exclude flood-

An excavated pond is created by hollowing out a depression to collect and hold water. As with any operation that requires stripping a large patch of earth, the immediate result can look pretty awful, but after the pond fills in with water and the banks fill in with grass, the result can be awful pretty.

water, and as long as water flows from the creek into the pond through the inlet pipe, inflow can usually be regulated to balance seepage.)

As already mentioned, dug ponds in areas where fields are tile-drained can be built to accept only tile water. Next to spring-fed groundwater ponds, tile-filled ones have the best water quality in most cases.

In flat country, the dug pond works best where the groundwater level is fairly close to the surface. When you scoop out the dirt, the pond fills automatically. Such ponds are almost trouble-free, the only problem being what to do with dirt dug out of the hole. Some can be piled around the bank to exclude all run-off water, but in flat country, that takes only a little. I've seen the waste dirt used very imaginatively. At one pond, the owner made a long, 6-foot bank of it between the pond and the road to give him instant privacy. In windy country, the waste dirt is almost always piled on the windward side of the pond to serve as a windbreak. Don't pile dirt high close to the banks, as the weight could crumble the sides of the pond or the dirt could wash into the pond.

On both embankment ponds and dug ponds, pond owners will line the bank with rock called riprap. Wave action, even in small ponds, will cause water to eat away the shoreline over the years, and the rock helps stabilize the banks. On a dam bank, riprap discourages (but does not necessarily prevent) muskrats from digging holes.

In most cases, you should figure a good tight fence around the pond area into the cost of construction. On a large pond, this can get expensive, but where cattle, hogs, or other livestock are raised, almost imperative. But I go a step farther. If possible, fence out humans too. If the pond is small, the cost of a chain link fence may not be insurmountable. On a larger site, a regular stock fence, equipped with posts with angled elbows at the top, will discourage trespassers. The fence is topped by a strand of barbed wire, then a second or third strand of barbed wire affixed to the top section of the post which is bent or angled to the outside of the fenced area. Such a fence is almost impossible to climb from the outside.

It's not that you hate humanity. But a pond does bring with it the chance of accidental drowning and the possibility that you could be sued for negligence. So trespassing signs help, but in today's goofy world, signs will not always relieve you of responsibility. Your homeowner's insurance should cover possible pond accidents.

Also, ponds attract fishermen you may not want to attract, not to mention all sorts of passersby who do not understand the meaning of private property except in the case of their own. Motorcyclists, snowmobilers, and 4-wheel-drive nuts believe they have a right to wreck any property they can get their machines on (but are not so broad-minded when you start wrecking their machines), and a fence can save you grief. Where fee-fishing is carried on, a fence may be imperative, or you may find yourself with more fishermen than you have fees.

A thick hedge of multiflora rose will stop children who may blunder or toddle their way to your pond and fall into the water. Such a hedge will stop most anyone, if it is pruned and cared for properly. And it makes an excellent bird shelter. Multiflora is now illegal in some states, like Ohio—you aren't supposed to be able to buy it. Some panicky politician decided multiflora was a noxious weed that would "take over" the state if allowed to spread uncontrolled. The same logic would declare automobiles illegal because they kill people by the hundreds. Multiflora will not take over anything except abandoned fields and then only for a time. When trees grow up through the rampant thorns, as trees will most assuredly do, they shade out the multiflora. In my multiflora hedge, I had to keep cutting tree saplings out that grew up and dominated the hedge. In cultivated fields, multiflora is no problem. In pastures it takes work to control it, but not half as much work as controlling whitethorn and thistles.

A hedge of whitethorn (wild hawthorn) can be pruned to turn even sheep and is very beautiful in all seasons—white with bloom in spring, red with fruit in fall, and delightful silver grey bark in winter. But controlling thorn trees demands a yearly grubbing of sprouts. Hawthorn is also good wildlife food and cover.

A final note to pond construction: The best detailed information on pond construction (without being confusing) that I have seen is *Ponds for Water Supply and Recreation* by the Soil Conservation Service, Agricultural Handbook No. 387, issued January, 1971, and available from the Superintendent of Documents, U.S. Government Printing Office, Washington, DC 20402.

POND MAINTENANCE: 9
CONTROLLING THE WEEDS 9

Probably the major problem in artificial ponds is weed growth that interferes with swimming and fishing or that simply runs against the grain of the modern human's idea of what is aesthetically beautiful. As modern man would brook no weed in his lawn, so he envisions, as the ideal pond, a body of diamond-clear water surrounded by an unadulterated sward of bluegrass exactly and evenly 1½ inches tall.

In the early days of a pond, this "ideal" can be almost achieved, once the water has settled and the grass is established. At that point you have a body of water similar to what would temporarily result if you could cover your lawn instantly with 6 feet of water. For awhile, that water would make a very nice place to swim. But quickly the grass beneath would turn to slime and mud and, before long, the water would stagnate a little, turn murky with pollen dust and other windblown debris dropping into it, bloom with algae, and in the shallow areas eventually choke with water weeds. That is how a pond ages. Nature means to fill every body of water with organic matter, eventually turning it into dry land.

In Minnesota, the land of ten thousand lakes, you can see bodies of water in all stages of life and death. The oldest are merely swamps with hardly any standing water remaining. This is the natural process. It well may be that the natural process of every planet is a slow descent from much water to no water, from steamy jungle to desert, and it is at least obviously true from archeology and geology that civilizations seem to dry up as environments do. Some historians are convinced that the civilization, by misusing its environment, hastens the natural aging process. The evidence is too clear to ignore, and we are seeing now our own Great Plains

169

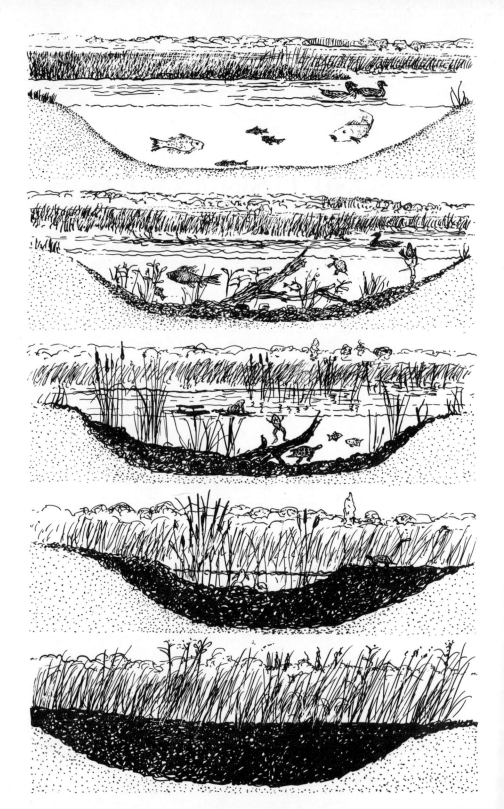

Pond Succession

farmers sucking up and dispersing groundwater at horrifying rates to grow crops for world markets. Our economists think we are so clever to trade food for oil, but all we are doing is committing slow suicide.

Be convinced, at least, of one fact: A farm pond ages by filling itself with organic matter that supports even more vegetative growth, that makes more organic matter, and so on until dry land is achieved after hundreds of years. If you try to stop this natural process, you are, in effect, trying to keep a pond from being a pond. You are trying to change it into a basin of water where some things are supposed to go on naturally while other things are not. This is impossible because the web of life in your pond is totally interconnected. If you kill plants you affect other plants and the animals that feed on them. Your success in maintaining one and killing the other will always be partial at best. You will spend a lot of money and not achieve the results you are led to expect. If you read the literature of pond maintenance closely, you will notice that the verbs used are almost always in the conditional form.

The truth is, that if you want to control weeds in your pond, and algae, and leeches, and other creepy-crawly things, the only way to do it effectively is to drain the pond periodically—every five to ten years—let it dry out awhile, and start all over again. This is precisely what pond experts are beginning to advise. It is the most, if not only, effective way to keep a pond from aging.

POND FERTILIZATION

Fertilizing the pond to increase the minute forms of life that feed on the nutrients causes the water to cloud, blocking sunlight to the bottom and thereby inhibiting weed growth. This practice will work, but, as more and more pond advisors are concluding, it is very difficult to practice right, and once started, it must be continued. If halted, the buildup of nutrients will make the weed problem worse than ever. Midwestern conservationists no longer advise fertilizing typical farm ponds—a point of view that would have been heresy just a few years ago. What's more, water biologists say that ponds in agricultural areas, fed by run-off water, usually receive enough fertilizer washing off cultivated fields.

On small ponds, a combination of mechanical weed control

171

along with natural predation works fairly well. But it takes work. It isn't easy to drag algae beds by hand or with cables.

On the other hand, some weeds are desirable in a pond. Many, as we have seen, are edible. The charge is made that they shelter small fish from predator bass, touching off population explosions. In our pond, the small fish are small bass, and some of them need that shelter if they are going to grow into a size we can eat. I'm extremely doubtful that weeds cause an overbalance of bluegills. That overbalance is inherent in the initial stocking rate of the pond, which we'll get to later.

The charge is also made that a large number of weeds in the water use up fertility when they grow and take oxygen from the fish when they die, perhaps initiating a fish kill. But weeds produce oxygen. When they die naturally, seldom do they contribute critically to oxygen depletion. About the only time I've seen enough weeds die to create a fish kill is when they are treated all at once with herbicides.

HERBICIDES

Herbicide recommendations direct you to treat early in the summer before weed growth is heavy. But if you treat when fish eggs are hatching, the herbicide can kill eggs or fry even at recommended safe levels for adult fish as specified on the label.

What's more, you are limited in what herbicide, if any, you can apply if the pond is used for irrigation (obviously, it can't have herbicides in it that would kill the plants you are irrigating). Some chemicals cannot be used if livestock are drinking the water, or may be used only after a waiting time has elapsed. All the more for humans, if the pond water is for domestic use. Swimming is often not possible for a prescribed time after chemical treatment, and fish should not be eaten within a certain number of days—this is specific information you can learn from the label. If you screw up, you can kill a lot more than just the weeds in your pond.

I can see no more use for herbicides in small farm ponds than in small gardens or on small farms. It's an expense you can do without. Weed your pond the way you weed the rest of your homestead.

There are four classes of plants that grow in ponds, and a fifth class might include all the ordinary weeds and brush that grow up on the banks. In the pond, the smallest plants are the microscopic planktons that make up a vital link in the food chain and are therefore beneficial. They also provide oxygen. The other three are: floating weeds like algae; submerged weeds like pondweed, coontail, and water milfoil; and emergent weeds like cattails. Let us say you decide to kill the algae with the usual chemical treatment of copper sulfate (which can also kill fish eggs and fry, tadpoles, and the like). What is that going to do to the even more frail microscopic plants? On your submerged weeds, you might try Diquat or Simazine or 2,4-D or some other toxic chemical that *might* kill the weeds (one weed family, *Chara,* is difficult to kill with any chemical and if you kill the other submerged weeds you are making it easier for *Chara* to increase and multiply), but use can be hazardous if you don't follow the label exactly. Some chemicals for submerged weeds react differently at different water temperatures, for example. Now ask yourself, what are these toxic compounds doing to microscopic plants and animals? Ask yourself especially when you are advised to make application first in the shallower water so the fish have a chance "to move into deeper water to escape the chemical"—a quote from the Ohio State Extension Service bulletin on herbicide use.

Even tougher chemicals are needed to down emergent weeds like cattails. Dowpon is one recommended for cattails by Purdue University. It is, says Purdue, safe for fish. But the label reads: "Do not graze livestock on treated areas during the application *season.*" (My italics.) What does such strong stuff do to lesser forms of pond life? Diquat, which works on cattails a little, has a label restriction cautioning against cattle drinking the water for ten days after application. What about other pond life, exposed to that water immediately after application? The best way to control emergent weeds on a pond of small size is to pull them by hand before they get established.

I've been to seminars and meetings where wildlife and fish biologists and other pond experts answer questions about killing pond weeds. They do a lot of shifting from one foot to the other. They speak with many ifs and maybes. And they are constantly cautioning against too great a reliance on toxic chemicals in ponds. Moreover, the bottom line on all treatments remains universally

173

true. *Chemical kills are temporary and must be repeated year after year.* All they are really doing is arresting the proper unfolding of the pond's life, not to mention some lightening of your pocketbook.

CONTROLLING WEEDS WITHOUT CHEMICALS

A combination of mechanical and biological control, certainly on ponds of no more than half an acre in size, is smarter. Certainly, you will *want* a few water lilies on your pond if they'll grow there. I sure would. If they threaten to choke the whole pond (very unlikely—yellow water lilies have always grown in our creek and on a nearby pond, and they never have choked the whole channel, but grow in about the same small patches they did when I was a kid), you can pull some out by hand, or with a rake. For large lakes or ponds, there are now mowers adapted to use in water to control emergent weeds. Cattails cannot be allowed to engulf the whole shoreline of a pond, but a small patch is desirable. Some biologists say cattails draw muskrats, but we had muskrats before we had cattails, and they ate up the cattails when the latter came, leaving none for us. We still have muskrats but, momentarily anyway, no cattails. Arrowhead seldom grows if the pond banks have the proper 3-to-1 slope that discourages shoreline weeds. But arrowhead is good eating and why not have a few? Why not a pond like a garden where a little of this and a little of that is grown, toward the ultimate goal of a variety of every plant and animal native to your area.

Dragging, pulling, carrying algae manually out of even a small pond is hard work—but work which, in my experience, kids who like to swim are willing to help with. I've paid them $10 for a pickup load and thought the money well spent: cleaner pond, nice garden mulch, and two kids learning the value of a buck.

Algae interferes with fishing and boating, but in the worst of times, deeper areas of our pond are free enough for swimming. If you know how, you can drop a line down between tufts of algae with a cane pole without snagging the bait. In fact, often that is where you will catch the bass, hiding under the algae. I've heard that fish avoid bait or hook on which algae is snagged, but that's not true in my experience.

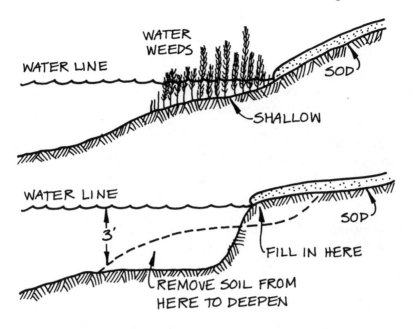

WATER
WEEDS

WATER LINE

SOD

SHALLOW

WATER LINE

SOD

3'

FILL IN HERE

REMOVE SOIL FROM
HERE TO DEEPEN

Grading Shorelines to Eliminate Weeds

If your pond sides have the proper depth, you can work a bit manually pulling some weeds—especially before they get a good foothold, just as you must do in the garden. Natural predators will take care of the rest of the excess if the pond is managed to encourage the presence of these predators. Muskrats are only one control. Ducks and geese can help. Wild ducks eat the floating weeds and other weed seeds. They should: Most often it is wild ducks who bring the weeds to your pond in the first place. If you have an excessive growth of duckweed, Pekin or Muscovy ducks, domestic species, can be kept on the pond to control it. Geese eat some of the underwater weeds like pondweed, muskgrass and majas. Don't expect miracles of weed control with ducks unless you really crowd a bunch of them on the pond, in which case the excess ducks will be as prohibitive of swimming as the weeds. Seek balance. A few of every creature, like the Ark. Control to maintain balance, not to extinguish certain species.

The most controversial biological control of weeds is the stocking of plant-eating fish. Carp, grass carp, and tilapia (the last in warm waters) are most commonly used. Carp have a bad, bad reputation with sport fishermen, and rightly so, because the critters overpopulate and muddy waters to conditions so turbid that other game fish are driven out. But carp are not by far all bad, and some species of Chinese carp may be all good for aquaculture. The grass carp, or white Amur, has proven abilities to clean vegetation from waterways and is used very effectively in Chinese polyculture of fish. But, not without reason, its introduction into the United States is being fought by many sportsmen and biologists and the fish is prohibited in many—but not all—states. (More on that later.) Israeli carp, a strain of regular carp, eat filamentous algae and are cautiously suggested even by the SCS handbooks as a possible control because they "do not normally spawn in fishponds with bass and bluegills." Nevertheless, the stocking of carp is regulated or prohibited in most states.

Crayfish eat some weeds, and, though it is not widely known, can be used in some situations on southern aquacultural farms for weed control. So says Stan Hudson (who himself relies on chemical weed control), a fish farmer in Kansas who writes a lively and practical column for commercial fish growers in the *Commercial Fish Farmer*.

Surface agitation can, surprisingly, keep wide areas of a pond free of scum. Pond scum may be algae, or it may be a combination of duckweed and watermeal or other floating plants, or it may be windblown dust from tree pollen, seeds, leaves, or dead flowering parts of plants. The latter, in particular, can make clean, sparkling water look temporarily dirty. My father noticed that on windy days, most scum on our pond was blown to the lee bank, leaving the main part of the pond clean and inviting for fishing and swimming. So he rigged up what looked like a miniature paddle wheel on a riverboat, attached it to the end of the pier, and powered it with a small electric motor. Sure enough, the movement of water generated by the paddle swept the scum to the opposite bank, clearing an area of about an eighth of an acre. Electric agitators and aerators used to increase oxygen supply in ponds for fish can be used more or less to achieve the same effect. In fact, some commercial manufacturers of agitators claim their machines will control the spread of algae in ponds, and agricultural research bears this out.

Underwater weed mowers are mostly big and expensive, but

at least one company sells plans for a weed cutter for small areas: Joe Morreale & Son of Richmond, Illinois, advertises the "Pond Sweeper" in *Farm Pond Harvest* magazine. I imagine there are others, or will be. I've not tried any of them and so can't endorse or criticize them. The weed cutters I've seen, homemade usually, are little more than a cable or wire pulled or seesawed through the water to cut off weeds, or drag them to shore, or both.

The use of fertilizer to increase plankton bloom and thereby cloud the water to prevent sunlight from reaching the bottom, is, as I have said, a proven weed control measure, but one that increasingly is not advocated for typical farm ponds. However, if you have the time and interest and the need, this method not only temporarily decreases weed growth, but ups the food supply of the creatures who feed on the plankton, which, in turn, increases the number of these small animals that the fish can eat. In other words, you fertilize for increased fish growth. If commercial inorganic fertilizers turn you off, you can fertilize for plankton bloom with manure. Commercial fish farmers prefer poultry manure, if available. The manure is scattered into the shallow water along the shore. Of course, this method won't enhance swimming for awhile, any more than chemicals that burn your skin.

Summing up, the best way to control weeds, in my opinion, is to drain the pond every five to ten years or lower the water level to expose the shallow bottom where the weeds are growing. Without water, the weeds die. The soil can be tilled, also, which is what many commercial aquaculturists do. The backyard aquaculturist can scoop up the surface layer of detritus and organic matter and soil from the pond bottom and use it effectively for fertilizer in the garden—as oriental farmers have always done. A five- to ten-year deposit can be quite significant.

If you irrigate from your pond, you can lower the pond level that way. The irrigation water will contain significant amounts of the fertility that has been accumulating on the pond bottom. Draining or lowering the level of the pond provides, at the same time, a chance to harvest the fish or to remove an imbalance of one species, or to get rid of undesirable fish altogether. If done only once every five to ten years, the pond will be out of ecological balance only a year or two during that time, but it will be a type of imbalance that benefits your recreation without poisoning the web of life at your pond site.

Finally, there are the weeds and brush that threaten to grow up on the land around the pond. Here, definitely, the typical farm pond needs no herbicide treatment. An occasional mowing plus a minimum amount of time spent grubbing out small trees and bushes before they get a start is all that's necessary. Biologists caution not to mow everything. Some tall grass at the pond edge, even some orderly bush growth, is beneficial to the fish. Such growth brings insects to the water for the fish to eat and encourages dragonflies that prey on mosquitoes—not to mention birds. Also, the taller grass will benefit other forms of wildlife. Best to keep the dam mowed close, however, because the lack of cover discourages muskrats and groundhogs from lurking there.

COMMON POND WEEDS

Bladderwort (*Utricularia* species)

Aquatic plants belonging to this genus are free-floating and without any visible roots. Some species have tiny bladders scattered on the leaf segments that trap small animals and aid in flotation. Stems float horizontally under the water surface and may reach up to 3 feet in length. When the plant blooms in late summer, yellow flowers extend above the surface of the water.

Bur Reed (*Sparganium* species)

Bur reeds are perennial plants that grow in shallow water and wet soil. They have long strap-like leaves 3 inches to 5 inches in length, and the giant species may reach 6 feet in height. Flowering occurs in early summer; the seeds are on stalks and are bur-like. Insect larvae and other small aquatic animals inhabit their underwater stems.

Coontail (*Ceratophyllum demersum*)

The common name for this plant is derived from the similarity of its leaves to a raccoon's tail. This perennial grows completely under water. Thread-like leaves are arranged in whorls around a central, hollow stem that can reach a length of 20 feet. The flowers are pollinated under water. The tough-covered seeds are eaten by waterfowl.

Duckweed (*Spirodela polyrhiza*)

Shallow waters of ponds and slow streams are frequently covered with a green blanket of duckweed. Frequently mistaken for algae, the tiny leaves are up to ¼ inch in diameter, with trailing roots 1 inch long. Waterfowl love these prolific perennial herbs. Dense layers can be up to 1 inch thick. Their ability to reproduce rapidly makes them difficult to control.

Common Elodea (*Anacharis canadensis*)

Elodea grows completely under water. Four broad oval leaves are arranged in a whorl around a center stem. These whorls are compact near the plant tip; the spacing gradually increases further down the stem. Leaf margins have microscopic barbs. Fragmented portions of the plant can develop into new plants.

Fanwort (*Cobomba caroliniana*)

A member of the water-lily family, fanwort has a slender stem that is covered with a gelatinous slime. The leaves, submersed in the water, are fan shaped and have many narrow segments. The small white or yellow flowers emerge above the water. Dense growths of fanwort may harbor many small animals.

Naiad (*Najas guadalupensis*)

The slender leaves of naiad are wider at the base and form whorls along the reddish brown stem. The leaves have sheaths at the base, and tiny seeds are located in the axils. Leaf margins may have visible spines and stems; leaves and seeds are favorite food for waterfowl. These plants provide shelter for many aquatic animals.

Pennywort (*Hydrocotyle* species)

A member of the parsley family, pennywort plants often form a dense mat along pond shorelines. Leaves of mature plants are approximately the size of a half-dollar, and are rounded with broad lobes. Small flowers are formed in the axils of the leaves. The plant stalk rises from horizontal roots buried in shallow water.

Curly Pondweed (*Potamogeton crispus*)

Native to Europe, this perennial has broad, membranous leaves with visible veins. The leaves are alternately arranged on the stem and have a row of small spines. These plants grow rapidly early in spring and will frequently inhibit the growth of other weeds. Seeds are beaked and grow on a spike above the water.

Grassy Pondweed (*Potamogeton pectinalus*)

Local conditions influence the form that grassy pondweed takes. Submerged leaves range from 1 inch to 6 inches in length. The many-branched stems resemble a fan, with leaves alternately arranged on the stem. Both tubers and seeds are popular waterfowl food.

Floating Pondweed (*Potamogeton natans*)

The submerged leaves of this plant are long and narrow or absent; the floating leaves resemble the shape of a heart. Floating pondweed grows in quiet water. Nutlets have almost no keel and appear above the water's surface.

Bushy Pondweed (*Najas flexilis*)

Actually a member of the naiad family, this annual submerged plant often grows in thick clumps. The ribbon-like leaves are wider at the base, forming whorls at the flexible, thick stems. The plant's shape varies with water depth. Stems, leaves, and seeds are prized by ducks.

Pickerelweed (*Pontederia cordata*)

These perennial plants grow in shallow water and damp shores. Leaves are broad and heart shaped, with long petioles. Showy blue flowers are produced on a spike. Rapid producers, these plants can render waterways impassible, and they frequently are nesting sites for mosquitoes.

Rush (*Juncus* species)

Members of this genus have cylindrical leaves, hollow or pithy stems, and flowers that form on stem tips. They grow in damp, poorly drained areas and in shallow water. These annual plants have tiny seeds with a projection coming out of the tip.

Spatterdock (*Nuphar luteum*)

Dense growth of this perennial plant often interferes with navigation. Spatterdock grows from the silty bottom of sluggish streams and ponds. The notched leaves are heart shaped and float or extend above the water. Yellow flowers have a single row of petals that curve inward and form a ball.

Spikerush (*Elocharis* species)

Approximately 150 species of spikerush grow in marshy areas and along banks and shores. The rootstock is matted, and the stem is mostly leafless, as the leaves are reduced to sheaths. Seed clusters emerge in a clump from the rootstock.

Water Milfoil (*Myriophyllum* species)

The hollow stem of water milfoil has feather-like, whorled leaves that may differ in size from the base to the stem tip. The entire plant grows under water with the exception of a stalk of tiny flowers that may extend above the water surface. Extensive patches of water milfoil frequently crowd out other plant growth.

Water Primrose (*Jussiaea* species)

This plant generally grows in shallow water along the shoreline of ponds and streams. Hollow red stems extend from the shoreline; an extensive root network extends under water from the main stem. Leaves are bright green; the plant has yellow flowers in the middle of the summer.

Watershield (*Brasenia schreberi*)

The common name of watershield is derived from the shape of its leaves—similar to a shield. The leaves float on the surface of the water, and may be 2 to 5 inches in length. Stems and the underside of the leaves are covered with a thick, gelatinous material. Dull purple flowers appear early in summer. Watershield is frequently eaten by waterfowl.

Water Smartweed (*Polygonum* species)

A widespread species, smartweed has glossy leaves and spikes of whitish green or pink flowers. The slender stems are jointed with leaf stiples located at these joints. Leaves are about 4 inches in length. Water smartweed is an emergent plant. Its seeds are wildlife food.

Water Stargrass (*Heteranthera dubia*)

Water stargrass is a rooted plant which is found submerged in still, shallow water. Leaves and stems are long and grass-like. The tiny, yellow flowers are shaped like a star.

Wild Celery (*Vallisneria americana*)

Waterfowl frequently eat the thick, fleshy stems of wild celery. The roots of this perennial are buried in the mud of both shallow and deep waters. Horizontal stems connect the tufts of thin, flaccid leaves. A flower supported by a coiled stalk is visible late in summer; after the flower is pollinated it is pulled under water to ripen.

MAINTAINING
WATER QUALITY 10

There's a certain amount of subjectivity involved in defining clean water. Water that a boy will swim in gleefully may be dirty enough to make his mother shudder at the thought. Water clean enough to satisfy a carp may kill trout. Water full of fish waste and rotting organic matter will invigorate a plant when it might very well sicken a man. Crystal-clear water looks great to swimmers, but fishermen prefer a cloudier water indicative of plankton bloom that means more fish and fewer weeds.

All of which is a roundabout way of saying that water quality in aquaculture depends upon the purpose of the water. In considering a homestead pond, which will be used for both recreation and fish production and perhaps irrigation and household use, too, the water must be quite clean to begin with, and very clean to end with. In later chapters, when we talk about more intensive types of food production, like raising carp in water heavily laden with hog manure, water quality will obviously mean something else.

For a general-purpose pond, the most important step in maintaining water quality is the one you take when you select the site and design of your pond. A small watershed, covered with pasture or woodland, or ponds fed by springs or other underground aquifers into which no industrial or residential sewage waste is seeping, will provide water as clean as you can get. Runoff from intensively farmed soil will bring mud and toxic chemicals into your pond on a continuous basis, and this pollution will be nearly impossible to control or neutralize.

If you (and your fish) don't like muddy water, don't keep carp, bullhead catfish, or other bottom-rooting fish in your pond, and don't let muskrats build up to high population levels. It should go without saying that you will not allow hogs or cattle free access to the pond. All these animals will keep your pond turbid even with the best antiturbidity treatments.

Protect pond banks from washing as much as possible. A good sod cover plus a layer of riprap where wave action is most troublesome will keep that source of muddiness controlled.

MAINTAINING FERTILE WATER

Water quality first of all is interrelated with water fertility if the water is to produce food. A pond can be made fertile and kept that way in about the same way you enrich and maintain a garden. An organically managed pond will, in fact, be easier to enrich because you will not normally "garden" it as intensively as your vegetable plots. Most plant life in a pond ends up dying and being recycled back through the pond life, and the pond bottom slowly increases in rich organic matter and plant food as time progresses. You can help that process along in exactly the same way you do in the garden, putting manure, compost, old hay, or any organic fertilizer along the shore in the shallow water. In fact, manure and especially old hay, weeds, grass, or similar sources of organic matter are recommended also for clearing up muddy water—so you get two birds with one stone. Best to fertilize in spring and fall when water is cool and full of oxygen. Too much manure applied on a hot, cloudy, summer day might, in a pond crowded with fish, lead to oxygen depletion enough to harm the fish. Or the feverish activity of bacteria at work in the manure may lead to deoxygenation. However, these are rare occurrences in most ponds.

What you do when you "fertilize" a pond is increase the growth of microscopic plants, which in turn increases the amount of oxygen in the water through photosynthesis. The increase in plankton increases the food supply for small forage fish and other marine life. In turn, these animals increase and provide more food for bass and other predator fish.

As pointed out earlier, many farm ponds receive enough fertilizer in run-off water to satisfy ordinary needs. These needs diminish as the pond ages and, even in intensive aquacultural production, the use of fertilizers tapers off, especially nitrogen. After three to five years, some fish raisers can apply only phosphorus at the rate of 40 pounds of superphosphate per acre. (I imagine that about 60 to 80 pounds of rock phosphate would accomplish the same purpose.) In a pond's early life, the guidebooks call for an application of 100 pounds of 8-8-2 commercial fertilizer or its equivalent in organic fertilizers. Cottonseed meal and manures encourage growth of filamentous algae, say the experts, but when you stop to think about it, *any* fertilizer is going to encourage algae and all plant growth.

How do you know if you need more fertility for intensive fish production? Farm pond managers rely on a simple stratagem. If you can see a light-colored object at a depth of 18 inches in the water, you don't have a good plankton bloom. You can make a simple testing device by nailing a white disk to the end of a stick. Mark the stick at 12 inches and at 18 inches. If the disk goes out of sight when you submerge it 12 inches into the water, the pond is assumed to be fertile enough to feed approximately 400 pounds of fish per acre and produce 150 pounds of harvested fish per year, without supplemental feeding. If the disk is still visible at 18 inches, you will be lucky if the pond produces half that amount per year.

Organic fertilizers can be simply tossed into the water along the shore. Chemicals are usually applied by pouring a bag onto a platform that floats just under the water surface. One platform will service up to 15 acres, as wave action and water currents mix the fertilizer through the water.

I write the foregoing with some hesitancy because I do not believe most typical, general-purpose ponds will need to be fertilized, unless you are putting some toxic chemical in the water to kill weeds that will also kill plankton. The first year or so, extra

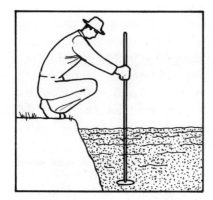 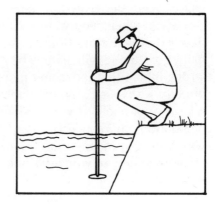

Checking Water Fertility

189

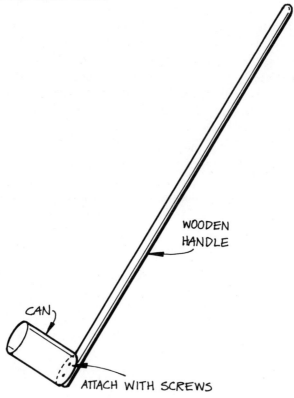

WOODEN
HANDLE

CAN

ATTACH WITH SCREWS

Soil Sampler

fertilizer might help, but after that, all you may be doing is encouraging the growth of emergent weeds.

Even where you want to raise more fish in a given water area than would naturally flourish there, I'm not so sure fertilizing as a matter of course will always be recommended by experts. I have a strong hunch that more and more, you will be told to feed the fish directly with some kind of supplemental ration and let the plankton take care of itself. If you feed directly a larger than "natural" fish population, there will be more fish-waste fertilizer in the water, which in turn means more plankton. And in many cases, supplemental feeding may be advisable or necessary no matter how good the plankton crop is.

Lime may be necessary in your pond as it often is in your garden. Fish, like most plants, like a pH of around 7, will tolerate water no higher than 8 or 9, and hardly lower than 4. Best to stay in the 6-to-8 range. Lime also makes water harder, and where water hardness is around 10 parts per million, a lime application can raise it up above 20 ppm. In University of Alabama research, fish grew better when water hardness was 20 ppm or more. Agricultural lime can also clear turbid water (see below).

A pond is tested by taking soil samples from the bottom in at least five different places per acre. A simple sample collector used by Alabama researchers is shown.

MUDDY WATER

In most properly designed and maintained ponds, muddy water will settle out less than six months after the pond has filled, though after hard rains, the water may muddy a little temporarily. However, I've often noticed that our pond, which has a very protected watershed, actually gets clearer after a hard rain. I'm not sure why. The water is generally clearer in early spring and late fall. In summer, the surface is always sprinkled with pollen dust, falling weed seeds, leaves, dead blossoms, and other kinds of windblown debris. Very often, the water looks dirty when, in reality, it is just covered with this surface scum. Rain and wind wash it away.

Where muddy water (turbidity) persists in a pond, it may be caused by very fine clay particles suspended in the water, too light to settle out. If so, any *one* of the following treatments will cause the particles to coagulate and settle: 1,000 pounds of agricultural gypsum, 1,000 pounds of agricultural limestone (calcium carbonate), 740 pounds of hydrated lime, or 250 pounds of aluminum sulfate (commercial alum)—*per surface acre*. Gypsum is the most commonly recommended treatment. It won't hurt fish. Sometimes the recommendation is given in acre-feet rather than surface acres, in which case the proper amount is 500 pounds per acre-foot, or if you want to be absolutely accurate, 523 pounds per acre-foot. That's about one-tenth of an ounce per cubic foot. If after six weeks the pond hasn't cleared up, do another treatment using one-quarter the previous amount. Don't expect gypsum to work if there are bottom-feeding fish at work, like carp, or if a lot of silt is being washed in off the pond's watershed.

Old hay will clear up muddy water too, as mentioned, and it is

Old hay spread in pond shallows can help eliminate muddy water.

a better recourse for organic-minded pond owners. For every acre of pond surface, use seven to ten bales and repeat the treatment after ten days if necessary. Break up the bales and scatter the chunks in the shallow water along the edges of the pond. Don't apply on hot, cloudy days when there is likelihood of oxygen depletion in your pond.

OXYGEN

That brings up another important aspect of water quality: the amount of oxygen present in the water. In a natural pond or a naturally managed pond, plant life will be abundant enough to produce the oxygen needed along with the stirring in of air on the surface from wind and wave action. If enormous amounts of vegetation should decay all at once in the pond, especially in cloudy weather when photosynthesis is decreased, enough oxygen might be sucked out of the water to cause a fish kill. Sometimes, with heavy weed decay and heavy fish populations, there's a shortage of oxygen in the late fall that can cause problems or set the stage for a more drastic fish kill in winter.

Regardless of weed decay, a winter freeze-over that lasts a month or longer may mean danger, particularly if the ice is covered with snow. Snow is the culprit more than ice, because sunlight cannot penetrate the snow cover, and the oxygen-producing process of photosynthesis by microscopic plants slows down. Oxygen depletion results.

In an earlier chapter, oxygen depletion from "turn-over" of the pond water was described. Turn-over is another cause of fish kill, and it can happen whenever temperature change is sufficient to equalize the temperature of surface water and bottom water. Bottom water, which has much less oxygen in it than the upper layers, mixes with top water and can temporarily cause a shortage of oxygen, especially where fish are crowded. The phenomenon occurs mainly in spring and fall, but it can take place in the wake of a summer storm and may produce what is usually considered a "mysterious" fish kill, since there is no apparent pollution problem.

A fish kill is a tragedy for a commercial producer. But homesteaders should note well: Invariably in a general-purpose pond, a die-off triggered by a natural shortage of oxygen means the pond was overcrowded, probably with an undesirable imbalance of the fish population. It is one of nature's ways of evening the score. If, however again, your pond contains undesirable species like carp and bullhead which can survive on less oxygen, an oxygen shortage may kill the "good" fish and leave the "bad." This is, of course, most true of trout, whose demand for oxygen is higher than other fish.

In ordinary homestead ponds not geared to intensive production of fish, oxygen depletion can usually be avoided by not setting the stage for a massive weed die-off, as by trying to kill the algae from the entire pond at once. In winter, keep the snow off the ice if you experience long periods of freeze-up. On our pond, this job is never a problem since whenever there's ice, there are hockey players, who keep the snow off their playing rink as a matter of course.

Removal of overabundant amounts of aquatic vegetation before winter is a cautionary preventive practiced by some pond owners. On a small, well-managed pond, a homesteader will not let the weeds run wild anyway.

Another excellent safeguard against oxygen depletion and the build-up of harmful gases like hydrogen sulfide in the bottom water is the aforementioned bottom-water drain. Draining off bottom water, especially while pumping fresh water in, is an effective way to arrest oxygen depletion.

Getting Food from Water

Commercial fish raisers always keep an eye out for an emergency. Fish can run out of oxygen very quickly, and when you see fish gasping at the surface, any way you can get oxygen into the pond will do. Run a stationary motorboat motor. Sprinkle water onto the surface with pump and hose. Recirculate or splash water over a baffle or through a coarse screen with a lift pump. Broadcast a quick treatment of 50 to 100 pounds of superphosphate per surface acre—it will stimulate microscopic plants to give off more oxygen within an hour.

But reacting to an emergency instead of acting correctly ahead of time is strictly flying by the seat of your pants. If serious fish production is your goal, you should get an aerator for your pond and use it to supply extra oxygen for your fish as assiduously as you supply extra food. Aerators (many models on the market) are easy to use and economical to operate. They float like a buoy on the water, the motor churning and lifting a spray into the air that falls back to the surface, mixing air into the water. Those models that have the motor underneath rather than on top will work well even in winter on ponds more than an acre in size with a good inflow of

An aerator enables a pond owner to increase the fish population density by making more oxygen available to the fish. It also turns the pond into a fountain.

Cut a hole in the ice and the aerator will continue to work.

fresh water. Just knock a hole in the ice and set them in. (Top-mounted motors can freeze into huge icicles.) On smaller ponds, it's better to circulate water without lifting it in this situation. Aerators promote the general health of fish by keeping high rates of dissolved oxygen in a pond. They also inhibit algal growth to some extent.

BUGS AND OTHER CREEPY-CRAWLY CREATURES

For some pond owners, water quality means an absence of mosquito larvae, leeches, snails, unsavory-looking water bugs, perhaps even snakes and turtles. For the most part, that view is wrong-headed. Snapping turtles aren't going to attack you and never have as far as I know, unless they are first attacked. The snakes you see in water, except for cottonmouths in the South, are rarely ever venomous. Rattlers and copperheads are not water-inhabiting snakes. Poisonous snakes might be found around a pond, but if so, they would be found there, pond or no pond.

Trying to rid a pond of mosquitoes by spraying is a thankless job. Better to rely on fish and dragonflies to control the hordes and come to peace with nature: a few mosquitoes you have with you always. The same is going to be true of leeches and water bugs. The latter are harmless, the former more loathesome in the mind than in the skin. I've had I don't know how many leeches attach them-

Leech

selves to me over the years, and I'm still disgustingly healthy.

But creatures like leeches can become pestiferous, especially to little children splashing in shallow water. If you can't abide them (the leeches, I mean), you may gain temporary respite with a treatment of rotenone, applied as described on page 211 at lesser rates by half. Copper sulfate at 5 ppm, which is about 14 pounds per acre-foot, is standard treatment for hard-to-kill algae, and at that rate you will also kill off many leeches and snails (and who knows what all—copper sulfate levels of 50 to 100 parts per billion cause deficiencies in reproduction and early growth of fish). Snails are generally good for typical all-purpose ponds, fitting well into the eat-and-be-eaten food chain. Some snails eat fish eggs, which may be an advantage in a farm pond, though not in intensive aquacultural production. Snails can be an intermediate host of the schistosome invertebrate that causes "swimmer's itch" in northern lakes, though I know of no farm ponds where this is a problem. In fact, many snails that are merely tolerated, if not considered pests, in this country are gourmet delicacies elsewhere.

What I'm saying (over and over again) is that trying to kill out one undesirable link in the pond's food chain is more trouble than it's worth. The way to avoid leeches is to build a pier or raft out to deep water and swim there instead of wading through the shore mud where these bloodsuckers lurk. Moreover, in ponds where fish are active, especially bluegills, leeches get eaten up before they get to you.

POND WATER FOR HOUSEHOLD USE

With proper filtering and disinfecting, pond water can usually be cleaned enough to drink safely, or used to clean food utensils in kitchen and milkhouse. Where good wells, springs, or city water are not available, homesteaders and farmers often convert to pond water. Local health authorities, extension service personnel, and manufacturers of filtering and chlorinating devices are all at your service when you need advice in this regard. A publication written jointly by extension engineers from thirteen midwestern universities I have found particularly helpful—*Private Water Systems,* available from your local extension office or from Midwest Plan Service, Iowa State University, Ames, Iowa. I'm sure extension engineers elsewhere have similar helpful publications. I am not going to go into great detail on filtering and disinfecting water, because you will need to consult local health codes anyway.

Your first step is to draw water as clean as possible from the pond. You do this with what is called a suspended filter intake hanging from a float about 1 to 2 feet beneath the surface where water is usually the cleanest. If at all possible, the pipe leading from the filter intake should go downhill out of the pond so that the water feeds out by gravity. The pipe leads first into a settling basin equipped with an alum feeder to remove turbidity. (If you can successfully treat muddy water in the pond with alum or gypsum, you don't need the settling basin.) Next water moves into another tank where it is chlorinated and then filtered slowly through sand and gravel to remove impurities. From there the water flows into a storage tank until pumped to house or dairy for use. Sometimes a carbon filter is placed in the line to the house or dairy to remove excess chlorine or off-flavor taste. See the drawing on the next page.

Before being put into use, a sand filter should be flushed with a

197

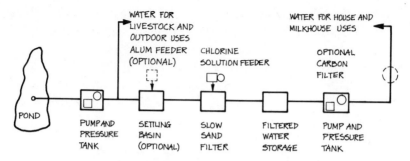

Filtering and Disinfecting Water from a Pond

strong chlorine solution. There are several commercial chlorine solutions that must be used according to the percentage of chlorine in them. In dairies, rather strong chlorine solutions are used to disinfect milk utensils and you would use less of these products in chlorinating water than say laundry bleach, which is a relatively weak 5 percent solution. But either can be used. The rule of thumb in flushing or shock-treating a sand filter is 1 gallon of laundry bleach for an 8-by-8-foot tank. Fill tank with water, pour in bleach, let stand for twenty-four hours, flush out. A smaller tank uses less bleach, a larger one more, of course.

The continuous chlorinator injects chlorine into the water as it

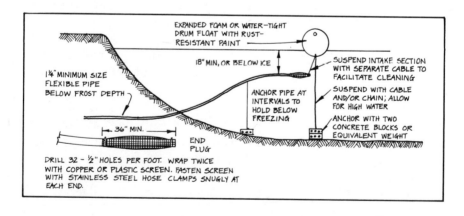

Homemade Suspended Filter Intake

enters the filter tank, or in a less desirable arrangement, as it leaves the filter tank. Your health officer and the man who sells you your chlorinator will tell you how to install everything to meet local health standards and codes. It is important to wire the pump motors so that a sensing device of some kind will turn off the pump when the chlorine solution container is empty.

RAISING FISH IN A TYPICAL ARTIFICIAL POND 11

There are still people who believe fish get into a new pond by falling with the rain. The idea is not quite as far-fetched as it sounds, because fish have been sucked up out of lakes by wind funnels, carried aloft for many miles, and then dropped far from their place of origin.

But that's a very rare phenomenon. If fish are going to get into your pond, someone—or something—is going to have to put them there. Heron and other waterfowl can carry fish eggs into a pond, but I daresay this does not happen as often as some new pond owners are led to believe. Fish that appear in a pond without the owner's involvement (or wish) usually get there by swimming up improperly designed overflow outlets, or down ill-conceived inlets, or perhaps more commonly, by being dumped in from some careless fisherman's minnow bucket. Since, nine times out of ten, the fish you get for free in these ways are not the kind you want, you should take steps to avoid their coming. Above all, do not allow indiscriminate minnow-bait fishing in your pond. In fact, don't allow minnow fishing at all.

Most ponds are built primarily for fishing. But for the homesteader, good fishing as such might be secondary to good production of fish for eating. The two purposes can be combined but are not necessarily the same. For example, you might crowd into a pond many trout and feed them a supplemental ration above and beyond what the fish would get naturally, and perhaps aerate the pond so the fish get enough oxygen. You can, in this manner, raise ten times as many trout as you could in the same pond without supplemental feeding and oxygen. But the smaller number of wild fish will make excellent sport fishing while the tame, supplementally fed trout will follow you up and down the shoreline waiting

201

(literally) for a handout. Somehow it is just not much fun to throw a line in and hook such fish. It's like shooting hogs in a pen as compared to tracking down a wild boar.

STOCKING A WARM-WATER POND

Much controversy still exists over what species of fish and how many ought to be stocked in an artificial pond, particularly a warm-water pond. The root of the controversy rests on the question of how much "management" a pond owner is going to exert over his fish population. State and federal recommendations are made on the usually correct assumption that *most* pond owners are not going to take the time and work necessary year in and year out to control fish population and, more importantly, do not intend to feed the fish supplementally. Federal and state biologists therefore recommend stocking rates that come closest, in their experience, to providing a pond with a supply of fish, and hopefully a balance of fish, eating only what the pond provides naturally in the way of food.

That being so, the most common stocking rate recommended for warm-water ponds is 100 largemouth bass fingerlings and 500 bluegill fingerlings per acre of surface water. Sometimes the recommended rate is 1,000 bluegills to 100 bass or again 400 bluegills and 100 redear sunfish per 100 bass. In ponds over a half-acre in size you can add 100 channel catfish per acre to the stocking mixture. For ponds a half-acre or smaller, many fishery biologists are now recommending either the bass-bluegill mixture *or* 200 channel catfish at the per-acre rate, not both.

Why largemouth bass, bluegills, and channel cats? Bluegills eat the insect life that lives on the plankton in the pond, and the bass prey on the smaller bluegills as well as their own offspring. Ideally, the two will work out a balance of population beneficial to the pond and to each other. Every conceivable combination of fish has been tried; none work as well as this one. Other kinds of basses will not forage the bluegills hard enough. Other kinds of sunfish, especially the green sunfish, multiply too fast. Perch and pike will live in farm ponds but not easily or well.

Catfish like farm ponds, of course; they eat food the bass and bluegill would let go to waste. Channel cats are the best choice as they do not muddy the water and will hardly ever reproduce in a

Bluegills ready for stocking. Bluegills can be stunted by too-dense populations, so don't overstock if you want the fish to grow.

pond, hence will never overpopulate. Overpopulation is the bane of farm ponds. Fish rarely starve to death when a pond becomes crowded, but they do not grow. You get a multitude of small fish, less fun to catch and tedious to clean for supper. Better that the channel cats get fished out and have to be replaced every three to four years than to have them overpopulate like bullheads and crappie are almost sure to do.

The trouble is, the bass/bluegill population will get out of

203

whack, too. The number-one problem in most farm ponds is too many bluegills, no big bass. The main reason this happens is that in the first two years, the owners fish too much and after that, not enough. Water biologists have worked out a simple but strict regimen for harvesting bass and bluegills, which, if followed, will provide good fishing indefinitely, they say, without further stocking or supplemental feeding. Their regimen goes like this:

1. The first year after stocking bass and bluegill fingerlings, return *all* fish caught to the pond.
2. The second year, fish out 80 pounds of bluegill per acre, but throw all bass caught back into the pond. (Incidentally, always handle fish with wet hands, as the slimy protective coating on a fish may come off on dry hands.)
3. The third year, and thereafter, take out 80 pounds of bluegill per acre and 20 to 25 pounds of bass per acre. *However* (and this is the real tricky part of management), bass caught between 12 and 15 inches in size should always be returned to the water, as this size largemouth bass preys most voraciously on the bluegills. Smaller or larger bass can be kept.

This regimen requires that all fisherpersons (I've waited a long time for an opportunity to use that word) keep records of the fish they catch—a task easier said than done. But unless you are willing to follow strict management control of fish population, you may be much better off never stocking bluegills with your bass at all,

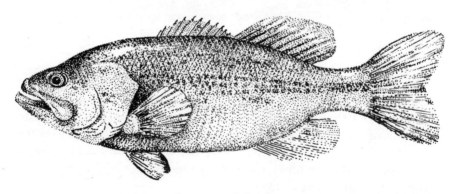

Largemouth Bass

because inevitably you will get a population explosion of bluegills—many, many small bluegills but no large ones, which, in turn, leads to a decrease in the number of bass even though the bass eat the bluegills.

Seldom does the imbalance go the other way—too many bass and not enough bluegills—but that can happen, too. Knowledgeable pond owners watch for signs of impending imbalances. If few bass are caught over a period of time when they should be biting, if no large bluegills are caught, if no apparent bass-spawning or new hatches of bass are noticed, or if a large number of tadpoles survive (without being eaten)—any or all signs may indicate too many bluegills, and not enough bass. But the only sure way to check population balance is to seine the shallow-water areas with a minnow seine between July 1 and September 1 to get an indication of the spawning success of the two fish. The following analysis prepared by the SCS is used in Ohio and will serve for any warm-water bluegill/bass pond:

Farm Pond Analysis To be used in ponds that have been stocked long enough for the bass to reproduce, usually during the third or later summer. In some southern Ohio ponds perhaps the second summer. Seine edge of pond between July 1 and September 1.

I. NO YOUNG BASS PRESENT:

1. Many newly hatched bluegills, no or few intermediate bluegills. (Bass slightly overcrowded.) Will usually correct itself.

2. No recent hatch of bluegills, many intermediates. (Unbalanced, bluegills overcrowded, insufficient bass.) Reduce bluegills and add bass.

3. Same as above, plus tadpoles and/or minnows. No young bass or extremely few. Reduce bluegills in fall and add bass. Sometimes best to start pond over.

4. No recent hatch of bluegills, few intermediates. (Unbalanced, due to crowding by other species; e.g., bullheads, green sunfish, small crappies.) Usually best to start pond over.

5. No recent hatch of bluegills, no intermediates. (Water too cold for bass-spawning—less than 68 degrees F [20 degrees C]—too saline, or too heavily laden with silt.) If too cold, start pond over and use trout.

II. YOUNG BASS PRESENT:

1. Many newly hatched bluegills and some intermediates present. In balance and producing according to its fertility. Fish hard.

2. Many newly hatched bluegills and no intermediates. Temporary balance, but bass overcrowded. Will correct itself. Fish hard for bass.

3. No recent hatch of bluegills.

   a. Few intermediate bluegills. Pond overcrowded after bass-spawning period. Usually due to being fertilized last year, unfertilized current year. Sometimes due to overcrowding by other species which reached a competitive size in late spring or summer.

   b. No intermediate bluegills. Bluegill absent or unable to reproduce. About only causes of no reproduction would be water too cold for spawning, or too saline—i.e., salinity = 0.5 percent or higher. Add bluegills if water is suitable.

   c. No intermediate bluegills, many newly hatched green sunfish. Add bluegills if few weeds occur.

   d. Many intermediate bluegills. Unbalanced, as 1-2 above, but less badly overcrowded by bluegills. Add bass or reduce bluegills.

In the table that follows, you will see other stocking practices sometimes recommended for farm ponds. Instead of bluegills, minnows can be stocked with the bass. But be forewarned that minnows, particularly golden shiners, can overpopulate as badly as sunfish and do not, of course, provide the fishing that bluegills will. Some pond owners have found that they can get rid of their excess minnows if there is a bait-minnow producer in the area. Minnow

STOCKING

Combination	Species	Number/ Acre*	Minimum Size	Date
Bass-Sunfish (Bream)	Bluegills	500	½″-1¼″	August to March
	or			
	Bluegills & Redear or Hybrid Green	400 100	½″-1¼″ ½″-1¼″	August to March
	Largemouth Bass	100	1″+	June to August
Bass-Sunfish (Bream)- Catfish	Bluegills	500	½″-1¼″	August to March
	or			
	Bluegills & Redear or Hybrid Green	400 100	½″-1¼″ ½″-1¼″	August to March August to March
	Channel Catfish	100	4″-6″	August to March
	Largemouth Bass	100	1″+	June to August
Bass-Minnow	Fathead Minnow or Golden Shiner	1,000	2½″-4″	August to March
	Largemouth Bass	100	1″+	June to August
Bass-Minnow- Catfish	Fathead Minnow or Golden Shiner	1,000	2½″-4″	August to March
	Channel Catfish	100	4″-6″	August to March
	Largemouth Bass	100	1″+	June to August
Bass-Minnow- Catfish (when feeding commercial fish ration)	Fathead Minnow or Golden Shiner	1,000	2½″-4″	August to March
	Channel Catfish	500-1,000	4″-8″	August to March
	Largemouth Bass	100	1″+	June to August

*These rates are the maximum recommended stocking rates for most situations involving one surface acre. Increase or reduce numbers to be stocked by percent of area; e.g., ½-acre pond, reduce by 50 percent; 1½-acre pond, increase by 50 percent. Successful pond fisheries can be produced using approximately ½ the recommended rate and stocking larger sunfish (bream) (2″-4″) and bass (3″-4″). Rates can be increased under exceptionally good management and written recommendations of a state or federal biologist.

dealers may be willing to seine your pond—even pay you for the minnows.

My personal experience with farm ponds is that largemouth bass should be stocked without *any* bluegills, sunfish, or minnows. My father stocked our family pond with bass only, and over the years we have found this arrangement best for us. The bass eat most of their own offspring, and no overpopulation occurs as long as we fish occasionally. A supply of growing fish remains in the pond—I think principally because most years we have allowed the algae to grow thick enough to protect some of the young from their voracious elders. We do not get good fishing as many days as we would if bluegills lived in the pond, but we get about as much fishing as we desire. And when the bass are biting, we can haul out in a day or two all the fish a family wants to eat in a year. Critics of the all-bass/no-bluegill stocking practice maintain that the bass will not grow big as rapidly as when foraging on bluegills, but we have caught many one- and two-pounders, and those are pretty big fish to me.

Some pond experts now advocate bass alone in farm ponds if you use supplemental feeding. Bass aren't supposed to take to supplemental feeding, but the staff of *Farm Pond Harvest* magazine has demonstrated that largemouths *can* be persuaded to eat a wide variety of artificial food, including commercial fish feeds.

Another method of rearing bass without sunfish or bluegills is to feed *a few* minnows periodically to the bass to increase rate of growth. I would think that channel catfish minnows would be ideal. If less than 6 inches long, adult bass will readily eat them, and if some channel cats elude the bass, so much the better. They will hardly ever propagate in a farm pond, and, as adults, make fine fishing themselves.

In the type of situation discussed earlier, where no supplemental feeding is planned, most fishery biologists do not recommend stocking any other kind of fish. Crappie overpopulate too easily. Bullheads do too. You can tell a bullhead from a channel catfish because the latter has a forked tail and the bullhead does not. In some instances, northern pike have been raised successfully in ponds, but they are not generally recommended. Carp are a no-no in many states or are heavily regulated. They produce very well but are usually raised in carp-only ponds because they muddy the water so badly. Israeli carp are sometimes recommended to control troublesome filamentous algae.

But in fish management, as in all things, there is little agreement among experts. Some aquaculturists, like the Zetts family, which operates the well-known Zetts fish hatcheries in Drifting, Pennsylvania, prefer a more encompassing approach. The Zetts advise in their catalog: "Stock any type of fish that you like best. Any breed of fish does well in ponds." Understood in that statement is that fish will receive supplemental feeding, that some kinds, like carp, will be isolated in their own special ponds, and that fish that won't spawn in ponds naturally will have to be restocked periodically.

STOCKING A COLD-WATER POND

With cold-water ponds, not so much disagreement exists on the kind(s) of fish to stock. Trout is the first and only choice. (If you can grow trout, why would you want to try anything else?) Generally speaking, rainbows are best for artificial ponds: They are more adaptable and readily available from nurseries. Brook trout can be and are raised with rainbows for variety. In the East, most hatcheries offer brook trout, but this species is harder to obtain in the West. Brown trout are not recommended for farm ponds; they are more cannibalistic and harder to catch (but often grow to a larger size).

No other kind of fish ought to be raised with trout, say the experts. Trout can't compete well in a pond for available food and oxygen. However, trout do live amicably with other fish in certain situations. The most famous example I know about was Louis Bromfield's experiments with pond-fish culture, mentioned in his book *Malabar Farm*. He stocked an old pond with trout where other fish were already established, particularly sunfish. The trout grew and survived, probably because, as Bromfield noted, the large pond was very deep—20 feet at the deepest—and the trout could live in the deeper water somewhat biologically removed from the sunfish which stuck to the shallower water.

An artificial trout pond of average fertility will support naturally about 100 pounds of trout per surface acre. Therefore you can stock about five hundred 2- to 4-inch fingerlings and the fish will each grow to from 4 to 8 ounces the first year. If you fish these smaller fish lightly the first year, there will be enough natural food in the pond to grow the others to 1½-pound weights the second year. That's a nice trout to catch. Waiting another year for trout to grow to 2 pounds and beyond is not worthwhile, say Soil Conservation Service biologists, because once they reach 2 pounds, the trout grow very slowly in a purely natural environment and the death rate is high. Better to fish the pond hard and restock it every other year with 4-inch fingerlings. Some trout-pond owners simply drain the pond every two or three years and take out all the fish and start over. This way, the large trout do not have a chance to prey on the restocked fingerlings.

Do not stock trout in water above 65 degrees F (18.3 degrees C). Don't dump the fingerlings directly into your pond, either, as the change in water, even cooler water, can be very shocking to sensitive trout. Add pond water slowly to the water in the shipping container until the water is within 6 degrees F (3.3 degrees C) of the temperature of the pond water. The easiest way to do this is to pour half the water out of the container and then fill

Stocking a pond. The recycled plastic bags contain catfish fingerlings. The bags are floated in the pond until the temperature of the water in them stabilizes with that of the pond water, then they are gently emptied.

it with pond water. Dump half the water out again and again refill it with pond water. Do that three times and your trout should be properly acclimated. If the trout start rolling on their sides in distress, delay further mixing until they act normal again. When mixing is complete, pour the trout gently into the pond. Or you can simply lower the fish in the plastic bag they are shipped in, into the pond and hold them there until the water temperatures inside and outside the bag equalize. Open the bag and let the pond water mix very gradually with the water in the bag. Then slowly release the fish.

Whenever trout dimple the water surface looking for bugs, you can usually expect good fishing. Worms and crickets are good bait. You can catch trout through a hole in the ice in winter too. Don't be afraid of taking too many out of the pond because you will probably have to restock every other or every third year anyway. The more fish you catch, the faster the ones remaining will grow—at least up to 2 pounds. Start fishing as soon as trout are 6 to 8 inches long, which should be about six to ten months after stocking.

POPULATION CONTROL

If your pond becomes hopelessly unbalanced, or if you acquire an older pond full of undesirable rough fish, the best way to get rid of the problem is to drain the pond and start over. You can poison fish—rotenone is the common method—and, if you do it right, get rid of forage fish like bluegill without affecting the largemouth bass population too badly. Rotenone is sold as an insecticide more commonly than as a fish toxicant. If sold as a fish toxicant, directions on the label will tell you how to use it. If you buy a 5 percent rotenone insecticide you can proceed according to these directions from the Extension Service at Ohio State University:

Use 1 pound of 5 percent rotenone for each 300 feet of shoreline to be treated (or 1¼ pounds of 4 percent, 1⅔ pounds of 3 percent or 2½ pounds of 2 percent or 5 pounds of 1 percent). Do not use rotenone that is mixed with other insecticides or herbicides. Only 1½ to 2 pounds of 5 percent rotenone are required to eradicate completely all fish from 1 acre-foot of water. Generally no more than half the shoreline should be treated at one time. The maximum safe length of

211

shoreline to treat in a 1-acre pond is 600 feet, 450 feet in a ¾-acre pond, and 300 feet in a ½-acre pond.

Water temperature influences the effectiveness of rotenone. It acts more slowly at lower temperatures. Do not use rotenone when water temperatures are below 60 degrees F (15.5 degrees C).

Treat the pond at midday on a clear day with no wind and no prospect of a weather change. Under these conditions bass will be in cooler water and will be outside the area to be treated. On a windy day, you will be unable to control the rotenone, and some of it may spread into deeper water killing large fish. You may treat the leeward side of a pond with some safety if there is only a slight breeze.

Mix the powdered rotenone with just enough water to form a stiff paste, or mix the emulsified form with about twice its volume of water. Next, apply a line of the rotenone under the surface following the shoreline of the pond 10 to 15 feet out from the bank. The rotenone will settle downward and mix with the water on each side of the line of application. Most of the fish between the line of rotenone and the bank will be killed, while those outside the line are likely to move away. If weather conditions are right and care is taken with the methods, only small fish will be killed. Larger fish killed with rotenone may be used for human consumption if collected while still fresh (gills still pink).

You can counteract or "neutralize" the rotenone by applying potassium permanganate, if the treatment affects too much of the pond surface. This method is expensive and should be used only in emergencies. [Even then, effective neutralization may take twenty-four hours or more—too slow to stop some undesired poisoning.] About 2 pounds of potassium permanganate should be used for each pound of 5 percent rotenone applied. It should be dissolved in water and sprayed on the area treated or broadcast with a pail or dipper. Potassium permanganate may be ordered from drug supply companies.

. . . Two or three treatments of rotenone at intervals of a week or ten days should correct a situation where forage fish but not bass are reproducing and where there are moderate numbers of intermediate forage fish.

Seining and trapping, where practical, are certainly to be preferred to poisoning. Smaller ponds can usually be seined quite successfully. The most effective seine will be one that is at least 20 feet long and 4 feet high or deep, with a mesh no larger than ½-inch size. I think the law everywhere prohibits transporting such a seine off your private property without a permit, but sporting goods stores can order one for you, and you can take it home legally without a permit.

When seining, you will have to stick to the shoreline somewhat, as it becomes difficult to walk a seine through water more than chest deep. Every sweep of the seine should end at the shore. Lift the seine up on the bank, sort out and throw back the large fish, and keep the little ones. Some you can clean and eat, some will be so small they are good only for fertilizer, or perhaps to be processed to fish meal for protein feed for other animals or fish.

How many fish should you remove? If the bluegills and sunfish are overpopulating, it won't hurt to take out 50 to 100 pounds per acre per year until bass are big and plentiful again.

Fish traps can help control population, too—and, where your time is limited, provide you with a good supper on busy days. You can buy several kinds of traps—advertised constantly in magazines like *Commercial Fish Farmer* and *Farm Pond Harvest*. You can build one, too. Use ½-inch-mesh welded or woven wire or hardware cloth. Form a cylinder with the wire about 2 feet in diameter and 5 feet long. Close one end of the wire cylinder with a piece of

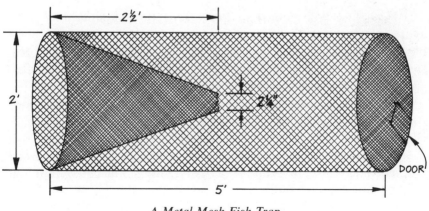

A Metal Mesh Fish Trap

the same wire. At the other end, place another cone or funnel-shaped piece of the wire with a 2½-inch opening in the small end. The small open end should be pointed into the inside of the trap. Fish will enter through the funnel, but are too stupid to find their way out. In the side of the trap, you may want to cut a door that you can open for easy emptying of the trap.

You can bait the trap with soybean cake, cottonseed cake, bread, or other food that will disintegrate only slowly in the water. We use stale sweet rolls. Cottage cheese in a cloth mesh bag works, too.

Set the traps in about 3 to 4 feet of water, parallel to the shore, and check them daily. Bass can be released and bluegills taken out.

Another way to control bluegill population is to destroy their nests during spawning time. If you watch the shallow water closely, you will discern shallow depressions over which the fish hover and into which they deposit eggs. Rake through the nests with a steel rake to destroy them. Make the rounds every day with your rake, and you will dent the bluegill population considerably.

Still another method works well on small ponds where the water level can be raised or lowered easily. Not many ponds are so equipped, of course, but if you can lower the water level at spawning time below the usual spawning grounds, the bluegills won't have enough shallow water to spawn plentifully. Even crappies can be raised in a pond in this manner because raising and lowering water level will effectively control their population.

GAUGING THE CATCH

How fast will your fish grow in a typical situation? With average fertility, availability of food, and density of fish, your bass, bluegills, and channel catfish should grow at the following rates, say extension wildlife biologists in Ohio. (In the South, fish often grow faster in the longer warm season.)

If you feed your fish to make them grow faster, the same common sense applies as when feeding chickens. Don't overfeed. Don't waste. You can prepare your own feeds from grains, fish meal, meat scraps, or whatever. Or you can buy commercial rations. There are a number of fish feeders marketed that cut wastage and feeding time.

AGE IN YEARS

	1	2	3	4	5	10	
Largemouth	6.3	9.0	11.6	13.5	15.8	20.7	Length/Inches
Bass	.13	.44	.75	1.13	2.0	5.5	Weight/Pounds
	3.2	4.6	5.7	6.6	7.4	8 +	Length
Bluegill	.03	.08	.16	.19	.31	.5+	Weight
Channel	6.4	9.6	12.6	14.3	16.7	26.6	Length
Catfish	.3	.5	.8	1.3	2.0	8.0	Weight

I'm not going to try to tell you how to catch fish with line and hook. Sometimes you can and sometimes you can't, and fishermen all have their opinions—as do the fish. Fish worms, and especially night crawlers, are a good all-around bait for bass, bluegills, and channel cats. Frogs and crayfish, especially in their soft-shell stage, will also tempt bass and channel cats mightily. Bass often feed about 20 feet off shore. Sometimes it pays to cast where you see the fish cruising, sometimes not. I usually catch bass and bluegills with a bobber on the line, but catfish off the bottom. Bluegills bite best during spawning time. I've experienced my best pond-fishing of bass around the first of June every year, on a day when rain is threatening.

Bass spawn earlier than bluegill, when water warms up in spring to around 60 degrees F (15.5 degrees C). Fingerlings take two years after stocking to reach spawning size, or a length of about 9 to 10 inches. If you watch, you can sometimes see them in mid-May (here in Ohio) fanning out nests in the shallow water. The female deposits up to twenty thousand eggs and the male guards them until they hatch in two weeks or less.

Bluegills and redears spawn the first season after stocking as fingerlings, when water reaches about 70 degrees F (21.1 degrees C) in spring. A female will lay up to sixty thousand eggs, they say, and these hatch in a few days. Some bluegills and redears spawn several times through the summer.

Channel cats hardly ever spawn in farm ponds, but you can sometimes induce them to do so following these directions from USDA.

Channel Catfish Spawning Devices
Channel catfish may be induced to reproduce in farm ponds by providing spawning containers. They do better in ponds 1 surface-acre or larger. In large ponds one spawning device per surface-acre is usually adequate. A coat of asphaltic paint on inside and outside will prevent rusting and provide a darker environment for spawning. Similar-type containers other than those listed may also be used.

1. Place the open end of the container toward the center of the pond and elevate it slightly.

2. Air pockets that form in containers with curved sides may be eliminated by drilling a small hole.

3. Containers should be kept at a depth of 3 to 4 feet. Move to water of this depth during period of low water elevation.

4. The location of each container should be suitably marked to facilitate annual cleaning and maintenance prior to spawning season.

Almost any 3-foot-long container, closed at one end, is a suitable catfish spawning device.

A box 1 foot square by 3 feet deep can be constructed from 1 x 12 rot-resistant lumber.

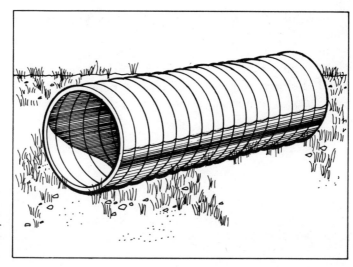

A yard-long section of 12-inch culvert pipe is usable if one end is closed.

Channel catfish usually reach sexual maturity in good-quality water at about three years of age or when they weight 3 to 4 pounds.

Extremely muddy and infertile waters usually produce such small amounts of food that the fish may never have enough nourishment to spawn.

217

Earthenware spawning containers are available commercially.

Hardly ever will fishing with line and hook alone take out as many fish as you want or need to harvest. Several kinds of commercial traps and netting devices are on the market. The simple trap described earlier will work quite well in a typical farm pond. Seining is more effective, especially if you can drain the water down to a small pool.

SPECIALIZED FISH PRODUCTION 12

Homesteaders who wish to produce more fish than are easily gotten from a typical farm pond, or in more intense concentrations, will do well to look to commercial aquaculture for guidelines. Catfish and trout are the two proven and popular fish to raise in this country and are the two species most readily available. Both are most acceptable in the marketplace, too. You will be wise to consider them first before casting an inquiring eye toward Chinese carp, tilapia, or other exotic species.

CATFISH

Catfish are not necessarily easy to raise, but they are easier to raise in homestead or backyard conditions than trout. The former tolerate lower water quality and grow best in temperatures from 70 to 90 degrees F (21.1 to 32.2 degrees C), so cold spring water is not necessary.

But catfish (or any fish) grown intensively will need extra oxygen, extra food, and sometimes extra filtration of the water. Catfish begin to die when oxygen goes below 1 part per million and, according to research reported in *Progressive Fish-Culturist* in 1976, need water charged with at least 3 ppm of oxygen. Many experts like to see water at 4 ppm for healthy growth of catfish. In intensively stocked ponds, bottom tube-drains draw off ammoniated water to keep ammonia content below 1 ppm. Above 2 ppm can be lethal. In raceways or tanks, the constantly flowing and/or recirculating water takes care of the problem. For catfish, water pH is best if slightly alkaline (7.5) and water hardness—the concentration of mineral ions, particularly calcium and magnesium—in the neighborhood of 50 ppm. Hardness can be

221

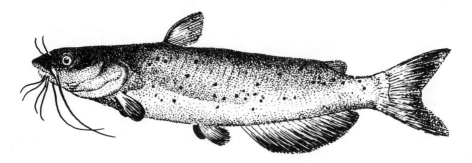

Channel Catfish

higher, however. If you lime to increase alkalinity, you will usually increase water hardness. Catfish can tolerate some muddiness in water, but will taste muddy unless kept in a freshwater holding tank a few days before processing.

Channel catfish are the preferred species, but blue catfish also respond rather well to artificial aquaculture.

Catfish need a feed ration that is about 30 percent protein, 5 percent fat, 10 to 20 percent carbohydrate, and about 10 percent fiber. The USDA recommends that 8 percent of the ration be fish meal and that the feed contains added vitamins. Intensively raised catfish can, for instance, become deficient in vitamin C rather easily when their natural sources aren't available. In a normal pond, catfish will get the .5 milligram of vitamin C per pound they need daily just from eating aquatic insects, but where production goes above 3,000 pounds per acre or where other fish compete too much (tilapia and green sunfish will), then extra vitamins in the feed are usually called for.

Commercial fish feed is usually pelleted, in floating or sinking form. Sinking pellets are cheaper. But many growers prefer the floating kind that give them an immediate indication of how well the fish are feeding. Channel cats aren't surface feeders but they learn soon enough. With sinking pellets, you can put some kind of tray on the pond, raceway, or tank bottom where you feed, and, by examining it after a feeding, see whether or not the fish are eating as they should.

A commercial fish food is much like the feed you buy for chickens or hogs. You can grind grains and add ingredients to make your own, as long as you adhere generally to the formula given above. Moisten the mash before feeding. The fish seem to like it better and you can handle it more easily—the wind can blow dry, powdery feed beyond your feeding area. The USDA recommends adding a jar of baby-food liver to each pound of mash when feeding the very young fish, which are called fry. Fry are usually fed in troughs available from aquacultural suppliers.

Start feeding about a pound and gradually increase the ration to the amount the fry will eat in half an hour. Daily ration after that should be about 3 percent of body weight of the fish in the pond. You have to catch and weigh a few fish every week for an accurate idea of total weight. Professional growers switch to a pelleted feed when the fish are about an inch long, but that is not absolutely necessary for a small-scale operation. Any wholesome food the fish will eat can substitute for commercial feed. You can feed worms and bread crumbs with good results.

Feeding guides for catfish all recommend feeding six days a week, either early in the morning or late in the afternoon. Why not seven days? The only reason I can figure is that everyone likes to have Sunday off, and the fish seem to endure it. Fish are not Christians, but on the other hand, they cannot bellow and squeal like other farm animals if you don't feed them on Sunday.

Scatter feed in ponds where water is 3 to 4 feet deep. Check after an hour, and if feed remains you are feeding too much or something's wrong with the fish. Overfeeding is wasteful and can lead to oxygen deficiency if more than 30 pounds per acre a day is being fed where water doesn't flow or circulate through the pond.

Large producers use self-feeders. The fish learn to bump the underside of the floating feeders to allow feed to fall into the water. Some auxiliary hand-feeding is usually necessary when self-feeders are used.

In winter, when water in outside ponds drops below 70 degrees F (21.1 degrees C), catfish stop eating, but not completely. The general rule of thumb is to feed ½ of 1 percent of the total weight of the fish every four to five days when water temperature is below 45 degrees F (7.2 degrees C), 6 inches below the surface. When the temperature is between 45 and 60 degrees F (7.2 and 15.5 degrees C), feed 6 days a week at the rate of 1 percent of the total fish weight. When the temperature is between 60 and 70 degrees F (15.5 and 21.1 degrees C), feed 2 percent for six days a week. In breeding ponds, some producers stock fathead minnows which the catfish eat for increased vigor and egg development. Cut fish or liver are other high-protein feeds for this purpose. A typical commercial catfish farm will contain at least 40 acres and, of course, there are many larger ones. In the 40 acres of surface water there may be five ponds of 1 acre each for breeding and raising fry, along with holding tanks. There may be as many as five production ponds of 7

Commercial catfish farming demands large-scale resources, from dozens and dozens of spawning containers to huge ponds. The investment necessary can be reduced by using land unsuitable for cropping and making multiple uses of the water. The operation shown is in Chico, California, a rice-growing area, where growers often irrigate their paddies with water from catfish ponds.

acres each. The ponds will usually (though not necessarily) be long and narrow and, if water flows through them constantly, the ponds will be called raceways. Catfish can be crowded more intensively in raceways than in ponds, just as is true of trout. But at any rate the long, narrow pond is easier to catch fish from and easier to observe fish in. The five production ponds in a typical setup should produce 1,200 pounds of fish per acre per year and, with good management, twice that amount.

Catfish can be raised indoors or in a semienclosed system in which case acre becomes a meaningless measurement of possible harvest. On 3 acres, mostly of buildings and raceways, John Greer Jr. reports in *Farm Pond Harvest,* production of 90,000 pounds of catfish in 1976.

The homesteader and backyard producer can scale down either the outdoor or indoor system, as we shall see. The cost of quarter-acre ponds for catfish came to $800 each for the University of Louisiana in 1975. A commercial catfish grower will tell you that to get into the business seriously requires an investment of $500,000. Pond culture need not take that kind of money, however. Some of the most successful ventures capitalize on waste land that can't be cropped and a good supply of water that can be used for many purposes. Rice growers, for example, first run the water they use to irrigate rice through their catfish ponds where it warms up and increases significantly in fertility from the catfish wastes.

Catfish can be raised in cages anchored in existing bodies of water where fish and game laws permit. Cages are made of corrosion-resistant wire on wood or metal frames, with a hinged door on top for feeding and harvesting. The cage bottom should be at least a foot off the floor of the pond or stream. Styrofoam blocks around the cage keep it afloat. The cages are stocked when the weather warms up. The fish must be fed a complete ration, as they will not get much to eat naturally.

Stocking rates in ponds are going to vary, depending on what system you use, how much oxygen you can charge into the water, how much food you want to feed. In ponds, the USDA recommends these rates:

1. Where water is solely from runoff and lift pumps aren't used, stock seven hundred and fifty to one thousand fingerlings (4 to 6 inches long) per surface acre.

Catfish can be raised in cages that are anchored in the middle of a pond or lake or stream. This commercially made model is fabricated of materials that will not harm the fish (the spiny fins of catfish could get caught in some mesh materials, injuring or killing the fish). The top provides access to introduce and remove fish and to feed the fish.

2. In ponds having a sure, controlled water supply, stock fifteen hundred to two thousand fingerlings, or twelve hundred fish of 10-inch size, or seven hundred to eight hundred fish weighing ½ to 1 pound.

3. In ponds through which water flows at the rate of at least 150 gallons per minute, you can stock thirty-five hundred to five thousand fingerlings.

It's not practical to count all those fish. Weigh out one hundred and multiply. If one hundred fingerlings weigh 1 pound, 20 pounds are roughly equal to two thousand fingerlings.

An ideal homestead catfish venture might consist of four ponds of a quarter-acre each, maybe 20 feet wide or preferably less, appropriately stocked. Ponds in the South need be no deeper than 3 or 4 feet, if that depth can be maintained through drought, but in the North the water should be 8 feet deep for winter protection. A commercial catfish grower would hardly consider an acre of water enough for an efficient operation, any more than a corn farmer would consider a 10-acre corn patch efficient, but homesteaders have their own yardsticks of efficiency.

You can raise your own fingerlings in a separate breeding pond, though it makes more sense in a small, part-time operation to buy fingerlings. A breeding pond should be stocked at the rate of ten to twenty pairs of breeders per acre, the lower number if the hatched fish will be held in the pond until they reach fingerling size. (You can spawn catfish in pens, but that's a rather sophisticated method best left to commercial producers.) Fertilized eggs can be left in the pond with male fish to fan water over them the natural way. Or the eggs can be transferred to special hatching "troughs" where the water is mechanically agitated. Where optimum harvest is the goal, young fry are removed from the breeding pond (so daddy won't eat them) and placed in rearing ponds to grow to fingerling size. Then they are transferred to grow-out or production ponds.

Other than greater ease of handling, the reasons for having several smaller production ponds rather than one large one are the capability of grouping fish by size and the security of not having all your eggs in one basket. If disease should strike where all your fish are in one pond, your budding sideline business might be stopped dead in its tracks. Fish are removed by draining or seining or a combination of the two. The ponds, especially the brood pond,

227

should be periodically drained, dried out, disked, and refilled. Refill at least thirty days before restocking.

TROUT

In a pond of average fertility where trout are raised without supplemental food, 100 to 200 pounds of fish per year are about all you can raise per acre. With supplemental feeding and perhaps supplemental aeration, you can increase annual production to 1,000 to 2,000 pounds per surface-acre. It takes about a pound of feed to produce a half-pound of trout. Commercial trout feeds are handy to use, but you can make up your own with grains and protein foods like worms, meat scraps, fish meal, and the like. Commercial growers use supplements as high as 40 percent and even 50 percent protein to speed growth. Feed only what the fish clean up promptly. Any that remains after fifteen minutes will be wasted and will use up precious oxygen as it decomposes. When water is above 65 degrees F (18.3 degrees C), it's not safe to feed trout.

In commercial trout production, much better yields are obtained in raceways than the 1,000 to 2,000 pounds per acre you can get from a pond. It is not unusual for a trout farm with 15 acres in raceways to produce 150,000 pounds a year. You can learn quickly what it takes to raise trout profitably when you see where the business flourishes. About 90 percent of the trout in commercial food trade is raised in Idaho—in fact, in a very small part of Idaho called the Magic Valley. Seemingly unlimited amounts of clear water at 55 degrees F (12.7 degrees C) issue from the earth in thousands of springs in Magic Valley. The water stays at good trout temperature—50 to 60 degrees F (10 to 15.5 degrees C)—summer and winter. Tumbling in large volumes over rocks or baffles in raceways, the water often maintains the 5 ppm oxygen content necessary for trout without added cost of aeration. There is little need to recirculate water. It's trout heaven.

But large and small springs exist all over the country, and many of them would serve easily for more or less intensive backyard trout culture. Many of them, in fact, do. Wisconsin farmers sometimes divert trout streams or spring water through small, homemade raceways where they raise a few fish for home consumption and to sell. Other folks simply dam up a spring into a very small pool and stock it. A trout pool should always be

Rainbow Trout

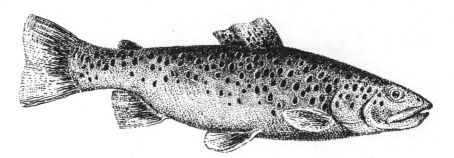

Brown Trout

Brook Trout

Getting Food from Water

The concrete raceways of a commercial trout hatchery.

designed to keep *out* normal run-off water. Silt and mud can kill trout. So can even minute amounts of some agricultural chemicals. Don't plant trees close to the pond, either—decaying leaves falling into the water might use up too much nitrogen if the supply is already critical. A trout pond of 1 acre is more than sufficient for any family. One as small as one-tenth of an acre can supply both good fish and good fishing.

In Ohio and surrounding states, if not elsewhere, some backyard aquaculturists are trying out a new idea for raising trout, promoted by fish consultant and trout breeder Jan Michalek, who operates an experimental research hatchery. Under Michalek's direction, the aquaculturists build small, circular, concrete pools like the ones in Michalek's backyard, from which they can produce enough trout for their families and as much as $1,200 worth extra to

230

sell. Michalek has been trying to sell the practicality of back-yard trout ever since he came to southern Ohio from his native Czechoslovakia as a political refugee years ago. With a background in fish management and production, he saw the numerous springs ignored in the United States as potential sources of high-quality, low-priced protein. USDA and wildlife biologists did not necessarily agree with him, so Michalek went to work building ponds according to designs he had used in Czecho-slovakia. What he accomplished was sometimes hard for fisheries biologists to believe even when they saw it with their own eyes.

"It works," say Michalek. "You can raise 1,000 pounds of trout in one of my circular pools measuring 16 feet in diameter. You can eat all the good protein you want and sell the rest to pay the fuel and utility bills on your home. You won't run into any problems unless you get greedy."

By greedy, Michalek means violating his key rule of success. You must have a spring with a flow-rate of 10 to 15 gallons per minute for *one* pool. "If you run another pool off that spring, as some try to do after they see the success of the first pool, then you get into trouble. If you want two pools, you need a flow-rate of 18 to 25 gallons. You can only raise so many fish in a given supply of water."

Michalek's pools are shallower on the outer edges, about 10 inches deep, dishing down to the center depth of about 30 inches. Each pool is equipped for artificial aeration. There's a drain in the center with a standpipe over it and a special filter—"My design," says Michalek. "The position of the holes is very critical, and I prefer to work with pool builders directly so the filter works right." (Michalek's present address is Rt. 1, 11830 Camp Ohio Road NE, St. Louisville, OH 43071.)

Caring for the fish is simple, says Michalek. They need to be fed at least twice daily. If you want a couple for dinner, you can dip them out in a net or catch them on a fly rod. "The fish are smart, though. If you start fishing for them, you will catch only a few and then the whole bunch of them in the pool get spooked and won't bite," says Michalek.

The spring water won't freeze in winter in the pools except for a thin ring of ice around the outside during very cold weather. Nor does water temperature rise much beyond 65 degrees F (18.3 degrees C) in summer if flowing at the adequate rate. "Actually,

Jan Michalek is a specialist at making the most of a given supply of spring water. He builds one 16-foot-diameter pool per 10 to 15 gallons per minute-flow and stocks each pool with up to one thousand pounds of trout. Michalek's pools are 18 inches at the perimeter and 32 inches deep in the center. The water enters at the edge and drains at the center, setting up a minor current. The fall of the water into the pools helps aerate it, and a commercial aerator is used in each pool to maintain high oxygen levels. Careful management is vital.

I've had water temperatures as high as 84 degrees F (28.8 degrees C) with no harm to the trout," says Michalek. "We don't know all there is to know about trout. With a flow-rate of 10 to 15 gallons of water per minute, I'm raising 1,000 pounds of fish in 1,000 gallons of water, and some of the experts find that hard to believe."

He doesn't advise homeowners to try to hatch their own fry. "That's ticklish work, even for the specialists. Buy your young fingerlings, 4 to 5 inches long, from a reputable hatchery or private breeder."

Would the concrete pools work for other kinds of fish? Certainly, says Michalek. Could you raise trout in the pools with recirculated well water? Possibly. He has one experiment going using recirculated water to which he adds just a bit of fresh water in the cycle. He's experimented with brown trout in particular, since they will tolerate warmer water than other trout.

Cost of a cement pool? Roughly one thousand dollars. If you built the pool yourself using Gunnite instead of regular concrete, you could get by with half or less of that cost.

Raising trout for food is only half of the commercial trout business. The other half produces trout for live sale to pay-lakes, clubs, and individuals. Production of live or recreational trout is not much different from that of food trout but less demanding, since most fish are sold as fingerlings. However, the market for large live trout is growing. A recreational trout producer may or may not hatch his own trout, but will usually be equipped to transport the live fish to customers within perhaps a 200-mile radius. Very small fry sell for about $10 to $15 per hundred on up to about $1 each for 10-inchers. Trout above a 12-inch length sometimes sell live by the pound, at a price equal to, or better than, the prevailing price of food trout. With live trout, you don't have the cost of processing the meat, but do have the cost of specially equipped trucks to haul the fish to customers. Trout hatcheries and recreational trout-raising facilities are found where large springs supply a steady, fairly heavy flow of water. The water runs through cement raceways and pools of various sizes by gravity, and fish are kept separated in raceways by size. The use of aerators allows heavier concentration of fish than would normally be safe, but commercial growers warn that the desire to make a few more bucks by overcrowding raceways is the beginning of many problems with trout.

TILAPIA

Three species of tilapia have been cultured successfully in the United States: Java tilapia, the blue tilapia, and the nile tilapia. They are hardy in warm water, easy to breed, extremely prolific, and, according to those who know, flavorful. (I've never eaten any.) They survive in water with as low as 2 ppm of dissolved oxygen. One pair can multiply to over one hundred thousand fish in six months. They can also survive higher ammonia levels than most fish.

Tilapia are mostly plant eaters and so are cheaper to produce than carnivores. Some eat plankton, others will eat even grass clippings and garden wastes. Soybean meal and ground grain make a good diet for them. Rodale Resources offers this formula for a good homemade feed: 35 percent coffee pulp; 24 percent ground corn; 20 percent molasses; 10 percent bran; 10 percent cottonseed meal; and 1 percent urea. In the absence of plant food, some tilapia become carnivorous.

Tilapia are a tropical fish, and their main drawback in the United States is that they will die if the water temperature drops

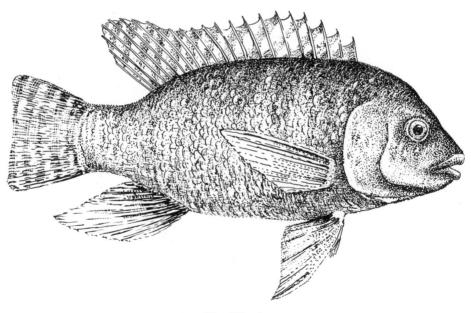

Blue Tilapia

234

much below 50 degrees F (10 degrees C). Laws ban them from some states because, where conditions are right, they can easily overpopulate and threaten other fish populations.

Tilapia breeders have developed a hybrid cross that produces nearly all-male offspring. Mike Sipe of Palmetto, Florida, one of the producers of the hybrid fish, says the hybrid is capable of producing 16,000 pounds of large fish per surface-acre of water. "We're developing a homeowner system that could fill the on-going protein needs of a family in just 100 square feet per person," he says. He raises tilapia in a greenhouse in tanks, over which hang houseplants grown for commercial trade.

The all-male hybrid would be one way to prevent multiplying the species in public waters. But scientists tell me the hybrid is not foolproof. An occasional female is produced, they say.

Dr. Boyd Kynard of the University of Arizona raised tilapia in cages anchored in a one-acre pond formed by strip-mining, only 4 feet deep. In a sixty-day test, survival of small fry was excellent and weight-gain a phenomenal sixteen times the weight of the stocked fry.

Sipe claims the fish are fifty times cheaper than beef to produce, thirty-five times cheaper than chicken, and four times cheaper than soybeans. "They feed on algae, some small aquatic animals, and organic wastes. Some sixty percent of the composition of bottom mud in a pond is usable as food by tilapia."

CARP

Most fish eaters and fish catchers scowl at the mere thought of carp, which litter (literally) many of our streams and rivers, muddying the water so that more desirable species are driven out. Even catching a carp is considered beneath a true fisherman's dignity. Still, for my own taste, smoked carp caught in clean water is not bad at all, and catching the lunkers can be lots of fun. I once hooked one so big and strong, it pulled the rowboat I was in upstream a few yards.

But even if the meat of rough common carp be deemed of poor quality, that judgment does not necessarily apply to the several species of Chinese carp—the silver carp, bighead, and grass carp, or even the strain of common carp called Israeli or mirror carp. The first three species have been raised in China for thousands of years,

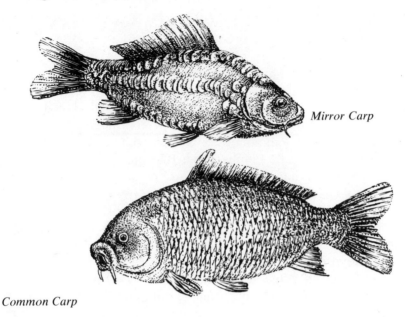

Mirror Carp

Common Carp

and if ten thousand Frenchmen can't be wrong, I doubt 100 million Chinese could be, either. The Chinese raise grass, bighead, and silver carp together in what aquaculturists call a polyculture. They feed the grass carp hay and green weeds. (Think how many tons of protein Americans could produce just with their grass clippings!) While the grass carp eat hay, bighead and silver carp feed on plankton in the middle depths of the pond, and mud carp clean up the wastes on the pond bottom. Aquaculturist Homer Buck of Parr Fisheries Research Center near Kinmundy, Illinois, visited China last year. He reported, "At one extremely impressive operation, the farmer was feeding grass carp in a pond of about one acre on grass only, which he cut and broadcast on the water twice a day. His figures showed an income per acre from carp sold at about $8,000, at least eight times better than our most efficient catfish farmers."

Buck was one of the first American aquaculturists to try feeding carp with manure, a traditional Chinese practice. Usually ducks, geese, or pigs are used in this kind of polyculture in China, but often any and all animal manure is fed to cultured fish. The water and bottom wastes are then recycled farther as highly fertile irrigation water for vegetables and crops. Buck, at Kinmundy, fed a typical commercial ration to pigs on cement floors, the manure being washed off directly into ponds of carp, catfish, and other fish. The manure stimulated algal growth, which the fish ate. "We were quite surprised at the high rate of fish production we got," says Buck. While gains in catfish and bass were negligible, the grass, bighead, silver, and common carp showed a gain of 2,514 pounds per acre in one pond, and 3,297 pounds per acre in the other. What's more, the carp controlled eutrophication and purified the water, maintaining its quality above EPA standards for clean water.

Nevertheless, grass carp, or White Amur, is banned in many states because many fisheries biologists and most sportsmen fear it would cause as much or more havoc than common carp has. Where allowed, grass carp are being used to control water weeds biologically. The outcome of the controversy awaits more evidence. Until then, grass carp are banned (except for approved experimentation) in Arizona, California, Connecticut, Florida, Georgia, Idaho, Illinois, Indiana, Louisiana, Maine, Michigan, Missouri, Nebraska, Nevada, New Hampshire, New Mexico, New York, North Carolina, Ohio, Oklahoma, Oregon, Pennsylvania, South Carolina, Tennessee, Texas, Utah, Vermont, Virginia, Washington, Wisconsin, and Wyoming.

YELLOW PERCH

Yellow perch or lake perch is a favorite fish in the Midwest and Great Lakes areas, its taste cherished above most other species. Walleye pike is a close relative but it's not quite as tasty in the opinion of most Midwesterners. The decline of yellow perch, if not walleye pike, in the Great Lakes has motivated concerned scientists and fisheries biologists to initiate aquacultural experiments with both fish. Results with yellow perch at the University of Wisconsin appear particularly significant. Using advanced technology, researchers produced weight gains in eight to eleven months that would take three to four years in the wild.

Wisconsin researchers decided to design a completely enclosed, indoor system for perch production. They grew fish in fiberglass tanks that measure 30 feet long, 6 feet wide, and 4 feet deep. The bottoms are on a slight incline to facilitate the movement of suspended solid waste out of the tanks. Water flows through the

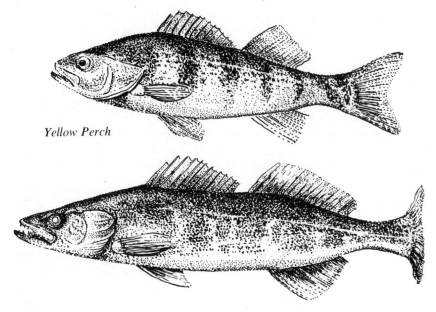

Yellow Perch

Walleye Pike

tanks and is recirculated to save money, since it must be heated to optimum temperature of 68 to 70 degrees F (20 to 21.1 degrees C). Fish density is ½-pound per gallon of water in the tanks. Oxygen is maintained about 5 ppm—4 ppm is good enough, but never below that. The researchers found that perch were very sensitive to light and grew faster when light was kept on sixteen hours and turned off eight. Only dim light proved appropriate, as the fish reacted adversely to bright lights. The pH of the water gave best results at 7.0 to 7.5. A successful feed formula proved to be 50 percent fish meal, 7 percent whey, 5 percent soybean meal, 10 percent fish solubles, 5 percent brewers' yeast, 10 percent bloodmeal, 9 percent soybean oil and a 4 percent vitamin premix. (In general, perch respond well to a 35 percent to 40 percent protein feed and can be fed worms, too. Minnows are okay for walleyes, but perch are too slow to catch them most of the time.)

For up-to-date information on the ongoing perch experiments in Wisconsin, contact the University of Wisconsin Sea Grant College Program, Sea Grant Communications Office, 1800 University Avenue, Madison, WI 53706.

Raising 500 pounds of fish in a 1,000-gallon tank begins to fall

Researchers in Wisconsin are experimenting with raising yellow perch in indoor pools.

into the realm of practical possibility for the backyard aquaculturist. Raising 250 pounds in a 500-gallon tank sounds even better. And most of us would settle for 100 pounds in a 300-gallon tank which would be a less-dense population and therefore that much less risky. As you can guess, raising fish in tanks in high densities with recirculating water requires very sophisticated filtration systems. But even in less complicated home production, filtration is the key to success when you want to produce a significant amount of food in comparatively small tanks, particularly since you will usually want to recycle the water, too.

To simplify (or perhaps to oversimplify), the problem is this: fish in crowded tanks produce, through their wastes and unconsumed food, excessive amounts of ammonia, phosphates, suspended and other dissolved solids, especially nitrogen in the form of ammonium nitrite. The nitrite form of nitrogen is toxic to fish and must be removed. The usual biological method is for water organisms to convert the ammonia to the nitrate nitrogen form. Fish are more tolerant of this mineralized form of nitrogen. This process is called nitrification. But in an enclosed system, the nitrates must be converted further to free nitrogen gas, a process

239

called denitrification. Microbes in the water perform this service if conditions are right for them and if given time to establish themselves before large numbers of fish are put into the tanks. In the perch experiments, a water temperature of 70 degrees F (21.1 degrees C) resulted in a good rate of nitrification.

This process is the primary function of a filter—the more surface-area the filter has for the growth of microbes, the better. Filters also may remove some suspended solids, but will quickly become overburdened if such solids are too plentiful. Sedimentation or screening ahead of filtering is a better way to remove solids, and it is necessary in a dense production system such as is employed on the perch. Sedimentation simply means holding the water motionless for the length of time it takes to settle out particulate matter.

Filters for fish tanks can be almost any material that is not corrosive or soluble in water, that the fish won't eat, and that offers a large amount of surface-area for screening the water and for microbes to grow on. A box of small rocks will work. Crushed limestone, the stones about the size of marbles, makes a good filter and the slightly soluble limestone can help keep the pH neutral to slightly alkaline. A box of sand is often used for a filter. Various commercial packages of plastic granules or chips are sold for filters. Clam shells make adequate filters. Some filters are gravity filters, the water flowing through them from top to bottom. Some are submerged filters, the water rising up through them from the bottom and flowing out the top. Whenever possible, make provision for back-flushing a filter so you can clean it easily if it gets overloaded with suspended solids.

The terminology of filtration makes it sound more complicated than it is. Anyone with experience with swimming pool filters understands the principles. A visit to a water treatment plant will aid your grasp of filtration too.

BLUEGILLS

In a previous chapter, I painted the bluegill as a necessary evil, if not a downright villain, in the farm pond. But in a more controlled aquacultural system—in backyard or in-house tanks, the bluegill's hardiness and prolific ways may increase its stature as a food in the future. Bluegills are easily fed, grow rapidly to a

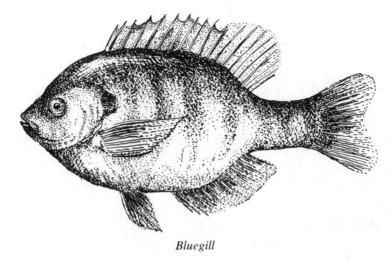

Bluegill

half-pound size, taste good, and if properly filleted, are not bony. Some bluegill lovers recommend cooking the smaller fish until the bones are crisp enough to chew and swallow safely. That works and I should know. One time in my season of wild oats, three of us vowed to "live off the wild" for a whole day. To make sure, we brought no food to camp. Total luck of the hunt that day was one (1) measly bluegill. We ate everything but the head.

Work with bluegills in backyard culture is being initiated at Rodale Resources, Emmaus, Pennsylvania. Dr. Joe Senft, who has been involved in the aquacultural research there, believes that the bluegill may be an overlooked practical source of food for the homesteader.

BULLHEADS

The bluegill is sometimes recommended for farm ponds; the lowly bullhead is a total outcast. It breeds too fast and overpopulates in farm ponds. Nevertheless, the bullhead, even more than the bluegill, is a hardy, resilient fish, easy to clean and debone, and excellent of taste in my opinion. Through flood and drought, chemical pollution and erosion pollution, the plucky bullhead persists in our creek. That's about all the proof I need that it would respond to backyard production.

Not much attention has been given the bullhead in this regard, but for the sake of any ideas it might give you, I'll recall how we

Brown Bullhead

used to raise this fish years before anyone ever thought much of growing fish, but only of catching them. We had a horse-trough, a cement tank about 8 feet long, 4 feet wide, and 5 feet deep, over half of which was covered with a roof—boards holding a foot of sawdust. The sawdust kept that end of the tank, where the float and inlet pipe were, from freezing. We threw bullheads in the tank that we caught in the creek and they flourished, even on our haphazard feeding of worms and bread crumbs.

When I think back on it, the tank was a pretty good production unit for catfish. As the livestock drank, more fresh water flowed in. The water was well water, pumped by a windmill into a wooden storage tank from which it fed by gravity to the stock tank. The system worked wonderfully well without the use of any energy other than the wind. I remember only once having to pump water by hand into the storage tank because of a lack of wind.

At any rate, the bullheads did just fine. They bred and brought forth clouds of black fry that seemed to hang in suspension in the water, there to be eyed curiously by cow and human alike. I don't remember what happened to all those small fish—we certainly didn't feed them to edible size. But if you own a homestead that just happens to have an old cement livestock tank, a windmill, and

242

a storage tank, you could be in the backyard aquaculture business in a very short time.

CRAYFISH

There are a score or more species of crayfish in the United States. The Louisiana red and the white crayfish have both proven themselves commercially practical for aquaculture, particularly the former. Almost all crayfish produced for market come from Louisiana, where the climate is favorable and where French tradition is still strong. (California is second in production.) Crayfish are a favorite food in France where they have long been cultivated as a backyard endeavor. "Small French farmers I visited were making $15,000 a year from an acre crayfish pond," E. Evan Brown, aquaculturist and economist at the University of Georgia told me. "Crayfish are very popular and the price very high, but even in the United States, you can make $1,000 to $2,000 on an acre of crayfish. If people learn that crayfish are just as good as lobster, demand could raise that value even more."

Fisheries biologist Andy Merkowsky, who works for Rodale Resources, is a firm believer in crayfish for the home grower in the South, though northern winters pose problems not yet worked out. "They are much easier to take care of than fish," he explains. "You need only 18 inches of water. They will thrive on grass clippings and other plant material and table scraps and an occasional meat or fish scrap. You don't have to worry about oxygen content in the water unless the pool is extremely crowded—crayfish can breath okay out of water. In cold weather, you can drain the pool because the crayfish dig down into the ground anyway. With experience, you should be able to produce 150 pounds of crayfish in the South, as tasty as shrimp or lobster, in a 12-by-12-foot pool only 18 inches deep."

Merkowsky says that if he were to start raising crayfish in his backyard, he'd dig out a shallow 12-by-12-foot pool, surround it with a galvanized steel or fiberglass wall sunk into the earth a foot or so, depending on winter severity, possibly insulate that wall to keep out cold, and cover the pool with a solar dome. If necessary to hold water, he'd use a plastic liner but with at least 8 inches of soil on top (or more, depending on winter severity and/or ability of the dome to maintain warmth) for the crayfish to burrow into. "If you

243

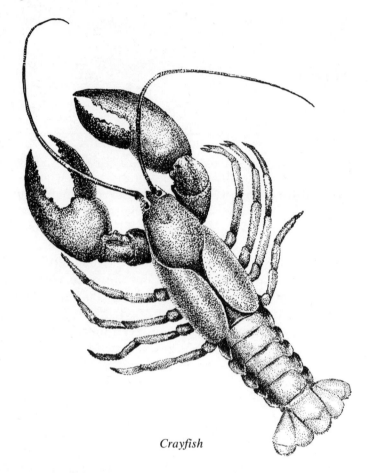

Crayfish

don't provide burrowing room for the crayfish, they will get out in the yard and make their burrows,'' says Merkowsky.

In the North, however, much more elaborate insulation in the ground around the crayfish pond would be necessary. Concrete and/or Styrofoam insulation to a depth below frostline, as in other northern winter fish tanks, might be necessary. These experiments have not been run yet in severe winters because crayfish are so much easier to raise in the South.

Crayfish grow rapidly in summer when the water temperature rises above 70 degrees F (21.1 degrees C). They will not eat as much, but will remain active at 55 to 60 degrees F (12.7 to 15.5 degrees C). ''With a solar dome, you could raise crayfish even in the North in all but the coldest weather. Since crayfish burrow into the ground when the temperature falls in winter and remain there for at least two months, you can drain the pond during that time and not have to worry about the crayfish. They will emerge when warmer temperatures return.''

It takes sixteen weeks for a crayfish to mature under ideal conditions. To harvest them, you can use a mesh trap such as used for minnows. "Use a mesh size that holds only the mature crayfish and then you don't have to sort and throw back small ones," says Merkowsky. Harvest is more or less continuous after sixteen weeks, as the crayfish do not all mature at the same time.

No work has been done with northern-type crayfish. With some two hundred species to work with world-wide, it seems possible—and Merkowsky agrees—that selective breeding could produce larger strains even for the North. Actually the Louisiana red isn't all that much bigger than some of the northern crawdaddies I've seen in our creek. But Merkowsky suggests using Louisiana reds, if you want to experiment. Contact the Louisiana Cooperative Extension Service at Louisiana State University for possible sources of crayfish stock. But you could be farther ahead in the North to catch a few of your local species out of the creek nearest to you and start selectively breeding them.

You can learn too, from the way crayfish are now being produced commercially. Aquaculturist Bill McLarney, who, with John Todd, heads up the New Alchemy Institute (more on that later), has a keen interest in the possibilities of crayfish for home production. In *Organic Gardening and Farming*® magazine, he described southern production methods this way:

> Some 2,500 acres of Louisiana rice fields are stocked with crayfish, but most of the farm production comes from shallow ponds constructed in marshy areas which are not well suited to most forms of terrestrial agriculture nor to fish culture. The most commonly raised crayfish in Louisiana is the famous "Louisiana red" (*Procambarus clarkii*) but some farmers also grow the white crayfish (*Procambarus blandingi*).
>
> The natural history of the two cultured species is similar; mating occurs in open waters in the late spring when the water level is high. The eggs are not fertilized at this time; rather, sperm is deposited in an external receptacle on the female. After breeding, the females come out on shore and dig burrows

Crayfish.

two to three feet deep near the water's edge. By the end of July, all the burrows are occupied by mated pairs and capped with plugs of earth. Soon the eggs and sperm are simultaneously released by the female, and the fertilized eggs are attached to the underside of her tail with a sticky substance called "glair." The several hundred eggs hatch in two weeks to a month, following which the adults die.

In normal years, hatching of wild crayfish occurs about the time the water in the Louisiana swamps rises, so the young are released. In dry years, the early part of the life cycle may be spent in the burrow, which may result in poor growth or mortality. Young crayfish at first stay in vegetation near shore, then gradually move out into deeper water to breed and die within a year. Crayfish culture ponds are constructed and managed so the vagaries of the weather play much less of a role in the completion of the life cycle.

The most productive Louisiana crayfish ponds are very shallow; when the highest point in the bottom is covered by 1 foot of water, depths of over 3 feet should not occur in more than 25 percent of the remaining area. The shallowness of the ponds calls for a relatively flat site, but the bottom need not be level; in fact small irregularities may be advantageous. Drains should be constructed so as to permit complete drainage in no more than thirty days.

As in all forms of aquaculture, a good water supply, preferably from a well, is crucial. Red crayfish do best at temperatures of 70 to 85 degrees F (21.1 to 29.4 C), with a pH of 6 to 8, a hardness of 50 to 200 ppm, and a salinity of no more than 10 parts per thousand, or approximately one-third the strength of ocean water. Would-be crayfish growers outside Louisiana who find that their water does not meet these specifications should look into the possibility of growing locally occurring species. A more general requirement, applicable to all species, is that the water be free of all contaminants. Crayfish are sensitive, not only to agricultural and industrial chemicals, but also to such more or less "natural" substances as creosote, nicotine, pine oil, and pyrethrum.

Pond construction and first flooding should be completed by mid-May and the water allowed to stand for at least two weeks before stocking. Even though wild crayfish may be present, it is necessary to stock the first year, after which the population should be self-sustaining. Freshly caught or purchased animals are stocked, at rates of 20 to 125 pounds to the acre, depending on the presence or absence of wild crayfish and the availability of shelter from predators.

Two weeks after stocking, gradual drainage is begun so that the females have an opportunity to burrow. Ponds are left nearly dry until September, when they are reflooded to release the young. From then on until the start of the harvest season in late November, the water level is left high.

Unlike lobsters, most species of crayfish are more or less herbivorous. While a number of plant species grow naturally in the shallow culture ponds, the most successful growers take pains to remove such hard, inedible plants as cattails and seed and encourage softer plants, notably alligator grass (*Alternanthea phylloxeroides*) and/or water primrose (*Jussiaea* spp.). Much remains to be learned about management and use of these and other plants.

Rice field culture of crayfish in Louisiana is similar to pond culture, but follows a two-year rotation schedule, as outlined below:

Plowing .... March 1-April 20
Replowing and planting rice .... April 15-May 15
Flooding and stocking .... May 1-May 31
Draining .... July 15-May 15
Harvesting rice and reflooding .. August 1-September 1
Harvesting crayfish .... December 1-June 15
Draining and use as pasture .... June 15-March 1

The average yield of both methods is 350 to 650 pounds to the acre, but some of the best growers achieve over 1,000 pounds. Some of the larger farms have hundreds of acres of ponds, but many large and small farmers also realize a supplementary income from small crayfish ponds built on land that would otherwise be unproductive.

. . . Other crayfish culture enterprises in the United States are designed to produce small crayfish for use as fish bait, but it is not difficult to see how some of the species and techniques involved could be adapted to the production of edible-size crayfish. Three to 3½ inches is considered the minimum marketable size wherever crayfish are sold in this country. I have contacted one bait grower who also markets a few crayfish for human consumption.

A. A. Headley, of Foster, Missouri, writes: ". . . There is considerable difference between propagating for human consumption and raising them for bait. I would recommend smaller, narrow ponds, not over 3 feet deep for bait propagation—40 feet by 20 feet is good. Climate or water temperature govern the spawning period; the females usually start appearing here in late May and early June, and by the last week in June the eggs and small craws are free of the female, and the adult crayfish can be removed from the ponds with minnow seines. Seines used for crayfish need more lead line weight than minnow seines to hold them close to the bottom of the ponds. I put the adult crayfish in larger, deeper ponds.

"Crayfish will eat and thrive on any kind of food, meat, or vegetable. We feed oatmeal mush and some fish food pellets early. Our fishing lakes produce an excess of crappies. We use a lot of these for crayfish food. Grind them with a chopper.

"We harvest some larger crayfish with traps—up to 8 or 9 inches—from larger ponds that contain quite dense aquatic growth. The demand seems to be picking up for the food craw. As yet I could, in one way, be considered an authority on crayfish for food, but I believe they can be produced in large numbers in the larger ponds by more intensive feeding and careful selection of stock."

Mr. Headley does not know the identity of the species he raises, but believes there are "at least three different kinds" in his area.

OTHER KINDS OF FISH

Certainly, as we have discussed, the largemouth bass will adapt to more intensive production. We should not pull the shade on any native fish. In fact, the danger is to become too intrigued with exotic fish like tilapia or Chinese carp because of what seem like advantages and overlook native fish. Freshwater prawns, for example, seem to have great promise to sophisticated, commercial aquaculture, but the backyarder will probably produce more protein with an unsung, common fish like the crappie in intensive pond culture.

New strains of largemouth bass are being sought and will certainly be forthcoming. Scientists want a bass that will adapt well to the warm water of electric power generating plants, in addition to strains that grow faster.

Muskies are being grown on artificial food in Wisconsin. Research into culturing northern pike continues at Minnesota and elsewhere. Striped bass, an ocean fish, seem, so far, to adapt well to fresh water.

As aquaculturists like to say: "We have only begun to scratch the surface."

DISEASES AND PARASITES OF FISH

In a farm pond where fish populations do not exceed natural levels, and where good management prevails, disease is not common and parasites seldom prevalent enough to cause trouble. When stress is placed on fish (or any other animal) natural resistance decreases, and trouble may occur. Lack of adequate oxygen and lack of proper food, especially in combination with higher than natural populations, are the major causes of poor fish health. In addition to good management, every effort should be made to stock ponds with healthy fish from sources uninfested with parasite problems. About the only way to do this, is to employ the knowledge of experts or to know personally the place your purchased fish come from. Though the occurrence is fairly rare, you can buy sick fish, or fish so weakened in shipment that they become sick. Commercial fish producers sometimes treat new brood stock with a one-hour bath in 10 ppm of potassium permanganate, then transfer the fish to a bath of 15 ppm of formalin for four to twelve hours to insure that no parasites are introduced into the pond.

In some cases, microscopic examination is necessary to diagnose a problem. But the backyard fish culturist ought to have at least a minimal awareness of the more common problems that can crop up, though for him the problems will be more rare than common. The Fish and Wildlife Service, at its Fish Farming Experimental Station near Stuttgart, Arkansas, issues a pamphlet, Bureau Resource Publication 76, that briefly describes "Parasites and Diseases of Warm-Water Fishes." The following information is derived in part from that pamphlet.

Fungal Diseases *Saprolegnia* fungi produce what look like tufts of cotton or wool on fish. Almost always, the disease attacks fish already weakened by some other problem. *Saprolegnia* will attack all species of fish in artificial ponds or reservoirs, but some species of carp are particularly susceptible. Gill rot is often associated with *Saprolegnia*. Gill rot, caused by *Branchiomyces sanguinis* fungi, begins with red spotting on the gills. The gills later turn grayish white and cease functioning. Drain-

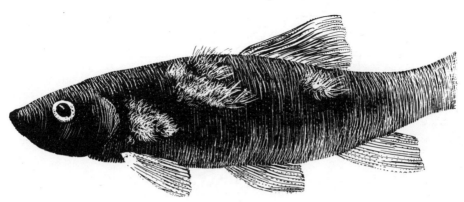

Fish with Saprolegnia

ing the pond and treating with quicklime in severe cases is one method of treatment, for both diseases. Removing infected fish may be enough to stop an outbreak if it is not bad. Other possible treatments listed by the Fish and Wildlife Service for *Saprolegnia* include copper sulfate, potassium permanganate and malachite green.

Bacterial Diseases   *Columnaris* looks like a fungal disease, and proper identification may require microscopic examination. Discolored patches appear on the fish's body and scales slough away, leaving lesions. Buffalo, golden shiners, bluegills, bass, crappies, and catfish get it. The best prevention is adequate oxygen in the water. Medicines that may help are the old-fashioned copper sulfate and potassium permanganate. Antibiotics are more modern remedies.

Furunculosis begins as abscesses in muscle tissue, the lesions finally working out through the skin where they become host to fungal diseases like *Saprolegnia*.

Parasites   Costiasis disease is caused by a protozoa of the genus *Costia*. It attacks channel catfish, bass, and bluegills, creating a blue gray film over the body surface. The fish won't eat and move jerkily and erratically about. Salt, acetic acid, formalin, and other treatments are prescribed.

Trichodiniasis causes irregular white patches to appear all

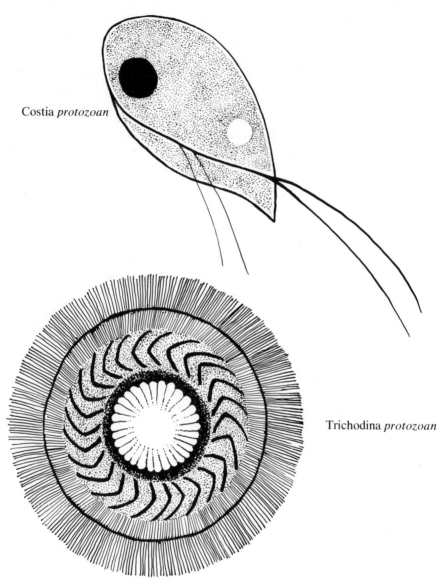

Costia *protozoan*

Trichodina *protozoan*

over the body of the fish. Frayed fins, sluggishness, and loss of appetite follow. All minnows, crappie, bass, and channel catfish are susceptible. The *Trichodina* protozoa, like the *Costia,* is microscopic.

Ichthiophthiriasis is a parasitical disease that fish experts have mercifully shortened to "Ich" disease. I suspect no catfish farmer in Arkansas would even try to wrap his tongue around the whole word, and after several college tries, I found it impossible to negotiate that "phth" myself. Ich disease forms white, pimplish spots on the skin and fins of fish, especially channel cats, bullheads, buffalo, carp, and sunfish. In a Peace Corps manual written by Marilyn Chakroff (Series No. 36E, September 1976), draining and liming the pond is advised for treatment. Or if chemicals are used, the following formulations are given as guidelines:

Formalin: 200 to 250 ppm as a daily bath, or 15 ppm in pond.
Malachite green: 1.25 ppm in a daily bath for thirty minutes, or 0.5 ppm in pond.
Methylene blue: 2 ppm in a daily bath.
Acriflavin: 10 ppm in three to twenty daily baths.
Salt: 7,000 ppm in several daily baths.

Black spot disease is caused by flukes in their larval stage. Small, black nodules appear on the flesh and over the body of the infected fish. Minnows, bluegills, sunfish, and bass are susceptible.

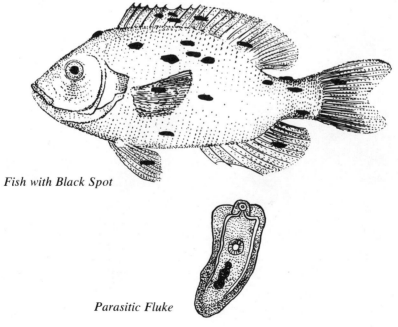

Fish with Black Spot

Parasitic Fluke

253

There's no cure for black spot. But it takes a combination of birds and snails for the fluke to maintain its life cycle and infect the fish. When a bird eats the infected fish, the adult worm eggs pass out with the bird's droppings into the pond. The eggs hatch, the larval worms enter snails, emerge as free-swimming flukes, and infest the fish. Removal of bird roosts around the pond or control of snails will help break the chain of infestation.

Intestinal flukes depend on snails for their life cycle, too. Eggs pass out of fish with droppings, hatch, enter snails, emerge as free swimmers, and enter mayfly naiads. The fish eats the mayflies and is infected. Listlessness and weight loss follow. Therapeutic agents prescribed include di-N-butyl tin oxide, kamala, and chloroxylenol.

There are tapeworms for every species of fish, just as for most species of other animals. They depend on other intermediate hosts—copepods and small fish—to keep their life cycle going, as is true of other tapeworms. The same controls as for intestinal flukes are advised.

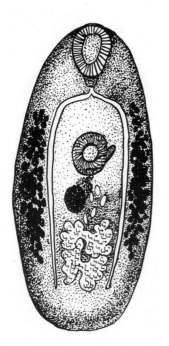

Intestinal Fluke

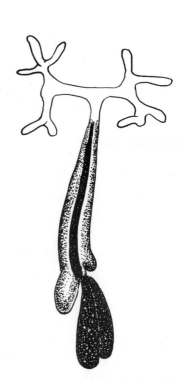

Anchor Worm

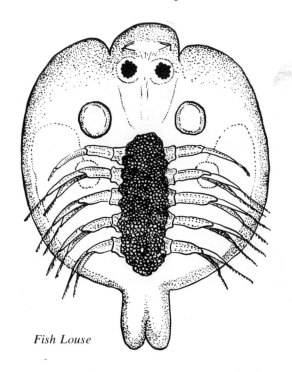

Fish Louse

The *anchor worm,* which is not really a worm but a copepod, *Lernaea cyprinacea,* is regularly giving fish farmers trouble. Most kinds of scaled fish are susceptible. The parasite resembles the shaft of a small barb inserted into the flesh of the fish and is difficult to remove. Lesions appear where the anchor imbeds itself in the fish; the sores then invite fungal infection. Benzene hexachloride, potassium permanganate, and Dylox are the chemicals commercial fish growers use to control anchor worms. Less toxic methods advised by Chakroff are adding castor oil to the pond, treating infected fish in a formalin bath, or removing parasites by hand—the latter method only practical for a few fish.

Fish lice are parasitic copepods of the genus *Argulus* and are closely related to the anchor worm. Listlessness, general discomfort, and in severe cases on young fish, death, follow infection. Most ordinary pond fish are susceptible. The parasite looks like a flat, pinkish red disc that clings to the skin, fins, or gills. It sucks blood and, while doing so, injects a poison into the fish. A bath of 3 to 5 percent salt, or of 250 ppm of formalin for one hour may bring control. Draining and liming the pond helps eradicate an infestation. Other chemical treatments include benzene hexachloride, potassium permanganate, and chlorine.

In addition to rotenone, other "natural" poisons that can be used to control undesirable aquatic animals are quicklime, teaseed cake, camelia seed cake, tobacco waste, and powdered croton seed. Most of these poisons break down within seven to twelve days, after which period new fish can be stocked. The Chakroff manual, cited above, gives these application rates:

Quicklime: 352 pounds/hectare.
Teaseed cake: 330 pounds/hectare.
Camelia seed cake: 110 to 440 pounds/hectare, depending on depth of water.
Powdered croton seed cake: 110 to 400 pounds/hectare, depending on water depth.
Tobacco waste: 330 pounds to 440 pounds hectare.

BACKYARD FISH
PRODUCTION EXPERIMENTS 13

A few private institutions and individuals maintain on-going research projects of interest primarily to small-scale, noncommercial aquaculturists. Among the better-known efforts are those pursued by the New Alchemy Institute at Woods Hole, Massachusetts, by *Farm Pond Harvest* magazine, Momence, Illinois, and by Rodale Press's Research and Development Group. Dr. Homer Buck and his colleagues at Parr Fisheries, Kinmundy, Illinois, conduct experiments of interest to both commercial and noncommercial growers—a statement that would, of course, hold true for many of the experiments conducted in universities around the country under the Sea Grant College Program. In addition, many individuals are at work perfecting fish production methods of their own. I will tell about only two of them: Robert Huke, a Dartmouth College professor, who has published an excellent booklet with Robert Sherwin, Jr., about his experiences—*A Fish and Vegetable Grower for All Seasons* (Norwich Publications, Box F, Norwich, VT 05055); and the previously mentioned Jan Michalek, a fish consultant, who operates an experimental research hatchery of his own at St. Louisville, Ohio.

THE NEW ALCHEMY INSTITUTE

In 1971, John Todd and Bill McLarney, who head the New Alchemy Institute, built their first semienclosed backyard fish system—part of their overall goal of perfecting low-energy, ecological, and self-sustaining life systems for small landholders. Because trout and catfish require relatively high amounts of animal protein in their diets, Todd and McLarney decided to experiment mainly with algae-eating tilapia, mirror carp, grass carp, bluegills, bull-

259

heads, and other fish, all in some way cheaper to feed than trout and channel catfish. Over a round pond 5 feet deep and 18 feet in diameter, they built a fiberglass-covered, geodesic dome. The dome retains the solar heat that streams through the fiberglass, and the water collects and stores that heat. Algae grow well in the warm water under the dome and provide the principal food for the tilapia. But in winter the dome cannot hold enough heat for tilapia. Without some other source of heat, these fish can be raised only through the six months of warm weather in the North. The best the researchers have been able to do so far is keep the fish alive over winter, but in water temperatures too cool for growth.

The algae also oxygenate the water a little and help purify it of some of the fish wastes and toxins by changing ammonia to nitrites to nitrates. The water is circulated by a small electric pump through a series of filters filled with clam shells to clean the water still more by the activity of the bacterial cultures.

Reporting on their work in the *Commercial Fish Farmer* of September 1977, Todd and McLarney wrote:

> The "Back Yard Fish Farm" has proven virtually problem-free. Routine labor inputs include only supplemental feeding and daily checking of the pump and filters. Failure to perform either chore results only in reduced growth rates, not in mortality of fish. Overpopulation by tilapia is prevented by netting the young at an early age when they aggregate on the surface.
>
> In the summer of 1976, the "Back Yard Fish Farm" yielded 55 pounds of tilapia, plus several thousand young fish which were used elsewhere at New Alchemy. The system is not capable of supporting tilapia through the winter, but it could be used to hold—and perhaps grow—fishes native to temperate climates. The dome also functions as a solar-heated greenhouse, permitting us to grow various types of vegetables the year-round in the space adjacent to the pond and on hanging structures.

The researchers next tried a different fish-growing system, one that involves three pools through which water circulates by gravity from the top pool to the bottom. The water then is pumped back to the top pool by a windmill or a ½-horsepower electric motor. The bottom and largest pool is 15 feet in diameter and 6 feet deep, covered by a plastic-covered greenhouse. In this pool, the researchers culture phytoplankton and zooplankton, which are pumped along with the water back up to the upper and middle ponds where fish are raised. The two fish ponds measure 5 feet by 15 feet by 1½ feet deep. As the water splashes from one pool to the next, it is oxygenated. Phytoplankton also help oxygenate the water, but the researchers, just to be safe, stock the middle pond only half as densely as the top one.

Bullheads in the ponds gained 50 percent in weight in one month with heavy supplemental feeding, report Todd and McLarney, while tilapia increased in weight by a factor of sixteen in two weeks with no supplementary feeding apart from bugs attracted by a bug light. The greenhouse adequately heats the main pond and is also used for vegetable production.

The third, newest, and in some ways most impressive installation at New Alchemy is what the researchers call their solar-algae ponds. These ponds are cylindrical tanks, 5 feet tall and 5 feet in diameter, made of .6-inch Kalwall fiberglass. The tanks admit 90

Solar tanks housing tilapia and carp at the New Alchemy Institute.

261

percent of the prevailing sunlight which encourages heavy algal bloom. The algae provide lots of food for fish and, by taking up ammonia directly, purify the water. The algal bloom darkens the color of the water, allowing it to absorb more solar heat. When one of the tanks was surrounded with another Kalwall skin with air space between and a Styrofoam-insulated lid, the growing season could be extended longer than in their other aquacultural greenhouses, say Todd and McLarney. They found they could also put reflective screens behind the tanks to increase the amount of light and warmth absorbed.

In addition to their articles in *Organic Gardening and Farming* magazine and in the *Commercial Fish Farmer,* the New Alchemists have written detailed and engaging accounts of their work in their *Journal of the New Alchemists,* particularly numbers 2, 3, and 4, which can be ordered through The New Alchemy Institute, Box 432, Woods Hole, MA 02543, if not available in your library.

RODALE PRESS'S RESEARCH

Robert Rodale, president of Rodale Press, has long been interested in backyard aquaculture as a logical and practical counterpart to the backyard garden. Impressed with the prodigious amount of protein that oriental farmers could produce from a combination of aquaculture and agriculture, Rodale wrote in 1971 that the whole world "must learn to walk through the water." He saw a new frontier in food production—"growing a variety of plants with aquatic and amphibian animals in a series of ponds on a small homestead." In addition to funding aquacultural research at other institutions, Rodale was able, in 1976, to begin his own serious experimentation through a new branch of his company called the Research and Development Group. A backyard pool and a farm pond were constructed at the New Experimental Farm. Then Mountain Springs, a small farm blessed with springs, was purchased and used for one year of aquacultural experiments.

From these beginnings there are evolving completely combined agri-aquacultural food production systems scaled for practical adaptation to the backyard and homestead. There's still a lot of work to do, and Rodale's researchers are reluctant to make broad recommendations based on their work. If there's one thing they've found, it's the one thing that the New Alchemists and other experimental aquaculturists have found: Raising dense populations of nonnative fish in artificial environments is very difficult.

A Farm Pond for the Backyard

Rodale's first experiment—one that continues—involved a series of small pools adjacent to the experimental gardens. The goal: to see if one such pond would be a practical way to produce just 50 pounds of cleaned fish a year, increasing a family's food supply by about as much as a dozen chickens or rabbits. How small could such a pond be? What equipment would be necessary? Could the fish be fed on fish, kitchen scraps, and other home sources of protein?

Native fish—channel catfish, buffalo, and mirror carp—were stocked in six pools each 12 feet in diameter and 3 feet deep. Native fish were chosen because they are more easily available to homeowners. The buffalo did not do well, mostly because they were not as available as had been anticipated and had to be shipped in from far away, but the catfish and carp performed quite well and

Rodale's backyard pond experiments begin with the fertilization of the small ponds with hog manure. One-and-a-half pounds of the manure are shoveled into a burlap sack and the sack is dropped in the pond, like a big tea bag. The resulting algae bloom isn't necessarily attractive, but it is a vital part of the food chain.

263

the experiment was considered a success. Here is the report of Jack Ruttle of the Research and Development Group:

Six ponds were dug and fertilized with 1½ pounds of hog manure. After an algal bloom was established, the ponds were stocked on May 22 with enough fish to grow 80 pounds in each pond. We planned two combinations of warm-water fish that would grow well together by using more of the available food in a pond than a single species would. Three replications of each of these polycultures were established. Three of the ponds got twenty catfish fingerlings each, to be fed a commercial trout ration. Ten mirror carp were stocked in each of the others. The carp would live on table scraps and some algae. All six ponds received ten buffalo fish apiece, which would feed on food scraps and waste from the other fish and on algae.

Caring for the fish was not demanding, but did require daily attention. Most of the time went to learning about water quality and cultivating a healthy colony of algae for oxygen

Topping up the pools was a several-times-a-week chore in the first rounds of experimentation, necessitated by the fact that the pond bottoms were not sufficiently impermeable. Efforts to seal the ponds with bentonite clay were not wholly successful.

production, fish food, and water purification. At the start, water was tested regularly and often for pH, temperature, ammonia, and oxygen. Of these, only oxygen levels became critical enough to merit constant checks. With a little experience, researchers learned to gauge oxygen levels by the color of the algae and the weather.

When photosynthesis stops at sundown, life in the pond coasts on the oxygen that accumulated during the day. And . . . there were often substantial variations between different ponds in algal growth. So for backup oxygenation, we used a Hush II aerator in each pond. Oxygen levels were very good for the first half of the season. However, long stretches of cloudy days coupled with cooling weather in late August and September didn't support enough photosynthesis to maintain adequate oxygen for the steadily growing fish.

Another complicating factor was leakage in all the ponds, which necessitated adding water constantly, and severely disrupted algal growth. The ponds need to be sealed with clay, creating a more stable environment for algae culture.

Feeding the fish took only minutes a day. Table scraps were blended according to a rule-of-thumb formula using 50 percent high-protein scraps, 25 percent green vegetable matter, and 25 percent high-carbohydrate foods. The fish were fed according to what they would take; occasional weight checks on these amounts provided an indication of how much they had grown.

By October 21, the water had cooled so that the fish weren't eating much, and the ponds were harvested. The late start had reduced the ideal season by about 25 percent and periods of low oxygen had inhibited growth. Still, the ponds produced fish of edible size. Overall conversion of feed to flesh was 2.2-to-1—very close to the 2-to-1 ratio hoped for.

The catfish grew especially well, averaging .8 pound apiece. The carp averaged 1½ pounds, a good pan size. The handful of surviving buffalo reached a little over half a pound apiece. Comparing these weight gains to the amount of feed given on an equal dry matter basis, shows that the table scraps nourished the fish as well as the trout chow.

Using water from the ponds, we irrigated a nearby vege-

Harvest is a simple job: The ponds are drained and the fish picked up.

table plot. At the end of the season, the nutrient-rich fish water had boosted yields in that plot 35 percent higher than in an identical garden watered directly from the spring.

A Fish Pool in the Basement

Could fish for table use be grown indoors, even in a basement where there was no sunlight? That's the second question Rodale researchers addressed themselves to. The answer is a qualified yes, though the experiment is far from completed. With proper filtration and aeration, fish will grow in basements, but the cost may be higher than for fish purchased at the market. However, since it is easier to control temperature indoors, pools can be used year-round, even in the North, for greater and more efficient production, reducing cost per pound to efficient levels.

The first basement pool used was built with plywood and a plastic liner. The pool worked adequately, but, inevitably, holes were punched into the liner. Sturdy cement-block pools, the insides coated with sealer paint, have proven more satisfactory, and in the long run, cheaper.

Several kinds of fish are being tested in several basement pools, each 18 inches deep and holding 600 gallons of water. The

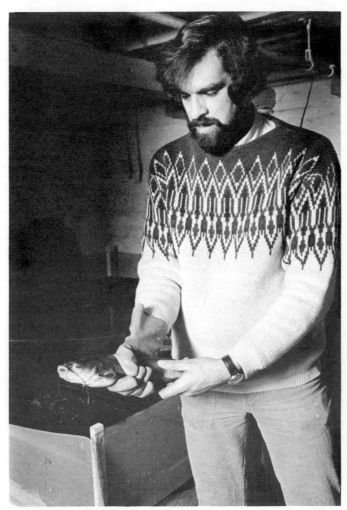

A Rodale researcher holding a 1½ pound catfish raised in an indoor pool.

267

goal is to raise 100 pounds of fish in each pool—a pound of fish per 6 gallons of water being a fairly dense population for a totally enclosed system. (Some commercial concerns claim to have achieved higher densities than that, but the cost and the management skills necessary would be beyond the means of most homeowners.)

Here's what researchers have learned so far:

1. Allow a minimum of 100 square feet of floor space for the pool and working area. Be sure the floor is strong enough to support the weight of the water in the pool (600 gallons of water weigh about 2½ tons) and that the floor is resistant to water damage.

2. Easy drainage is a must.

3. Pools should be no less than 64 square feet with a depth of 18 inches. It appears that this is an adequate size for the production of 100 pounds of fish twice a year, although the researchers have not yet reached this production goal.

4. Both commercial pellets and blends of various table scraps and other food wastes can be used successfully. To make sure fish are feeding and not wasting food, use some kind of feeder, such as the one described on page 274.

5. Test the water regularly. Test kits are available from commercial suppliers. You can put together your own kit by purchasing just the materials you need and save money. These materials can be purchased individually from some companies like the Hach Chemical Company (see Appendix for list of suppliers). Oxygen and ammonia kits, along with a thermometer, are all you are likely to need. The tests are simple to perform, requiring only that you not be color-blind. In a kit there's a test tube and some little porous sacks of powder (which Hach calls pillows).

Put a pillow in the tube, add pond water according to directions included in the kit, shake, and match the color that results with the color chart included to find oxygen level of the water. Kits for other tests are equally simple to use. If you've learned how to run your own soil tests, you can test your water with ease.

6. Since algae will not grow well with little or no sunlight indoors, you must provide for all the oxygen input and ammonia removal. Rodale researchers are working with a biological filter that converts ammonia to nitrate. The biological filter is a colony of

Careful records of water quality measurements are kept.

A Yellow Springs oxygen meter is used to measure oxygen levels in parts per million, and a Hach water quality test kit provides ammonia level and pH readings.

bacteria that clings to limestone rocks in the filter bed. Water from the pool continually circulates through the rocks. To build such a filter, you need a 55-gallon drum (or similar receptacle) for every 100 pounds of fish you plan to raise. Remove the lid of the drum, and perforate the bottom with ¼-inch holes. Set the drum on wood crossbars (2-by-4s will do) over one corner of the pool, and fill with crushed limestone rock. It takes about one-half ton of rock. Two-inch-size stone is the best. Over the top of the drum, position a galvanized pan, 10 inches in diameter by 3 inches or more deep, drilled with ⅛-inch holes. The pan distributes the recirculating water evenly over the limestone rock in the filter. Drilling the holes

269

Early in the indoor fish-farming experiments, pools were constructed of plywood and lined with plastic, and the water was filtered through home-brewed biological filters housed in 55-gallon drums.

is kind of tricky. You should have just enough holes to allow the water to drain through at the same rate as your circulator pumps it in. Inside the pan, stack two layers of fine mesh screen to sift large particles that might clog the fish's gills. Clean the screens off regularly, before the particles dissolve. A cloth on top of the screen helps considerably.

To lift water from the pool to the top of the drum, use a pump that moves water at the rate of 400 to 500 gallons per hour. As the water trickles through the stone, the bacteria remove the ammonia. The pumping can be reversed to backwash the system every month or so. Water and particulate matter from backwashing make excellent irrigation water and fertilizer for garden or potted plants.

The filter must be activated, starting about four weeks before fish are stocked, so that at stocking time, the bacteria have multiplied enough to handle the cleaning load. Either put a pound of manure in a burlap sack and suspend it in the water, or add five drops of cleaning ammonia daily to the water. Every day perform

270

the water test for ammonia. In the first week or so, the ammonia level should go up, then level off for awhile, and then drop to less than one part per million, an indication that the bacteria in the filter are ready to support a growing fish population. After harvesting fish and cleaning the pool, be sure to remember to allow time to activate the filter again before stocking with fish.

The filtering process mixes some oxygen into the water, too, but not enough for densely stocked fish. An aerator should be put into operation in the pool, too. A 1/20-horsepower bubbling or surface aerator should recharge enough water for 100 pounds of fish. With lesser amounts of fish, you may be able to get by with a small bubbler like those used in aquariums, but it's risky. The only oxygen you have to work with is what comes from the aerator and filter.

Periodically skim the surface of the water with a flat board when large bubbles of foam appear, say researchers. These bubbles are really large particles of waste mixed with air.

Fish in the indoor pools have been fed commercial fish feeds, but the researchers hope to test supplementary feeds such as fresh worms; grains, including amaranth, which is high in protein; and midge larvae. Aquaculturists are learning how to grow the midge larvae on burlap sacks in fertilized ponds, then allowing the fish to "graze" on the sacks suspended in their pools.

Like all other animals, fish react favorably to vitamin supplements, especially in an enclosed system where they have no source of natural vitamins. Rodale researchers intend to investigate this field, too—trying brewer's yeast, a good source of B vitamins; and amaranth, for vitamin C.

Which kind of aerator should you use in an indoor pool? Air compression units that pump air into the water rather than moving the water are more cost-efficient, but aerators that lift the water on the surface give greater surface-area for oxygen transfer and also help circulate the water. In very small tanks, air pumps seem to give the most efficient oxygenation, but on larger pools, most aquaculturists are using aerators that lift, spray, or churn surface water. One man I know uses an ordinary sump pump to lift the water. Another uses a set of nozzles with a lift pump, the water squirting with some force from three nozzles back against the water surface.

Cage Culture of Fish

Growing fish in cages in large, existing bodies of water is a third area in which Rodale experimenters are active. From a practical point of view, cage-culturing of fish has distinct advantages, especially for the home producer. As we have seen elsewhere, cages may be the only way a homesteader can practice controlled fish production if he lives next to a larger river or lake. Even in his own farm pond, cage culture is more convenient and reliable than seining or hook and line. Cages certainly are cheaper than building a special pool for fish production.

Rodale researchers built their own cages of Vexar netting over a wood frame. Each cage measures a cubic yard and is topped by a Styrofoam float. In the first attempt (1977), the cages were stocked late, July 11, and harvested October 7. Growth rates were highly encouraging, however, with catfish increasing in weight on the average from 50 grams to 83 grams, and bluegills, in another cage, from 45 grams to 116 grams. However, most of the bluegills were lost when the wind blew their cage over. Another problem was that muskrats in the farm pond liked to gnaw on the Styrofoam floats.

The fish were fed floating-type commercial feed. Each cage was initially stocked with 200 small fish. Indications are, if I may draw a conclusion as an outside observer, that if a cage is stocked at the beginning of warm weather, a very adequate poundage of fish for the table could be produced—100 pounds per cage being entirely within reason in one summer season.

Feeding Fish

Rodale researchers follow the general rule of feeding fish 3 percent of their total weight. As the fish grow, you can estimate the change in weight and the change in ration without having to weigh the fish regularly.

Change the ration weekly, not daily. Assuming that water conditions are right and the fish eating and growing normally, and assuming a pound of flesh produced for each 2 pounds of feed, you can proceed in this fashion. For the second week's ration, take half the weight of the first week's ration (2 pounds feed becomes 1 pound fish), and calculate 3 percent of that. Adding that amount to the first week's feed gives the new ration. For the third week, begin with the total for the second week.

For example, if you stock 10 pounds of fingerlings, they should get .3 pounds of pellets each day for the first week, or a total of 2.1 pounds. Next week assume that they have gained 1.05 pounds. Round that down to 1 pound for convenience; it is better to underfeed slightly than to overfeed. Three percent of 1 is .03. Add that to the .3 for the first week and the fish get .33 pound of feed daily for the second week. For the third week, begin with 2.3 pounds, the previous weekly total, assume the fish gained 1.1 pounds, and so on.

Feed the fish at the same time every day.

A feeder is useful because it helps you check on how much the fish consume. The feeder can help you gauge whether your method for estimating the proper amount of feed is on target. Clean excess feed out of the feeder regularly.

A researcher rigs a homemade fish feeder.

273

FEEDER

Materials

4—1" x 3" x 12" for the inner frame
2—1" x 3" x 26" for the outer frame
2—1" x 3" x 36" for the outer frame
1 floating device
1 piece screen 34" × 44"
1—3" stone
5' heavy nylon string
paint

Construction

1. Construct the square wooden inner frame and the rectangular outer frame. Paint it for durability.
2. Staple the screen onto the outer frame so that it forms a concave catch basin.
3. Hinge the inner frame to a narrow end of the outer frame. See picture.
4. Tie a piece of rope to the opposite end. Attach a small float to the other end of this rope. To remove the feeder from the water simply grasp the float and the rope.
5. Place a rock in the end of the catch basin which has the float. The rock should be just heavy enough to sink the catch basin, so it is at a 45-degree angle to the surface. Sinking feeds placed in the floating inner frame will drop onto the catch basin. Floating feeds will stay in the frame.

Homemade blends of 50 percent high-protein food scraps, 25 percent high-carbohydrate food scraps, and 25 percent moist, vitamin- and fiber-rich vegetable trimmings made a good fish food after being run through a food grinder. But homeowners do not usually have nearly enough table scraps to feed many fish. Restaurants are the most likely source. You still might want to add a balanced vitamin feed supplement, available at farm supply stores.

Insect traps are being used successfully to provide outdoor pond fish with supplemental protein. If bugs are not plentiful, however, you may spend more on electricity than the value of the insects caught. But most summertime ponds have bugs aplenty. You kill two birds with one stone, so to speak: You feed the fish and you get rid of unwanted bugs.

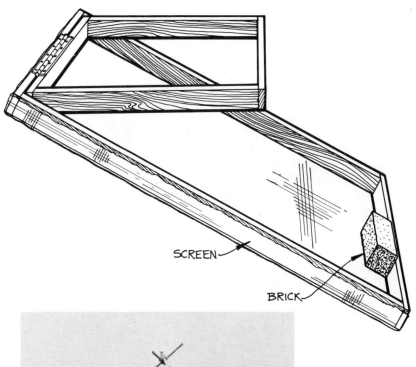

SCREEN

BRICK

The bug light suspended above a pond, ready for use.

BUG LIGHT TRAP

Materials
  1—15¼" diameter circle, ½" ext. plywood
  1—15¼" OD, 13¼" ID ring, ½" ext. plywood
  4—15¼" x 1⅜" x ¾" white pine
  4—6" x 19" x ¼" ext. plywood
  8—1" #10 wood screws
  1—18" black light, starter, and holder unit
  1 plug and screw-eye for top
  1 length of electric cord
  flat black paint

Construction
  1. Start by cutting four pieces of ¼-inch exterior plywood 6 inches by 19 inches. These will be used for the baffles.
  2. The next step is to cut frame and lamp holder supports. Using ¾-inch white pine, rip four pieces 15¼ inches long and 1⅜ inches wide and cut a ¼-by-½-inch-deep dado lengthwise down the exact center of all four pieces.
  3. Cut cross-lap joints at the center of each of the four pieces. Glue the pieces together to form two Xs.
  4. Apply glue to the ¼-inch grooves and insert the baffles into the cross frames. Paint the unit a flat black.
  5. When the paint has finally dried, position and glue the lamp holders onto top and bottom cross supports with an epoxy or other waterproof glue. Be sure the lamp holders are placed so that the bulb will be in the exact center of the baffles.
  6. Cut two 15¼-inch-diameter circles from ½-inch exterior plywood. Cut out the interior of one circle to leave a 1-inch-thick ring. Paint both pieces flat black. Using 1-inch #10 screws, attach the solid circle to the top of the baffle supports and the 1-inch ring to the bottom. Fasten a screw eye to the center of the top for hanging.

Commercial bug traps are available. If you want to make your own, a homemade design was built and used by Rodale researchers. In this trap, bugs circling the light strike the baffles and fall into the water.

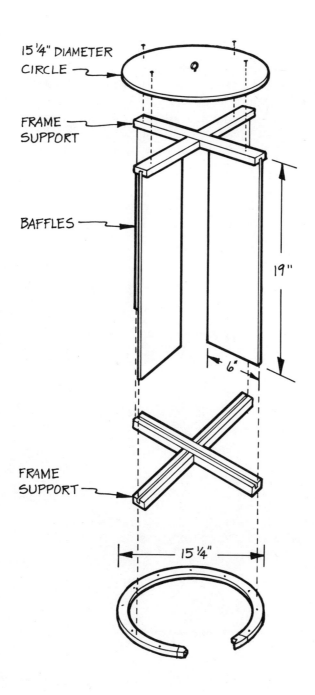

15 ¼" DIAMETER CIRCLE

FRAME SUPPORT

BAFFLES

19"

6"

FRAME SUPPORT

15 ¼"

Spring-Fed Pools

The work at Mountain Springs passed through only one season before the property was turned over to the Lehigh Valley Conservancy, a local land trust. Like all pioneering effort, it saw good days and bad days. "One thing you should tell homesteaders for sure," says Joe Senft, who headed up the project, "if you have a spring on your place, observe it closely for *a whole year* before you build your fish ponds. Flow-rates may vary with the season. If you stock fish based on a spring flow-rate, and the flow decreases in the fall, you're going to have a problem."

A second caveat researchers gave me had to do with sealing earthen ponds. Soil types and admixtures of types can vary within a given area so much that even soil experts can misjudge the sealing capability of the clays. Make sure your soil or subsoil holds water,

Several of the pools at the Mountain Springs research site were created by Gunniting the cellar holes of derelict farm buildings after the frame superstructures were removed. A constant dribble of water from the inlet valve countered evaporation loss.

Stocking one of the Mountain Springs pools.

and if it doesn't, be ready with some sealing material to plug the leaks. Bentonite is the sealer most often advised for leaky ponds. "But find out how much montmorillonite is in the bentonite," says Senft. "That's the stuff that does the job." A supplier he used was Volclay Soil Laboratory, American Colloid Co., 5100 Suffield Court, Skokie, IL 60076.

The pioneer aquaculturists found a nifty use for old shed foundations at Mountain Spring. Using Gunnite to plug cracks in the old stone foundation walls and to put down a concrete apron over the clay floors (laying down old wire fencing for reinforce-

279

ment), they built useful trout ponds. Being below soil-surface level for the most part, and downhill from the springs, the ponds were easy to fill by gravity.

Nevertheless, they advise would-be pool builders to place pools for trout where there is some shade in very warm weather, unless flow-through rate of water from the spring is abundant.

The researchers also advise fish-pond builders to take a good look at where their water is coming from and where it will go. Spring water, just like run-off water, though to a lesser degree, may have contaminants harmful to fish in it. If the water passes on to the property of another, make sure your use of it doesn't interfere with his rights.

Be extremely careful of the usual human inclination to make your pond water clear and free of algal growths, they warn. Algae is a sign of healthy water. It promotes fish growth. Killing it with algicides will deoxygenate the water twice—once because the algae produce oxygen, and the second time because the dying mass of algae consumes oxygen. "Copper sulfate is recommended by many extension workers as a safe chemical to control algae," says Senft, "but extremely low levels of copper have recently been shown to impair fish development. In hard water, you might get away with copper treatments, but where there is no great flow-through of water, copper levels may build up. The long-term effects are bad. Some of the newer materials like Cutrine and Aquazine have lower levels of copper and are thought to be safer. But they stay in the water a longer time, which could add up to the same result as using plain copper sulfate."

BOB HUKE'S BACKYARD FISH POND-GREENHOUSE

What Bob and Ellie Huke are doing in their Vermont backyard is an almost-perfect example of homestead fish production. In a greenhouse they built, which is heated only by the sun, the Hukes are raising catfish in summer, trout in winter, and fresh vegetables nine months a year. The sun provides the heat that grows the vegetables. The tank of water in the center of the greenhouse acts as a heat sink, releasing the stored warmth at night and on cloudy days, while keeping water temperatures high enough in winter so the trout remain active. The fish, in turn, enrich the water with

Bob Huke originally conceived of his geodesic dome greenhouse as a place to raise vegetables out of season. As an afterthought, a water tank was added, and it now is home for catfish in summer and trout in winter. The reflector panels on the north wall help keep temperatures above freezing over the winter.

their wastes, and the water can be used to irrigate and fertilize the vegetables.

The greenhouse is a two-frequency geodesic dome, shaped roughly like a hemisphere, with a diameter of 17½ feet on the ground. The enclosure provides about 225 square feet of soil surface under cover. The dome is set on twelve cedar posts that anchor it in place. Around the outer perimeter, 3-inch-thick sheets of foam insulation extend 4 feet into the ground. This insulation prevents winter loss of soil heat to the frozen ground outside. The framework for the dome comprises a series of triangles made of 1½-by-1½-inch knot-free pine. The triangles with southern, eastern, and western exposures were initially covered with 10-mil plastic film stapled to the outside. This proved too flimsy, and the plastic was replaced with sturdier fiberglass—Kalwall Sun-Lite Premium. The six north-facing triangles are filled with 1½-inch foam insulation board with aluminum foil on the inside to reflect the sun's rays. The tank measures 6 by 12 feet on the sides and is 34 inches deep—actually the bottom half of a prefab, concrete, 2,000-gallon septic tank.

Water in the tank circulated through a filter made of two connected 55-gallon drums filled with a matrix of plastic rings (available from aquacultural supply houses). The filter was designed by Enertech Corporation, a Norwich, Vermont, business. Water is pumped through the filter and aerated by dropping in a cascade from the top of the second drum back into the tank.

Water temperature rises as high as 90 degrees F (32.2 degrees C) in summer, which the catfish don't mind, and falls only to a low of 35 degrees F (1.6 degrees C) in winter, which the trout can tolerate. The Hukes put about seventy-five catfish fingerlings in the 1,400-gallon tank on April 15 and harvest them on November 15 at an average weight of three-quarters of a pound. A dozen or so trout are stocked in the pond within a week after the catfish are gone. When harvested in spring, they have averaged 12½ inches long—from 5 inches initial stocking size.

Catfish eat algae, fish scraps, and a commercial trout chow. Trout fatten almost exclusively on commercial feed. Bob Huke admits that, so far, he could have bought his fish cheaper, but when he adds in the quality of the food, the entertainment value of the project, and the many years the pool and greenhouse should last, the venture is profitable indeed.

JAN MICHALEK'S BACKYARD TROUT POOLS

When Vaughn Taylor of Frederickstown, Ohio, wanted to raise fish in the springs his homestead is blessed with, he couldn't find much help from the usual state and university sources of information. Then he heard what Jan Michalek was doing (see pages 230-33 in previous chapter) and contacted him. With Michalek's help, Taylor was soon raising trout successfully. When I visited him, his fourth "crop" of over one thousand rainbow trout was fattening in a pool outside the kitchen door.

The concrete pool is round, 16 feet in diameter, with a water depth of 18 inches at the outside wall and about 30 inches at the center. Water from a spring enters the pool through a pipe, spills over a baffle board, and falls into the water at the outer edge. At the center, the water drains out through a special filter designed to empty water at the same flow-rate as it enters the pool. Once water froze on the standpipe-filter and wind knocked it over. The Taylors found most of their fish on the ground where the drain pipe empties below the pool, dead or dying. Quick work saved some fish, but the rest had to be immediately cleaned and frozen. Fortunately, the Taylors have experienced no other accidents, and the filter is now anchored.

Water moves in the pool in a circular path as it drains through, much like water draining out of a sink. This movement creates a current, which trout prefer over motionless water.

For extra aeration, Taylor uses a sump pump that lifts the water into the air and lets it splash back into the pool. When the

Vaughn and Bonnie Taylor stock 1,500 trout in this 16-foot spring-fed pool in their backyard.

pool is full of fish—1,000 pounds—the aerator must operate almost constantly. Taylor has had to agitate the water manually during brief power failures and is trying to figure out a way to employ a hydraulic ram for agitating the water in emergencies. Also, any pump that compresses air (mechanical tank-sprayer or a tire pump) could be used to pump air into a pond.

He sells fish for fifteen cents an inch of length, plus twenty-five cents each for cleaning. So far he has had no trouble selling all he raises. "In fact, our problem is that we do not have enough fish. If we went commercial, there are restaurants which would buy from us regularly. Right now, we can't supply them regularly enough," says Taylor. But to 1,000 pounds of fish, he feeds, as a rule of thumb, about seventeen hundred pounds of feed. On sales of $1,500, he figures less than half as cost for feed, fingerlings, and electricity—worthwhile profit for a sideline, family enterprise.

Michalek's pools need a flow-rate of at least 10 to 15 gallons per minute. Orville Coffman of Lancaster, Ohio, another Michalek customer, wanted to expand from two pools to a commercial operation, but found that his spring wasn't adequate to support dense trout populations in more than two pools. So he dug two wells, one producing 100 gallons per minute and a second yielding nearly as much. With this much water, he now raises over twenty

thousand fish per year in eight pools and a concrete raceway. Most of the fish he sells through his pay-fishing pond next to the pools. Fishermen pay twelve cents per inch of length for the fish they catch. Coffman's basic advice: Make sure of the purity of your water. He tried to use supplemental water from a nearby, clear, fast-running creek in his trout pools. The water was cold enough for trout and would indeed support a few naturally in the stream. But there was enough agricultural pesticide and fertilizer runoff to poison fish when the water was used in a closed, dense-production system.

Orville Pierpont of Utica, Ohio, raises backyard trout strictly for his family's enjoyment. He likes to fish and so do his sons and their children. Having a spring flowing through a narrow ravine in his backyard, Pierpont decided to make a small pond with an earth

A battery of concrete pools, fed by springs and wells, is the heart of Orville Coffman's commercial fish-raising operation. Predators are fenced out of Coffman's pools with covers made of conduit pipe and chicken wire. A pulley and weight setup makes removal of the cover a simple proposition.

285

dam. He stocked the pond—about a tenth-acre in size—with bass and bluegills and crappie and even a few perch. But he wanted trout. Lots of trout and big ones, too. The water was cold enough and clean enough. He talked to Michalek who persuaded him to spend $400 he had saved for a vacation on an aerator and some trout food. Now the Pierponts pull trout that weigh nearly 2 pounds from the pond. "If you take a two-week vacation, you'll spend more than $400 and hardly ever catch fish like these," he says.

Because his fish can get some food naturally in the pond, Pierpont needs to feed them only once a day. If algicides aren't used in the water, "moss" or algae from the pond makes excellent garden mulch, but it is hard work to rake out, says Orville's son, Jim, an avid organic gardener.

In their concrete pools, Taylor and Coffman feed the trout twice a day. Mostly they stick to the more convenient commercial feeds, but Taylor hopes to raise worms as supplemental feed. Michalek encourages fish growers to use homemade sources of protein feed whenever possible along with commercial feeds. Beef

Orville Pierpont stocks trout in a spring-fed embankment pond beside his home.

liver is a good feed, he says, but not pork liver. Taylor has tried feeding Japanese beetles, which have become all too numerous on his farm. "The fish seem to relish them," he says. "Don't feed too many, though," counsels Michalek. "They can impart a disagreeable taste to the meat if fed in excess."

Pierpont, with his larger, natural pond (it's 16 feet deep in the center), doesn't have to run his aerator constantly, as do the others. He turns it on a couple of hours in the evening and leaves it on longer than that only on the hottest summer days and nights. "When you see fish gulping at the surface, get that aerator going immediately," he says. Coffman, as a commercial producer, has a standby generator to run the aerators in his pools. He can't afford a power failure—"It could wipe us out," he says.

Predators can be a problem, too. Be assured that if there are wild birds or animals in your area that like trout, they will find yours, even in the relative security of your backyard. Kingfishers and raccoons are the most troublesome, says Taylor. In his natural pond, Pierpont has learned that snapping turtles will take a toll of the trout population. He caught a turtle once that had a 7-inch trout in it. Of course, turtle is so delectable, who would mind losing a few trout in return for gourmet meals of fried turtle?

Coffman devised an effective protective wire cover for his pools. The cover is a huge ring of conduit pipe fitted with chicken-wire mesh. It fits neatly over the whole pool and can be raised or lowered easily by means of a rope and pulley attached to a tall post next to the pool.

RAISING CATFISH IN A BARREL

Philip and Joyce Mahan of Alabama tried raising catfish in a barrel in 1971, starting forty fish on commercial catfish feed and then feeding them almost entirely on fish worms which they raised. Here is their story, from their article in *Organic Gardening and Farming,* November 1973:

> After some study and experimentation, we have set up a productive food chain—table scraps to earthworms to catfish—in our backyard. The project is satisfactory in many respects, utilizing waste materials to produce fresh fish for food and at the same time yielding ample compost for a small

287

garden. The material cost is minimal. The whole operation can be set up for less than $15. The equipment occupies only about 12 square feet of space, and the entire assembly can be easily moved if necessary.

The materials can be very simple: two 55-gallon steel drums, three panes of glass 24 inches square, and a medium-size aquarium air pump. One of the drums will serve as a tank for the fish, oxygen being supplied from the air pump, and the second drum should be cut in half to provide two bins for the worms. The panes of glass are used as covers for the worm bins and fish tank, and, for ease and safety in handling, can be framed with scrap lumber.

We chose channel catfish because they are readily available in our part of Alabama, and reach eating size in a summer. Various small members of the sunfish family, such as bluegill or bream, would also be suitable.

For information on raising channel catfish, we relied on studies made at Auburn University in Alabama, as well as on the work done at Skidway Institute of Oceanography for the Georgia Fish and Game Commission where fish were raised in tanks. The commercial growers from whom we got our fry and fingerlings raised their eyebrows considerably at the idea of growing fish in a barrel and feeding them earthworms; but they did not actually discourage us. While we readily admit that our plan has no commercial possibilities, we know that we can produce, for our own table, tasty fresh fish that is uncontaminated and costs practically nothing, both considerations being highly relevant at this time.

Fish are usually efficient food producers; a 1-pound fish yields approximately 10 ounces of food. Further efficiency is indicated by the fact that fish fed on commercial fish ration convert about 85 percent of their food to meat. While we are not prepared to compute the technical data about food conversion in fish on an earthworm diet, we can readily state that the fish relish earthworms and do grow well on this food.

The Auburn experiments showed that fish could be grown in large numbers in confinement, and the Georgia study confirmed these findings. Although there is some relationship between the number of fish and the volume of water in which they are grown, the most important variable, according to the

Georgia study, was the rate of water turn-over. Spraying the water back into the tank aerates the water and at the same time releases the ammonia produced by excretory matter in the water. Because the oxygen requirements of fish are quite high, the faster the circulation of the water, the faster the growth of the fish.

We decided to keep our equipment as simple and inexpensive as possible at the beginning, but to use the maximum stocking density of the Georgia experiments, keeping forty fish in a 55-gallon drum. Although inexpensive circulation pumps are available, we chose to use a Metaframe Hush II aquarium bubbler for oxygenation and a garden hose to siphon off water from the bottom of the barrel.

We took off 15 gallons of water per day, but as we run the waste water onto the worm beds and adjacent garden, the cost is negligible. Although we have creek water close at hand, we were advised to use city water to avoid the introduction of undesirable algae and fungi that might be harmful to fish. Because city water is usually quite highly chlorinated, it is necessary to draw the water in 5-gallon buckets and let it stand for a day in the sun before emptying it into the drum to replace the water siphoned off. We have seen no evidence of oxygen starvation in the fish with this method of water circulation.

The most important variable we have found is water temperature. Catfish will feed at temperatures as low as 40 to 45 degrees [F (4.4 to 7.2 degrees C)], but their greatest growth is achieved at 84 degrees [F (28.8 degrees C)]. We noticed a decided increase in feeding activity when we painted the barrel black and moved it into full sun. Leaving the buckets of water in the sun not only speeds chlorine dissipation, but warms the water as well. In areas where city water temperatures are close to the growth optimum, the chlorine can be removed by setting the hose nozzle at fine spray, and the barrel can then be filled directly from the water supply. Although summer growth is greatest, the project continues through the year. By judicious use of sun when possible, plus auxiliary heat when necessary, winter growth can be kept at a fairly high level.

When water temperatures are right, the fish will feed so enthusiastically that they may leap completely out of the barrel. For this reason, the top of the barrel should be covered

Philip Mahan's experiments with backyard catfish-raising were carried out in a plastic-lined wooden box and a 55-gallon drum. Catfish fry were purchased and stocked in the wooden pool. When they reached fingerling size, they were transferred to the drum, where they were kept until they had reached eating size.

completely with a pane of glass which will also help in keeping the water warm. Because fish feed most eagerly in late evening and early morning, we feed them at these times of the day. As with earthworms, care must be taken not to overfeed. In warm water and bright sunlight, any uneaten worms will die and decompose rapidly, giving off gases which are poisonous to fish.

Transferring any grown animal to a confining environment produces the equivalent of cultural shock, and is followed by a period when feeding is light and growth is slow. At this time special care must be taken not to overfeed. Unless fish can be found that have been hatched and grown in a tank, small fish should be selected to stock the barrel, as their adaptation time is proportionally shorter than that of larger fish. To eliminate as much transplanting shock as possible, we use a large wooden box, lined with two layers of polyethylene sheeting and covered with an old door, to stock with fry. By the time the fry reach fingerling size, they can be transferred to the barrel as replacements are needed, and very little shock is evident. An insect lamp over an opening in the cover of the fry tank permits the small fish to eat at night, while ridding the garden of night-flying pests.

The Mahans did not keep detailed records on how many earthworms they fed nor the weight of the fish. They estimate they fed an average of seventy-five to one hundred worms per day, the worms weighing not more than an ounce per hundred. Nor did they weigh the fingerlings, or the fish they ate later. "We didn't know this thing was going to work," says Mahan.

DUCKS AND GEESE 14

You can raise ducks and geese without a pond or pool, but not very well. Waterfowl belong in water, at least part of the time, and not to indulge their waterfowlish instinct is asking for trouble. Water seems to increase the fertility of the birds, not to mention their health and happiness. And with a pond available to them, the amount of care you have to give is greatly decreased.

The number of commercial duck farms is declining in this country, overtaken by climbing costs and lack of consumer interest. Used to be, a farmer could raise a large flock of ducks cheaply by using natural streams. No more. Ducks in high concentrations, like any other animal, are messy and will pollute a stream quickly.

Large duck factory/farms today use artificial pools, usually of concrete, through which they pump many gallons of water each day. Such operations think nothing of feeding out two-hundred-thousand ducks a year, purchasing day-old ducklings and fattening them to market size in seven to eight weeks. Ducklings are kept inside for about three weeks, then penned in large outdoor lots equipped with pools and self-feeders. Diseases, some spread by starlings, are a normal worry. Foxes, coons, and great horned owls take their toll, also.

Good duck farmers do combine aquaculture into their operation at least one other way. The pond water, laden with duck manure, is pumped into a lagoon for storage, then used to irrigate and fertilize nearby farmland.

POLYCULTURE SYSTEMS

Duck production in Europe and the Orient is far more efficient, however. Duck or goose farms are combined with fish raising, the ducks fed over the pond, their wastes dropping into the water. The enriched water produces increased amounts of the algae and planktons fish eat. Usually several kinds of fish are stocked, each feeding on different types of wastes and water life so that nothing is wasted. Dr. Homer Buck, the aquaculturist mentioned in chapter 12, was extremely impressed with the high amounts of protein small farmers in other parts of the world obtained from ponds where waterfowl and fish production were combined. Reporting on several of these operations (see his *Report of Participants in the FAO Technical Conference on Aquaculture and Subsequent Visits to Various World Centers in Aquaculture,* published by the Illinois Natural History Survey and the University of Illinois at Urbana; this small but informative booklet gives convincing evidence that small-scale aquaculture can be practical), Buck reported:

> . . . We observed a duck-cum-fish operation having a feature new to me, but said to be common in Hong Kong. The fish farmer owned ponds and fish, but no swine or poultry, and so he built a duck-feeding platform and a duck-sheltering house over the fish pond and invited a neighbor who owned only ducks to put his birds over the fish pond. A wire fence in the pond confined the ducks to the feeding platform and shelter, and to about one-third of the pond area, thus preventing them from damaging the pond banks. Unfortunately, the fish farmer was not available to supply details on the number and types of fish stocked, the number of ducks, et cetera. I did learn, however, that such ducks are fed twice daily with boiled grain (usually sorghum) plus a small daily ration of dried, chopped fish. The ducks are placed on the pond at an age of three to ten days, and are ready for market in seventy days. We were unable to estimate the density of the ducks, but my hosts told me that the number used was highly variable. They had no firm knowledge of what constituted "too many" ducks, but believed that anything over one hundred ducks per acre might be too many, although they knew that the duck farmers usually exceeded this number. I was further told that the Hong Kong farmers prefer using ducks to pigs as a source of manure, because ducks are easier to care for, less expensive to feed, and require less investment in the form of housing or pens. . . .

And of geese, Buck observed in Taiwan:

> I was particularly impressed by one operation featuring geese over a polyculture pond, for which some statistics were provided. The pond appeared to be slightly larger than 1 hectare and received all of the wastes from fifteen hundred fattening geese. The farmer owned a large, modern incubator for the production of his own goslings. He fattened fifteen hundred geese at a time, and the geese were ready for market in three months. Each goose brought an average of $12.50 U.S., and the investment for feed was at the rate of about $2.50 U.S. per goose. Thus, this farmer was selling fifteen hundred geese four times a year at a gross profit of $10.00 U.S. per goose and turning a total gross profit in the vicinity of $60,000 U.S. per year. He had the additional profit from the sale of fish, but the amount of such profit was not learned.

Buck visited similar ventures in Hungary:

> The Hungarians have long received special recognition for their expertise in the combined culture of ducks and fish, and at my request, we next visited a neighboring state farm having such a duck-cum-fish operation. This particular farm was raising eleven thousand ducks on one 47-hectare pond, and sixteen thousand ducks on another pond of 43 hectares. The ponds were stocked with common carp, silver carp, and grass carp. Bighead carp would have been used if available. The duck raising is fully coordinated with the fish-growing season. This permits the production of three crops of ducks and one crop of fish between late April and late September. The ducks used here were the English breed, called Cherry Valley, which mature to a weight of 2.5 kg. in fifty-one days. Mr. Csávás [the guide] told me that most farms used a hybrid duck developed in Hungary which attains a weight of 2.8 kg. in only forty-six days. Mr. Csávás further stated that it was common practice to hold between five hundred and six hundred ducks per hectare of water in a pond having an optimum polyculture of fishes, and that this could yield as much as 2.5 tons of fish per hectare in the period from April through September. At the time of my visit, the gross from the ducks was about $2,000 U.S. per hectare.

Getting Food from Water

There are several sound reasons why ducks or geese can be produced efficiently in combination with fish. Feeding is cheaper, for one thing. You don't have to add as much protein to the feed ration because the ducks get some protein eating frogs, tadpoles, insect larvae, mollusks, and aquatic weeds. In fact, ducks will eat any small fingerlings too slow to escape them, which is why ducks should not be allowed on spawning grounds. Second, a duck raised on a pond is freer of parasites and diseases than a pen-reared duck. Also, feathers from pond ducks are cleaner and of higher quality— the feathers (about 4 ounces per bird) usually worth around 10 percent of the value of the meat. Third, as the ducks swim over the water, they distribute the manure as evenly as any device of man could do it, but without any cost or labor. What's more, the manure is distributed fresh when its carbon content is highest. According to Dr. E. Woynarovich, in a paper presented at the FAO Conference on Aquaculture in 1976, more carbon compounds are released when the manure is spread fresh over the water, resulting in higher primary production of fish and less pollution problems. Fourth, by feeding the ducks on platforms over the water, any feed they waste falls into the water and is eaten by the fish. Fifth and most important in such a system, says Woynarovich, the use of fertilizer or supplemental fish feed is not necessary, thus greatly reducing the cost of fish production.

At least five hundred ducks can be kept on 1 hectare of water for one year, says Woynarovich, amounting to 36 tons of manure. According to his figures, 3 tons of duck manure will produce 264 to 396 pounds of fish meat.

RAISING DUCKS

Whether or not you want to get that serious about fish and waterfowl combinations, such enterprises provide plenty of good reasons for keeping a few ducks or geese around if you have a pond. Even if you don't, a dozen ducks will be happy with no more water than you can easily provide them in a child's plastic wading pool. Clean the wading pool often and pour the nutrient-rich water on your garden.

With a pond, a dozen ducks will take care of themselves if they have room to roam on the land surrounding the pond.

A doghouse is all the shelter four ducks need, with extra grain in

A piebald Muscovy and her young 'uns.

winter, when there is no plant material for them to eat. Mature ducks are extremely hardy. One winter day I walked over our family farm pond when the temperature was 10 degrees F below zero. I had a bucket of water which I hoped to pour in the cracks that had appeared in the thick ice due to settling. The cracks were interfering with our hockey games. When I started pouring the water, my sister's ducks, watching from the shore, came waddling joyously out to me. They tried their best to swim in the miniscule stream of water I poured in the ice crack, thrashing and wallowing around with joyous quacks, scooping the bit of water into their beaks. They had been given water to drink; I guess they just wanted to splash and play, never mind the 10-below-zero temperature. I had to give up my crack-sealing task. When I left, the ducks gathered around the little hole I had made in the ice to get my water and quacked happily away like neighboring housewives over ten-o'clock coffee.

Normally you should try to keep some open water on your pond, if ducks are out in the winter. They will themselves keep a spot free of ice in all but the coldest weather.

Pekin and Muscovy are the two most common kinds of ducks raised for meat. Runner ducks and a few other kinds are kept for

Muscovy Duck

Pekin Duck

An ideal, work-free homestead duck-raising setup gives the ducks free access to the pond and surrounding land and provides a simple pondside shelter.

egg production. If you get serious about ducks, you will find a great number of exotic and not so exotic breeds, but for practical homestead production, Pekin or Muscovy are to be preferred.

You can maintain a breeding flock and hatch eggs along stringent, no-nonsense commercial guidelines, or you can buy ducklings and fatten out batches every eight weeks. But as a start, you might prefer just a few ducks and let them breed and hatch naturally. You need a drake for every five or six hens, more or less. Ducks are not always good mothers, but they will brood a batch of ducklings on their own, even outside in a fence corner. Best to provide a shed, though, where dogs, cats, and other predators can't get to the ducks. Plan for at least one nest for each three to five breeders. Make nests of 12-inch boards, each 12-by-16 inches with a partition between each nest. Place the framework of nests on the floor and nail the back to the wall so the framework can't move. The floor serves as the bottom for all the nests. Runs outside the shed should end in a stream or pond, an artificial one if not a natural one.

You can gather eggs and sell them like you do hen eggs. For incubation, better to let the duck do it. In an incubator, you have to turn the eggs four times a day. Eggs under a substitute mother hen, or under a duck without access to water, have to be sprinkled with water daily between about the fifteenth and twenty-fourth days and again just before the ducklings are ready to break through the shell. Incubation is twenty-eight days for Pekins, and thirty-three to thirty-five days for Muscovies.

Ducklings need protection just like baby chicks. They shouldn't get wet until their feathers develop, in about six weeks.

When high-level egg or meat production is desired, you have to feed grain, usually as a mash, about the same kind of ration you would prepare for chickens. Through summer, ducks on the homestead can get along fine on the vegetable matter and other natural food they find when roaming fields and swimming on the pond.

RAISING GEESE

Geese will take care of themselves pretty well, too, in a homestead situation, grazing pasture just like livestock. The two common types of geese available are the Toulouse and the Embden. Geese never appear to me as affable as ducks. But I'm prejudiced. A Toulouse drake chased me clear across a sheep pasture when I was about six years old and not much taller than he.

Geese are particular about the company they keep, I guess. They usually mate for life, a gander and one hen, or as many as five hens, if you divide them off that way before they get to thinking too much about it. Mate your flock in late fall, feed a little grain commencing in January, breeding to follow in February and eggs in March. Don't try to break up established families or harems half-way through the breeding season or resulting eggs may be sterile.

Geese may start breeding in their first or second year, but serious producers like to use fowl three to five years old for best results. Gives you a good chance to select birds on the basis of fast growth and good size, too. Females will go on producing for ten years, but ganders should usually be replaced about the sixth year.

It's not easy to differentiate sexes. Ganders are usually slightly larger. Unlike the human species, the gander has the high, shrill voice, the female, a harsh, coarse call. To be really sure, says the book, lay the bird flat on its back (a formidable task, believe me).

Embden Goose

Toulouse Goose

Getting Food from Water

In the female, the sphincter muscle that closes the anus appears folded if stretched. But slight pressure around the gander's anus will cause its sexual organ to protrude.

Goose eggs under mother goose (or clucky chicken used as a substitute mother) have to be sprinkled with water, unless the goose has access to water herself. I prefer to let Mother Nature take care of these things her way, except when said geese are being raised with the serious idea of making money or paying bills. Incidentally, reaching for an egg under a duck or goose can be a dangerous occupation. A duck can swat you with a wing so hard you'll think your hand is broken in five places.

Tender grass and succulent weed growth are the goose's favorite food, and, as is well known, geese make pretty good weeders in strawberry and mint fields, if handled correctly. They have to be penned in the field. But a fairly large number of geese,

Embden geese.

running out of weeds to eat and water to drink, and especially if confined to a fairly small strawberry patch, will trample said patch to destruction.

Grain fed before egg laying and to fatten goslings should be about the same mixture you'd feed chickens under similar circumstances. Do not, however, feed a lot of corn. For breeders, limit corn to one-fourth of the ration. Otherwise they get fat and lazy.

Books tell you how to defeather ducks and geese at butchering by using the melted wax method. The homesteader, butchering just a few, will be better off scalding, like he does chickens. It's harder to get the water to penetrate to the skin, but if you ruffle through the feathers with a stick while the goose or duck is submerged in the scalding water, you'll do okay.

Duck and goose down are salable, if you want to squeeze every possible cent out of the enterprise. Better yet, save up your feathers and make a good down pillow for yourself. To clean the feathers, put them in a loosely woven bag and dunk into warm water and detergent. Slosh around awhile, rinse, and hang on the clothesline to dry. Drying may take three weeks of sunlight.

Meanwhile, the days your ducks and geese spend on your pond will make your fish grow faster at no expense to you.

GARDEN POOLS AND WATER GARDENS 15

Even the smallest garden pool can provide some of the benefits (and all of the pleasures) associated with a larger, aquaculturally managed pond or stream. While too small for very much food production, the garden pool, like the small kitchen garden, can produce more than its size would indicate because its very smallness allows you to maintain complete control over it. You can decide exactly how much of which aquatic plants and animals you want in your pool down to the last fin and rhizome, and maintain that amount fairly easily.

The main purpose of a garden pool in a backyard ought to be landscaping beauty and personal enjoyment. The pool area, surrounded by its own special flora and fauna, hidden from public view by hedge or trees, can be "a magic land of sweet repose," just steps from your back door. Some water gardens are so cleverly designed as to transform a niche in a suburban lawn into an enchanting glade of a forest or tropical island. With equipment available at garden stores, you can build authentic-looking waterfalls, rock-ledge pools, even tiny, rippling creeks. You can grow flowers as exotic as the lotus and lure to your garden more beneficial birds and animals than you thought existed in your neighborhood.

The latter advantage is the reason every serious organic gardener, even if not particularly interested in aquaculture, ought to consider a garden pool. The pool can at least double the usual variety of plant and animal life in a backyard. The more variety in the biological food chain, the more chance of maintaining an equilibrium where no one organism can overpopulate and become a pest. For example, the fish in the pool keep the mosquitoes from becoming numerous. The toads, sure to be attracted, will eat mosquitoes, too, and will hop over into your vegetable garden and consume cutworms and slugs. Last summer, I had a chance to observe rather closely the eating habits of a toad who took up residence alongside our house near the drainpipe from the roof eaves. An examination of its droppings (left regularly on the patio) revealed an enormous appetite—the mere volume of droppings surprised me. The feces was composed entirely of the remains of insects. The number consumed each night I'd guess at between fifty and one hundred. Toads are the nicest thing that can happen to a garden pool; their music during mating and egg-laying season is sweeter than birdsong.

BUILDING A GARDEN POOL

In formal gardens there are "right" and "wrong" designs for water gardens. The rules are thought up by landscape designers as a way to make their work seem more complicated and therefore more expensive than it really ought to be. And the rules, like those for clothing styles, keep changing. If you want to worry about how fashionable and arty your pool looks—whether, for instance, fountains are "in" now or whether kidney-shaped pools are passé—there are heaps of garden books to help you worry, and many landscapers willing to settle your doubts. I don't know if kidney-shaped pools are passé this year or not. Nor do I care.

There are, however, practical considerations to keep in mind before forging ahead on a pool-building project. Catharine Osgood Foster, in her book *Organic Flower Gardening* (which has an excellent chapter on water gardens), says a garden pool should not measure less than 50 square feet of surface water, and preferably more. If the pool contains 100 square feet, the depth should be at least 18 inches; from 100 to 300 square feet, 24 inches deep; 300 square feet, 30 inches; and 1,000 square feet or more, 36 inches. The first reason for these guidelines has to do with algae. In the normal history of a garden pool, algal growth explodes into overpopulation when the pool is new. Then when the other organisms that normally inhabit pool water gain a good foothold, the algae comes into balance, and the green, murky water clears up again. But where the amount of water is too small, balance will not be reached, or will be reached only after a long time, and the green water will persist.

A second reason for not making a pool too small is that a small amount of water will suffer too great and too abrupt a rise and fall in temperature from day to night, a variation potentially harmful to both fish and water plants.

The slope of the pool walls is important, too, in regard to temperature because slope, to a large extent, governs the surface-to-volume ratio in a pool. A saucer-shaped bottom is most apt to warm and cool too much. A square bottom is better, if you are forming the pool out of concrete. But with fiberglass, or particularly plastic film, some slope is desirable, or else the vertical earthen side will eventually crumble into the pool. Trial and error has determined that a slope of 20 percent is best.

Beyond these guidelines, size of the pool is up to you and your pocketbook. However, I think it will pay you to make the pool rather larger than smaller as long as you're going to the trouble to build it. Fish are essential for mosquito control, so why not make the pool large enough to fatten a few for eating. A pool without water lilies is like a horse without a rider, and for three water lily plants you ought to have a water surface of 50 square feet at the least. And why not a pool big enough to fall into when you come home hot and tired from the garden? I thought I was the only one dumb enough to consider that idea, but if an eminent and respectable gardener like Catharine Osgood Foster thinks that is a point worth mentioning, I'm emboldened to put it in print too.

For the fishes' sake, as well as for other considerations, the garden pool (which by definition here is totally artificial) should be designed so that water can be recirculated through it. A small circulating motor runs on very little electricity. All kinds of designs are used. Almost any kind of waterfall or fountain will suffice to mix oxygen back into the water in an artful way. If a hillside site is available, water can be pumped from a lower pool back up to a gurgling waterfall that spills water down through a series of tiny pools into the main one again. A necessary detail you may overlook is to be sure that the rocks used to form such waterfalls or cascades are undercut at the lip so water falls directly over instead of dribbling down the underside of the rock.

The backyard food producer who wants his garden pool to serve as many purposes as possible might want to combine a pool with a small artificial stream. I know a family who constructed a very attractive water garden this way, in a relatively small area that

307

Garden Waterfall

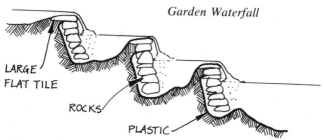

LARGE
FLAT TILE

ROCKS

PLASTIC

didn't even have a natural slope. First, they dug out the pool and used the dirt to build up a low mound about 25 feet away. At the top of the mound, they built a waterfall that concealed a pipe that led back, underground, to the lower pool. From the waterfall, they built a stream with concrete and stones of various kinds that led by a circuitous route to the lower pool. Rocks and plants bordered the little stream. In fact, what they created was a rock garden with a small creek through it and a pool at its foot. The flick of a switch turned on the pump that started a gush of water over the rocks of the waterfall, the water splashing on down until it reached the pool. When the pump was turned off, the water all drained into the lower pool and the creek dried up. The pool in this case contained only

308

goldfish, which can get along fine in 30 inches of water even with 6 or more inches of ice over it. Had the pool been enlarged to, say, 10 feet square and 3 feet deep, the owner could have fattened a few carp, catfish, even bluegills over summer, with no great problems. Whenever extra oxygen was necessary, all they would have had to do was turn on the recirculating pump.

Building a "creek" out of concrete is most difficult, since unless you really sink some kind of solid footing under it (way out of proportion to the cost of the creek itself) the concrete will crack and break up in a few years from the heaving effect of freezes. Cascades that consist essentially of a series of small fiberglass or plastic pools, each pouring water into the one below it, but all edges concealed cleverly with rocks and sand, are a better solution. The sound of the little waterfalls is heavenly. Plants that like a few inches of water can be grown right at the edges of the cascade pools.

A bog or swamp or small seeping spring in your yard may be an excellent candidate for a pool. All you have to do is dig it out. At least some, if not all, of the peaty mud from the pool excavation can be used as fill around the pool. Often a dug-out bog will not hold water very well. Since your pool is small (compared to a farm pond), you can rather easily put a 3- to 4-inch layer of clay on the bottom, and tamp it down hard when it's moist to form a fairly watertight floor. Other sealants mentioned elsewhere in this book can be used, too. If you use clay, cover it with the sphagnum moss or peaty soil originally in the bog so fish don't stir up the mud. Around the edges of this pool you can grow some of the rarer marsh plants like the sundew, an insectivorous plant that traps bugs in the hairs that grow from its leaves. The more common, but beautiful, marsh marigold is another choice. Other bog plants you might try are cardinal flower, jack-in-the-pulpit, pitcher plant, ferns, and water iris.

Other than bog ponds, most garden pools call for the use of concrete, or, increasingly today, fiberglass or plastic film. Gardening stores carry a variety of precast fiberglass pools, most of them too small (but usable for cascades). The very largest ones, with proper 20 percent slope, are what you want. They need only be dug into the ground, with rocks and plants judiciously placed around the brim, and you have an instant pool.

Plastic film is more popular because it's cheaper and versatile.

Plastic-lined Garden Pool

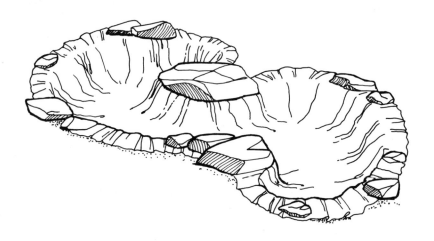

You merely dig a hole—any shape you desire—and cover the excavation with a sheet of plastic. Around the edges of the pool, put rocks over the plastic to hold it firmly in place and to hide the edges. Fill it with water. The plastic liner will last a year, maybe two ("you gets what you pays for"), and then it must be replaced. But for the price, most users don't mind. The only caution: Be sure when you put the liner down that there are no sharp rocks in the floor of the pool to puncture a hole in the plastic immediately.

In former times, the Cadillac of garden pools was made out of sheets of lead soldered together. Lead will give without cracking under pressure of the freezing and thawing soil around the pond, which is not necessarily true of concrete. The use of lead today would be questionable from a health standpoint, even though lead is amazingly inert to water corrosion. I know families who are still drinking water from lead pipes and seem to show no ill effects in the third generation. But just the same, health authorities might frown on using lead where food is being produced.

Copper was also used (by the rich) for garden pools, the sheets soldered together in much the same way lead was. Old copper apple butter kettles are being recycled into tubs for water plants. But if fish are part of your plans, don't use copper. It may not hurt plants, but it will surely poison fish.

The first garden pool I built, I simply buried a stock watering tank so the brim was level with the ground. The tank measured 6-by-2½-by-2½ feet. I had to put a brace into the middle of the tank to keep the two long sides from pushing inwards from the pressure of the soil, but otherwise the tank worked fine. Since we moved a year later, I don't know how long that tank would have lasted before rusting through, nor how much of a problem it would be to get the old one out and a new one in without harming plants close by. Galvanized tanks like that are good for about ten years, even with being banged around by cattle. In the earth and full of water and therefore not exposed to air so much (which is what really makes rusting severe), I figure the tank would last at least that long.

But all things considered, concrete is the best choice, and, built right, a concrete pool is worth the money you spend on it. Take extra pains in mixing cement, if you want the concrete to hold water well and long. Mix one part cement, two parts sand, and three parts gravel. Don't use limestone or sandstone which are somewhat porous. Mix the ingredients dry first, then add water sparingly. You want the concrete wet enough to work, but not sloppy wet. Runny concrete may not hold water well when it dries.

Pour the whole pool at once and that ain't easy. At least pour all the walls at the same time before the floor is dry so that a tight bond forms. If you pour floor and walls at the same time so there

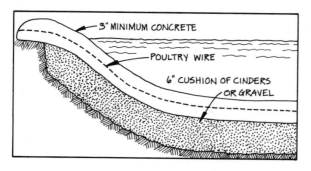

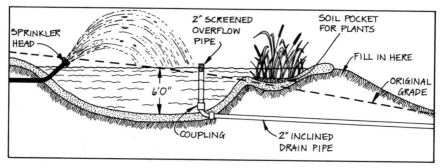

Concrete-lined Garden Pools

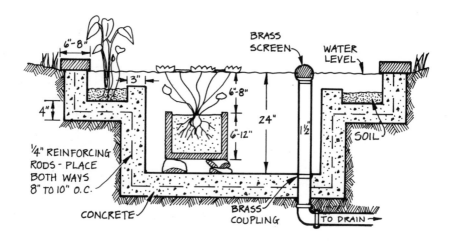

are no seams to crack later on, you have to suspend the inner wall form, which means beams or boards must be extended over the top of the pool site to fasten the form to. If you dig the pool excavation carefully, so the earthen sides are fairly smooth and vertical, you won't need an outer wall form. In any event, use reinforcing rods throughout for a good, stout pool. Try very hard to keep all the rods within the concrete. Any that stick out can rust and make a hole in the cement eventually. The walls and floor of the pool ought to sit on about a foot of gravel or cinders underneath for drainage.

Before the concrete dries but after it is firmed up, take off the forms and give the surface a coating of cement mortar, one part cement to two parts sand. Finishing cement this way requires a plasterer's trowel. You may want to hire an experienced cement finisher for this job.

Don't put water into the pool until the concrete is completely cured—three weeks is not too long to wait. Then, after water has been in the pool a couple of weeks, drain it out and refill before putting in fish. Alkalies, which can be harmful to fish, are drawn out of the cement and collect in that first water. If you have installed a drain in your pool, this will be the first of many times you will thank yourself for doing so. (But if your pool is not the lowest point in your yard, you can drain it by using a garden hose as a siphon. Fill the hose with water, hold both ends shut with your hands so no air can get in, dunk one end in the pond *first*, then drop the other end of the ground at a point lower than the pool bottom. The water in the hose will begin to run out and start the siphon working.)

Some gardeners (and fish growers) have used precast concrete septic tanks, or the bottom halves thereof, for garden pools. I believe this is the easiest way to install a pool, though not the cheapest. A good septic tank installer can put one in for you in half a day with his backhoe.

Around the edges of their pools, most water gardeners want a shallow ledge to grow plants that require only a few inches of water. It is difficult to form such a ledge with cement. When pouring your walls, you need to build the top of the form on the inside to allow for a shelf jutting out into the water. Make sure when you are pouring the walls that you get the concrete worked back well into the shelf form. With precast cement, about all you can do is suspend redwood shelves on hangers hooked over the top rim of the pond. Then pots of shallow water-loving plants can be positioned on the shelf. The effect is less natural, but most shallow-water plants should be confined to pots anyhow, as they spread very fast if given the chance.

WATER LILIES

Water lilies are the most interesting aquacultural plants you can grow in your water garden. They are among the most attractive of flowers, certainly, and they're available in a great variety. And finally, water lilies are most useful plants. Every part of the water lily is edible and is eaten by humans in some part of the world. Gourmets say the tender young leaves can be used to cook meat in, as we do with grape leaves or cabbage. The tubers are nutritious, raw or cooked. The seeds are eaten in some countries, sometimes dried, ground, and baked into bread. In our country, only the aquatic animals know how nutritious the water lily is, and it provides a key link in their biological food chain, as we have seen.

Water lilies are much more manageable if grown in pots

Water Lily

submerged in the water. Like most water plants, they grow and spread rapidly in a natural pond—too rapidly, if not thinned out. Tubs avoid the problem and, in any event, are necessary in a cement-bottomed pool. In preparing the soil in the tub, don't be afraid to add some well-rotted manure if available, as the lilies feed on soil nutrients as greedily as corn. Cover the soil in the pots with a layer of gravel or sand to keep water from washing the soil and stirring up mud. The water lily tuber should be planted right in the surface soil, barely covered. Set the tub(s) in water deep enough to allow 12 to 18 inches of water over the brim of the pot (unless specific directions for a certain variety call for more or less water depth than that). Good tubs can be made from wooden barrels cut in half. Cypress is better than oak, but either will do fine. Plastic and fiberglass tubs are okay, too, if large enough. A water lily ought to have about 3 cubic feet of soil to grow in. Plant in early spring.

You can start water lilies from seed sometimes by placing the seeds in a pan of sand and then soaking the sand with water at 70 to 80 degrees F (21.1 to 26.6 degrees C). After a day or so of soaking, carefully lower into 18 inches or more of water in the pool. As the plants grow, transfer them to suitably larger pots.

There are so many varieties of water lilies that a list is almost meaningless. Some are hardy; some are tropical and have to be stored in a greenhouse over winter. Some are night blooming; some day blooming. The common white pond lily of the North, *Nymphaea odorata,* is a good one to start with; it's hardy, dependable, beautiful, and now available in many fragrant and colorful hybrids.

If under water, the hardy varieties require no attention over winter. If the pool is to be drained, the plants should be covered with a thick layer of leaves or straw. Those growing in tubs can be moved and stored in a cool place.

The common yellow water lily grows wild along our creek and has to endure cruel winter conditions and sometimes ravaging spring floods. And still it flourishes. Its blossom is not as showy as other water lilies but I love it. All it requires of me is my delighted surprise at its yearly regrowth.

The lotus is an extravagantly showy water flower that responds well to tub culture, too. There are several main species, the Egyptian (*Nelumbium nelumbo*) and the American yellow

315

Lotus

(*N. pentapetalum*) being the best known. Lotuses aren't very hardy, but a tubful on your patio or in your pool are worth the bother of indoor storage over winter. Lotuses only require about 3 inches of water above the soil in the pot. They are often grown in tubs sunk in lawn or garden, as long as there's a hose handy to keep those 3 inches of water in the top of the tub.

   Water lilies are available from larger fish hatcheries and specialized nurseries. The ones I see advertised in garden magazines are: Zetts Fish Farm & Hatchery, Drifting, PA 16834; Three Springs Fisheries, 1644 Hort Rd., Buckeystown, MD 21717; Paradise Gardens, Bedford and May Sts., Whitman, MA 02382; and Tricker's Waterlilies, Saddle River, NJ 07458 or Box 7845, Independence, OH 44131.

316

OTHER AQUATIC PLANTS

There are other flowers to plant alongside your pool that are much easier to grow. Water irises like the yellow water flag, *Iris pseudo-acorus,* will grow in shallow water or on a bank very close to the water. My favorite for the same environment is the little purple wild iris. Whole clumps of this iris grow at the edge of our creek, as if someone planted and tended them. The sweet flag (*Acorus calamus*) has a fleshy rhizome that is edible. An essence extracted from the aromatic rhizome is used as a digestive tonic and to flavor wines. Certain kinds of water arums grow well in shallow water and produce showy blossoms, like *Calla palustris* which resembles its close relative, the calla lily. It needs full sun.

Sedge grass, bulrushes, and cattails can all be grown at the edge of pools, but will have to be thinned and controlled so their clumps do not get too large in relation to the size of the pool.

One of the best water plants to grow is a type of water plantain, arrowhead (*Saggitaria* spp.) which has edible rhizomes, is quite attractive, and is a good oxygenating plant. Other oxygenators recommended by water gardeners are cobomba and anacharis, rather tiny plants that float on the water surface. I am leary of tiny floating plants, however, because if the situation is to their liking, many of them will soon clog the pool. That is why I wouldn't use knotweed, waterweed, duckweed, water milfoil, or water crowfoot, although these plants are quite attractive, to say nothing of water hyacinth which is now such a problem in Florida.

With circulating waterfalls and some oxygen-giving plants in the water, your fish may do nicely, if stocked only thinly. With a small aerator or even a bubbler like those used in aquariums, and some kind of filter built into the recirculating system, you could add many more fish than would normally be recommended. But in doing this, you'll be traveling new pathways. Go slow and experiment. When the fish gasp for air, you know you've gone too far for the space and/or equipment you have in operation.

Keep your pool clean. Don't let old leaves, twigs, et cetera, sink and rot in the water. Rotting vegetation in a small pool can be critical; it won't do you any good and could do harm by removing too much oxygen. Experiment with a variety of fish; don't just

317

Water Iris

assume goldfish are the only proper species for garden pools. Encourage snails (the kinds that don't move into your vegetable garden), frogs, turtles, crayfish, and especially toads. Snails and crayfish are good scavengers of rotting vegetation. If possible, maintain an unmowed area between pool and vegetable garden to protect toads, especially in spring when the little ones are emerging from the water. Toads are more apt to travel to and from their moist daytime retreats to your garden when they have a route through protective high grass. The same goes for garter snakes, which are tremendous slug eaters, too. At least refrain from mowing in the dusk of evening when toads are most active. Mow around the pool only in the early afternoons of hot, dry days.

The birds, of course, will love your pool, and so will the bees. Birds, however, are often frightened by free-standing fountains, preferring small, natural-looking waterfalls or quiet water. If possible, plant shrubs and trees nearby that have food for birds—but don't plant trees that shed lots of leaves where they will fall into the pool. Elderberry, wild cherry, chokecherry, autumn olive, holly, dogwood, nandina, crabapple, oaks, sumac, pyracantha, pokeberry, red cedar, are all very good for birds. Oaks? Squirrels aren't the only animals that like acorns. Woodpeckers, jays, nuthatches, titmice, chickadees, catbirds, brown thrashers, and towhees go for acorns too.

Envision your garden pool first as a place of quiet beauty, a place for pleasant contemplation. But as you live with this miniature pond, learn to make of it an integral part of your food garden—a horn of plenty in its own right.

Ohio's Agricultural Research and Development Center has a pool to collect solar heat for greenhouses.

WEIRD NEW (AND OLD) IDEAS FOR THE FUTURE 16

The University of Delaware is developing a closed system for the production of oysters that is suitable for use virtually anywhere. That's a much more remarkable claim than it might seem, not unlike science promising a moon walk back in 1960. If you can raise fresh oysters in Indianapolis, then there seems to be hope for the most visionary ideas in food production short of pie in the sky. What's more, the Delaware aquaculturists say they can produce the oysters feeding only various algae, or even protein yeasts grown on petroleum extracts—both of which would put no strain on conventional sources of food. And as if that is not hard enough to believe, the researchers further confound us by claiming they will raise marketable oysters in this controlled system in one year!

ALGAE: FUTURE FARM CROP?

Even more wondrous projections for protein production are being made for algae. Scientists at the Los Alamos Scientific Laboratory in New Mexico have been studying, with the aid of laser beams, the still mysterious process of photosynthesis. In 1975, they announced the astounding deduction, based on their work, that it was entirely possible to produce 1,460 tons of protein-rich algae in a one-acre pond. The pond would be covered with plastic so that temperature could be maintained at 100 degrees F (37.7 degrees C), and carbon dioxide could be fed artificially to the crop. At 1975 prices, the scientists said the algae could be raised at an average cost of fifty cents per pound. If sold at $1 per pound (much less than the price in health food stores now), the algae would net the producer $1.5 million per acre! No one is going

321

to really believe that kind of rosy accounting, but the important point is that mankind has not really begun to produce food in the quantities or with the efficiencies that are possible. For the backyard producer the possibilities seem infinitely optimistic. Granted that algae ain't prime steak, it *is* edible and nutritious. If its domestication is perfected, there should be no reason for acute hunger anywhere the sun continues to shine.

Also intriguing is the fact that the scientists at Los Alamos produced algae in airtight containers much faster than in nature and think the process could be used commercially. Not only that, but some algae, when deprived of oxygen, produce hydrogen, which could be used for fuel.

And of course, algae produce methane gas as they rot, or make good fertilizer for conventional crops.

DEW PONDS

Not all the weird and wonderful ways to get sustenance from water come out of technological progress. Some ideas are very old and are just now being rediscovered or adapted to modern conditions. The controversial dew ponds or fog ponds of England and other parts of Europe are known to date back to the Bronze Age and earlier. As far back as neolithic times, man discovered that ponds on hilltops, where heavy mists were frequent, could be replenished by condensation. A pile of rocks, for example, might catch and condense considerable quantities of water, enough to provide water for soldiers in hilltop fortresses. Historical records show that down through the ages, when droughts dried up valley ponds and streams, the hilltop dew ponds held steady, replenished by nightly mists. Walter Johnson, an English anthropologist writing at the turn of the twentieth century (in his book *Folk-Memory*, published by Oxford University Press in 1908), reported experiments in 1901 at Lockinge, on the Berkshire Downs, with regard to the effectiveness of dew ponds:

> On the night of January 18, 1901, a rise of 1½ inches was recorded, on the following night, 2 inches, and a little later, on January 24, there was an increase of another inch. During one particular fog, occurring even in May, the level rose 1½ inches. Five nights of winter fog gave a total accession of 8

inches. . . . The results obtained by Mr. Cornish, though at first sight startling, will not altogether astonish those who have had occasion to spend several hours in a fog-laden atmosphere on a moderately high hill.

The effectiveness of dew ponds is disputed, and their practicality has not been demonstrated in drier desert regions. Nevertheless, areas like the California coast experience considerable fog and mist, and it would be particularly sad if Californians in the recent drought had suffered unduly for lack of technological know-how that was common knowledge to Bronze Age man.

Even in the Midwest, where heavy mists are rare, the amount of water deposited on plants in a night of heavy dew is considerable. I've long believed that corn's ability to catch and hold as much as a spoonful of water in the base whorls of its leaves relieves some of the stress the plants would otherwise suffer in dry periods between rains. On dewy nights in August, even in driest weather, water will catch in considerable quantities and actually drip steadily off the plant onto the ground once the little hollows in the whorls of leaves are full. I've never measured the amount of water exactly, but I'm sure a mature corn plant catches at least a fourth of a cup of water on such a night. At twenty-five thousand plants per acre, that's nearly 400 gallons of water per acre per night—insignificant in terms of irrigation value, but interesting nevertheless.

SOLAR STILLS

All good Boy Scouts learn another fairly old method of obtaining safe drinking water where none seems to be available—by solar distillation. The sun's rays are made to pass through some kind of transparent membrane (plastic works fine) onto a source of brine. Water evaporates from the brine and the vapor condenses on the membrane, which is so shaped to collect the condensation. Solar stills are practical enough to supply water for small towns and camps in isolated areas in Australia and in both Mediterranean and Caribbean communities. A solar still at Caiguna, in western Australia, uses waste heat from a nearby motor to supplement the solar heat—a practice markedly increasing the still's efficiency. (See *More Water for Arid Lands,* National Academy of Sciences, Washington, D.C., 1974, reprinted 1976, page 64 ff.)

RUN-OFF AGRICULTURE

Another water management method from the ancient past is being revitalized in arid desert regions, especially by the Israelis. Biblical and other ancient historical records gave evidence that the Negev Desert in Israel once supported fruitful farms at least as far back as 1000 B.C. Yet with a scant rainfall of from 5 to 7 inches per year, the area has, for centuries, barely provided sustenance for far-ranging nomadic herds. The assumption has always been that the weather was wetter in earlier times.

Michael Evenari and his fellow scientists in Israel have proved rather conclusively that such an assumption was wrong. The weather has not changed, but agricultural methods that incorporated elaborate and sophisticated systems for catching and using water were allowed to lapse when nomadic tribes overran the ancient farming culture. Crumbling remains of terraces and channels still exist in the Negev Desert and about all Evenari and his coworkers have to do is rebuild them. Then when rain falls, it gathers in the large hillside catchments that channel it to valley lands where crops are planted as in ancient times. In effect, a rainfall of 5 inches per year becomes, in the cultivated fields, an annual rainfall of 30 inches, enough for many kinds of field crops and orchards. The system is now called "run-off agriculture," and it can make a desert bloom. A catchment area on the Negev Desert needs to be about thirty times larger than the farmed area it feeds water to.

Evenari and others have developed a refinement of run-off agriculture that works even better than the ancient method. Instead of large catchment areas feeding large fields, they built smaller catchments to funnel water to smaller plots, which resulted in less total water-loss. The most efficiency was gained by building or shaping a very small catchment area for each tree or bush in an orchard. As much as 62 percent of the rainfall in one of these "microcatchments" could be saved and utilized by the plant. Microcatchments are inexpensive to build—costing from $5 to $20 per hectare, says Evenari. (See M. Evenari, L. Shanan, and N. Tadmor: *The Negev: The Challenge of a Desert,* Cambridge, Mass.: Harvard University Press, 1971.)

ICE FOR THE ICEHOUSE

Ice harvesting for refrigeration is a type of aquacultural production that seems obsolete today, but in the light of fossil fuel shortages, the technique should not be allowed to lapse into total obscurity. On some homesteads, the old icehouse has, in fact, already made a comeback, its low-cost practicality apparent to anyone willing to do the work of hauling in the ice.

An icehouse can be the simplest of buildings. It doesn't necessarily need a roof—in fact, some authorities believe ice will keep better in a roofless house where rainfall periodically moistens the sawdust on top of the ice. Wet sawdust is better insulation than dry. So all you really need is a big bin—floor and walls, and lots of sawdust. Two feet of sawdust below the blocks of ice and 2 feet above, with at least 1½ feet packed on each side, will keep the ice through summer. Put the icehouse on the north side of another taller building, if possible, or under trees—the more shade, the better. Use old sawdust if possible. Either old or new will insulate, but old insulates better, says folklore.

Most icehouses, at least the ones that remain standing, are roofed. M. G. Kains, in his now classic book *Five Acres and Independence*, prescribed a roofed icehouse, built with conventional concrete footing and wood-shaving insulated stud walls. In such a well-built house, you need only a foot of sawdust above and below the ice and only 6 inches worth on the sides. The plans call for a gravel floor in the icehouse with a 4-inch drain tile under the gravel to carry away melting water.

Kains estimated a family needs about 5 tons of ice per summer. One ton of ice, he said, requires about 45 cubic feet of space in the icehouse (a ton of solid ice would measure about 36 cubic feet). Five tons are about equal to fifty cakes, 22 inches square and 12 inches thick, allowing for some melting.

Cutting out 12-inch-thick blocks of ice is hard work, but Liz Buell, a homesteader writing in *Farmstead Magazine* (winter 1976), said a chain saw can make the job considerably easier. The idea is to cut two-thirds of the way through the ice blocks with a chain saw. (The blade will churn up too much slush if it dips through the ice into the water below.) Then finish the longitudinal

325

cuts with a conventional ice saw. Individual chunks can then be broken off by plunging the long-handled ice chisel into cracks between each block. Buell said that about eighty blocks weighing some 75 pounds each are enough to last her family in Maine until the following October.

Of course, your icebox will determine the size your blocks have to be cut. Antique iceboxes are sometimes available from antique dealers, but the price is usually high. You can build a wooden cabinet with a watertight tank under the ice compartment. Styrofoam insulation will cover a multitude of cabinetmaking sins, if you are not a professional carpenter. You have to insulate the box anyway. Make sure the door is as airtight as possible. If the tank that catches the melting ice water is not large enough to hold the whole ice block, you would be wise to run a tube from it to a drain. Otherwise, the tank will overflow and make a mess of your icebox.

Clear ice, which forms on still water, is solider than white ice and will last longer. If you are fortunate enough to have unpolluted water, you can chip off chunks to use directly in foods or drinks. Since this is rarely the case, you should take advantage of freezing weather by setting out cardboard milk containers full of water. Store the frozen containers in a separate part of the icehouse, and use in summer for ice cubes. The cardboard is easily removed from around the ice, readily identifies your "edible" ice, and keeps it from getting dirty while buried in the sawdust. Best to break up the ice cake with a hammer *before* removing the cardboard.

USING MARSH PLANTS TO CLEAN SEWAGE WATER

One of the interesting new discoveries about water is the use of marsh-growing rushes and reeds to filter and clean out toxic bacteria and chemicals from polluted wastewater. The process was reported at the Biological Water Quality Improvement Alternatives Conference at the University of Pennsylvania a few years ago. The feasibility of using bulrushes to clean polluted water was first demonstrated in Germany by Dr. Kaethe Seidel at the Max Planck Institute. Following her experiments, Dr. Joost De Joong, a Dutch chemist, is applying the principle successfully on a larger scale. He reported to the conference that a 25-acre marsh, in operation since

1967 at a summer recreation area, handles raw sewage from some three hundred thousand daytime swimmers and seven thousand campers each summer. Phragmites reeds (*Phragmites australis*) and bulrushes (*Scirpus lacustris*) are the plants he uses. The reeds reduce solids and sludge rather quickly because of the plants' high rate of transpiration. The bulrushes, into which the water flows, next remove minerals and chemicals. At the end of two weeks and a 400-yard journey through the marshes, the water is clean enough to release back into natural bodies of water. The only disadvantage is that the system cannot function when the plants aren't growing.

Experiments in filtering sewage water through man-made marshes are also being carried out at the Oshkosh campus of the University of Wisconsin.

PONDS TO COLLECT SOLAR HEAT

Ponds may someday be built in backyards as collectors for home and greenhouse heating—just as they are now built for swimming. At first glance, the experimental solar heat-collecting pond at Ohio's Agricultural Research and Development Center at Wooster looks like an Arab oilman's swimming pool. In fact, it looks that way at second glance, too. The pool measures 60 by 28 feet by 12 feet deep, and has been covered, at least temporarily, by a plastic bubble. Even on a sunny day in December, the temperature under the bubble gets up to a warm 75 degrees F (23.8 degrees C) or more, tempting one to dive in.

If anyone were so foolish as to do that, the resemblance to a swimming pool would change quickly to a similarity with the sea. The water is salty, and the deeper you'd go, the saltier you'd find it. Also unlike a conventional pool, the water gets progressively warmer with its depth. In fact, on a very hot day in late summer, the water at the bottom of the pool might approach the boiling point, though in December, the pond is doing well to maintain temperature at the lowest level at 100 degrees F (37.7 degrees C).

The reason for the salt is to make the water denser, and therefore heavier, at the bottom of the pool. The water has been literally laid in the pool in layers, using a complex method worked out by Dr. Carl Nielsen of the Department of Physics at Ohio State. In the lower 6 feet, the water contains 20 percent salt, with the salt content gradually decreasing to zero from the 6-foot depth to the surface. In other words, the top layer is lighter than the layers below it—the key to how the water can hold and store the sun's heat. Only the bottom 6 feet of water are convective; when heated, the water will circulate only up to about the 6-foot mark, rather than continue up to the top and dissipate the heat. So the lighter top layer of water acts as an insulator, holding the heat in, while the water, being nearly transparent, allows the sun's rays to go through. One meter of nonconvective water has an insulation value equivalent to 2⅓ inches of Styrofoam.

The sunlight penetrates to the black liner on the bottom of the pool, which absorbs the heat and transfers it to the water. The ground under the pool stores some heat, too, and can transfer it back to the pool in winter. The sides of the pool are insulated with Styrofoam.

The plastic bubble over the pond, composed of two layers with air space between, was originally intended to increase the insulating efficiency of the pool, but tests have so far shown no increase in efficiency during the winter months. The plastic diffuses the sunlight too much, which offsets the heat retention gained by using the plastic. Nor has the shiny, aluminized cloth reflector on the north wall increased the total accumulated radiation during summer, as it was intended to do. However, it appears that the reflector could increase effective pond area up to 160 percent in winter, if the plastic cover is removed. Final results await further testing.

The long-range goal of the experiment is to see if such a solar pond can collect and store enough heat to warm a house of 2,000 square feet of living space comfortably through a northern winter. Presently, the experimenters intend to use the heat to warm a 1,000-square-foot greenhouse located next to the pond. Heat can be transferred from the bottom of the pond to the greenhouse in two ways: either by running fresh water through pipes in the bottom of the pond, where it would be warmed and then pumped back to the greenhouse, or by circulating the salty water itself back and forth between pond and greenhouse through the underground pipes. The addition of a heat pump improves performance considerably.

Could a fish pond or swimming pool double as a solar heat collector? Scientists at Wooster won't say yes, but they won't say no, either. The salt solution in the water might preclude fish, or even swimming, but the saltwater is at the bottom and there is not much at all in the top of the pool. So double use of the water is not entirely out of the question. Another potential problem is that even larger swimming pools are too small to heat a house or large greenhouse, if converted to a solar pond.

Nevertheless, the mad scientist in all of us knows there are definite possibilities for *small* projects. A swimming pool is large enough to heat a small greenhouse or a basement room or two. Perhaps such a pool might serve as a swimming or fish pool in warm weather, then a salt solution could be added in cool weather after fish are harvested, to convert the pool to a heat collector until summer again.

WATER BUFFALO

The University of Florida should get credit for the wildest idea yet. Florida has a problem with aquatic plants, particularly the water hyacinth, which clog canals and lakes in the state. Florida spends some $20 million annually, trying to kill the water weeds with poison sprays, to no avail.

What to do? Well, how about bringing in some water buf-

Water buffalo are a mainstay of peasant agriculture in the Far East. Florida researchers believe they could be raised on water weeds in the United States.

329

faloes? The water buffalo is as much an aquatic animal as a duck. It spends its life normally lolling in the mud and water, grazing aquatic plants. What's more, the water buffalo is a very highly prized domestic animal in many parts of the world, supplying both milk and meat. Why not increase the food supply and control water hyacinths at the same time?

A water buffalo is not easy to find when you want one, but the university finally located four in Toronto (of all places) where a zoo was closing, and brought them down to the land of the pestiferous water hyacinth. Under close observation, they have been chomping away on the wicked water weeds ever since. So far, results are inconclusive. You can't just let water buffalo wander freely around the countryside looking for water weeds. Newly discovered fungal diseases and insect predators of water hyacinth now give more promise of controlling the plant biologically than the buffalo. But the fact remains that water buffalo could be raised economically on a diet mostly of water weeds. As Florida researchers point out, the animal could be raised on a farm without competing with beef for ordinary pastureland.

But if water buffaloes are not enough of a mind-boggling aquacultural vision to leave you with, consider the alligator. Hardly a backyard aquaculture project, but remember; there *are* such things as alligator farms. For the few people properly situated, alligators are more profitable than steers have been for most cattlemen!

APPENDIX

FISH COMMISSIONS

Alabama Dept. of Conservation
and Natural Resources
64 N. Union St.
Montgomery, AL 36104

Alaska Dept. of Fish and Game
Subport Bldg.
Juneau, AK 99801

Arizona Game and Fish Dept.
2222 W. Greenway Rd.
Phoenix, AZ 85023

Arkansas Game and
Fish Comm.
Game and Fish Bldg.
Little Rock, AR 72201

California Dept. of Fish
and Game
The Resources Agency
1416 9th St.
Sacramento, CA 95814

Colorado Dept. of Natural
Resources, Div. of Wildlife
6060 Broadway St.
Denver, CO 80216

Connecticut Dept. of
Environmental Protection
State Office Bldg.
Hartford, CT 06115

Delaware Dept. of Natural
Resources and Environmental
Control
Div. of Fish and Wildlife
D St.
Dover, DE 19901

District of Columbia
Metropolitan Police
300 Indiana Ave. N.W.
Washington, DC 20001

Florida Dept. of Natural
Resources
620 S. Meridian St.
Tallahassee, FL 32304

Georgia State Game and
Fish Div.
Trinity-Washington Bldg.
270 Washington St.
Atlanta, GA 30334

Getting Food from Water

Hawaii Dept. of Land and
Natural Resources
Div. of Fish and Game
1179 Punchbowl St.
Honolulu, HI 96813

Idaho Fish and Game Dept.
600 S. Walnut St., Box 25
Boise, ID 83707

Illinois Dept. of Conservation
State Office Bldg.
Springfield, MO 62706

Indiana Dept. of Natural
Resources
Div. of Fish and Wildlife
608 State Office Bldg.
Indianapolis, IN 46204

Iowa State Conservation Comm.
State Office Bldg.
300 4th St.
Des Moines, IA 50319

Kansas Forestry,
Fish and Game Comm.
Box 1028
Pratt, KS 67124

Kentucky Dept. of Fish
and Wildlife Resources
Capitol Plaza Tower
Frankfort, KY 40601

Louisiana Wildlife and
Fisheries Comm.
P. O. Box 44095
Capitol Station
Baton Rouge, LA 70804

Maine Dept. of Inland Fisheries
and Game
State Office Bldg.
Augusta, ME 04330

Maryland Fish and Wildlife
Administration
Natural Resources Bldg.
Annapolis, MD 21401

Massachusetts Dept. of
Environmental Resources
100 Cambridge St.
Boston, MA 02202

Michigan Dept. of
Natural Resources
Mason Bldg.
Lansing, MI 48926

Minnesota Dept. of Natural
Resources
Div. of Game and Fish
301 Centennial Bldg.
658 Cedar St.
St. Paul, MN 55101

Mississippi Game and
Fish Comm.
Robert E. Lee Office Bldg.
239 N. Lamar St.
P.O. Box 451
Jackson, MS 39205

Missouri Dept. of Conservation
P. O. Box 180
Jefferson City, MO 65101

Montana Fish and Game Dept.
Helena, MT 59601

Nebraska Game and
Parks Comm.
P. O. Box 30370
2200 N. 33rd St.
Lincoln, NE 68503

Nevada Dept. of Fish and Game
Box 10678
Reno, NV 89510

New Hampshire Fish
and Game Dept.
34 Bridge St.
Concord, NH 03301

New Jersey Dept. of
Environmental Protection
Div. of Fish, Game,
and Shellfisheries
Box 1390
Trenton, NJ 08625

New Mexico Dept. of
Game and Fish
State Capitol
Santa Fe, NM 87501

New York Dept. of
Environmental Conservation
Fish and Wildlife Div.
50 Wolf Rd.
Albany, NY 12201

North Carolina Wildlife
Resources Comm.
325 N. Salisbury St.
Raleigh, NC 27611

North Dakota State Game and
Fish Dept.
2121 Lovett Ave.
Bismarck, ND 58501

Ohio Dept. of Natural
Resources, Div. of Wildlife
Fountain Square
Columbus, OH 43224

Oklahoma Dept. of Wildlife
Conservation
1801 N. Lincoln Blvd.
P. O. Box 53465
Oklahoma City, OK 73105

Oregon Fish and Wildlife Comm.
Box 3503
Portland, OR 97208

Pennsylvania Fish Comm.
P. O. Box 1673
Harrisburg, PA 17120

Puerto Rico Dept. of
Natural Resources
P. O. Box 11488
San Juan, PR 00910

Rhode Island Dept. of Natural
Resources
Div. of Fish and Wildlife
83 Park St.
Providence, RI 02903

South Carolina Wildlife
Resources Dept.
Box 167, 1015 Main St.
Columbia, SC 29202

South Dakota Dept. of Game,
Fish and Parks
State Office Bldg.
Pierre, SD 57501

Tennessee Wildlife Resources
Agency
Box 40747
Ellington Agricultural Center
Nashville, TN 37220

Texas Parks and Wildlife Dept.
John H. Reagan Bldg.
Austin, TX 78701

Utah State Dept. of Natural
Resources
Div. of Wildlife Resources
1596 W. North Temple St.
Salt Lake City, UT 84116

Vermont Agency of
Environmental Conservation
Fish and Game Dept.
Montpelier, VT 05602

Getting Food from Water

Virginia Comm. of Game and
Inland Fisheries
4010 W. Broad St.
Box 11104
Richmond, VA 23230

Washington Dept. of Fisheries
115 General Administration Bldg.
Olympia, WA 98504

West Virginia Dept. of Natural
Resources
1800 Washington St. East
Charleston, WV 25305

Wisconsin Dept. of Natural
Resources
Box 450
Madison, WI 53701

Wyoming Game and Fish Dept.
Box 1589
Cheyenne, WY 82001

Canada

Alberta Dept. of Lands and
Forests
624 Natural Resources Bldg.
Edmonton, Alberta T5K 1H4

British Columbia Dept. of
Recreation and Conservation
Fish and Wildlife Branch
Parliament Bldgs.
Victoria,
British Columbia V8W 2L9

Manitoba Dept. of Mines,
Resources and Environmental
Management
1007 Century St.
Winnipeg, Manitoba R3H 0W4

New Brunswick Dept. of
Natural Resources
Fish and Wildlife Branch
Fredericton,
New Brunswick E3B 4Y1

Newfoundland Dept. of
Tourism, Wildlife Div.
Confederation Bldg.
St. John's,
Newfoundland A1C 5T7

Nova Scotia Dept. of Lands
and Forests, Wildlife Div.
Box 516
Kentville,
Nova Scotia B4N 3X6

Ontario Ministry of Natural
Resources
Div. of Fish and Wildlife
Parliament Bldg.
Toronto, Ontario M7A 1X5

Prince Edward Island Dept.
of Fisheries
P. O. Box 2000
Charlottetown,
Prince Edward Island C1A 7N8

Quebec Dept. of Tourism,
Fish and Game
150 St. Cyrille E.
Quebec City, Quebec G1R 2B1

Saskatchewan Dept. of Tourism
Renewable Resources
Government Administration Bldg.
Regina, Saskatchewan S4S 0B2

Yukon: Game Dept.
Box 2703
Whitehorse,
Yukon Territory Y1A 2C6

BOOKS

Bardach, John E.; Ryther, John H.; and McLarney, William O. *Aquaculture: The Farming and Husbandry of Freshwater and Marine Organisms*. New York: John Wiley and Sons, Inc., 1972.

Bennett, George W. *Management of Artificial Lakes and Ponds*. London: Reinhold Publishing Co., 1962.

Hickling, C. F. *The Farming of Fish*. Elmsford, NY: Pergamon Press, Ltd., 1968.

Huet, Marcel. *Textbook of Fish Culture. Breeding and Cultivation of Fish*. Surrey, England: Fishing News (Books) Ltd.

Scott, W. B., and Crossman, E. J. *Freshwater Fishes of Canada*. Fisheries Research Board of Canada, Ottawa, 1973, Bulletin 184.

Spotte, Stephen H. *Fish and Invertebrate Culture: Water Management in Closed Systems*. New York: John Wiley and Sons, Inc., 1970.

MAGAZINES

The Commercial Fish Farmer and Aquaculture News. Subscription Section, P.O. Box 2451, Little Rock, AR 72203. Buyers' guide, which lists suppliers of equipment and fish, is also available.

FAO Aquaculture Bulletin. Fishery Resources and Environment Division of the Food and Agriculture Organization of the United Nations, Rome, Italy.

Farm Pond Harvest. Professional Sportsman's Publishing Co., Rural Route 2, Momence, IL 60954.

Fisheries. American Fisheries Society, 5410 Grosvenor Lane, Bethesda, MD 20014.

The Progressive Fish-Culturist. Superintendent of Documents, United States Government Printing Office, Washington, DC 20402.

GOVERNMENT BOOKLETS

The following are available from United States Government Printing Office, Washington, DC 20402.

Getting Food from Water

Catfish Farming. Farmers' Bulletin No. 2260—40¢.

Trout Ponds for Recreation. Farmers' Bulletin No. 2249—no charge.

Warm Water Fish Ponds. Farmers' Bulletin No. 2250—no charge.

BIBLIOGRAPHIES

Aquaculture and Related Publications of the School of Forestry and Wildlife Management. Publications Clerk, 249 Ag. Center, School of Forestry and Wildlife Management, Louisiana State University, Baton Rouge, LA 70803, July 1974.

Aquaculture Bibliography. Organic Gardening Readers Service, Rodale Press, Inc., 33 E. Minor St., Emmaus, PA 18049.

Trout Ponds and Farm Ponds, a List of References. Royal Ontario Museum, Dept. of Ichthyology and Herpetology, 100 Queen's Pk., Toronto, Ontario, Canada M5S 2C6.

SOURCES OF FISH

These sources were listed in the *Commercial Fish Farmers Buyers' Guide.* (For a copy, write to Subscription Service, P.O. Box 2451, Little Rock, AR 72203.) For more sources consult with your state fish commission.

Carp Family

Common Carp
(*Cyprinus carpio*)

Arkansas Fisheries, Inc.
P.O. Box 14
Fargo, AR 72049
(501) 734-3727

Avis Lake
RFD 1
Caruthersville, MO 63830
(314) 333-1819

Beck's Fish Market
Route 1
Genoa, WI 54632
(608) 689-2302

Bowerman Distributors
1442 N. Summers Rd.
Imlay City, MI 48444
(313) 724-2185

Clear Creek Fisheries
Route 4, Box 60
Martinsville, IN 46151
(317) 342-2973

338

Fish Breeders of Calif., Inc.
P.O. Box 918
Niland, CA 92257
(714) 348-0547

Fish Breeders of Idaho, Inc.
Route 3
Buhl, ID 83316
(208) 543-6645

Fish-Gro Fisheries
P.O. Box 87
Everett, PA 15537
(814) 652-2319

John B. Fitzpatrick
214 E. North St.
Dwight, IL 60402
(815) 584-2545

Giesler Live Fish Co.
Route 1, Box 53
W. Columbia, TX 77486
(713) 345-3577

Greenfield Fishing Lakes &
Hatcheries
Route 8, Box 127
Greenfield, IN 46140
(317) 326-2496

Hoeft Enterprises
Route 1, Box 237B
Milton, WV 25541
(304) 743-9806

Hurricane Hill Fish Farm
Route 6
Ripley, TN 38063
(901) 635-1347

Lakeland Trout Farms
Route 1
Nunnelly, TN 37137
(615) 729-3731

Martin Fisheries
Route 7, Box 386
Fulton, NY 13069
(315) 593-2251

Oakland Bio-Aquatics
1840 Thunderbird St.
Troy, MI 48084
(313) 362-3199

Opel's Fish Hatchery
Route 1, Box 51
Worden, IL 62097
(618) 459-3287

Pappas Fish Co.
P.O. Box 8802
Toledo, OH 43623

Parks Lake
P.O. Box 7231
Shawnee Mission, KS 66207
(913) 764-1024

Peterson Trout Farm
Peterson, MN 55962

Schulty's Place
Route 3, Box 103C
Troy, MO 63379

Grass Carp or White Amur
(*Ctenopharyngodon idella*)

Arkansas Fisheries Inc.
P.O. Box 14
Fargo, AR 72049
(501) 734-3727

Cleveland Fisheries
P.O. Drawer 460
Cleveland, MS 38732
(601) 843-8174

Leon Hill Catfish Farms
Route 2
Lonoke, AR 72086

J. M. Malone & Son Enterprises
Box 158
Lonoke, AR 72086
(501) 676-2800

Ross Fish Farm
Star Route 1, Box 46
Mountain Pine, AR 71956

Bighead Carp
(*Aristichthys noblis*)

J. M. Malone & Son Enterprises
Box 158
Lonoke, AR 72086
(501) 676-2800

Silver Carp
(*Hypothalmichthys molitrix*)

J. M. Malone & Son Enterprises
Box 158
Lonoke, AR 72086
(501) 676-2800

Catfish Family

Channel Catfish
(*Ictalurus punctatus*)

Acadiana Fish Farm Ltd.
Route 1, Box 35-A
Branch, LA 70516
(318) 783-4313

S. S. Allison
Route 2
Pocahontas, AR 72455

Aquatic Control, Inc.
P.O. Box 100
Seymour, IN 47274

Aquatic Environmental
Controls Co.
44625 Tonopah St.
Newberry Springs, CA 92365
(714) 257-3588

Arkansas Fisheries Inc.
P.O. Box 14
Fargo, AR 72049
(501) 734-3727

Arms Bait Co.
Route 2, Box 115
Dublin, TX 76446

Battle Fish Farms
Route 1, Box 180
Tunica, MS 38676
(601) 363-2445

Bernbet Farm
Route 6
West Monroe, LA 71291

C. H. Block & Co.
P.O. Box 847
Tunica, MS 38676

Blue Ridge Fish Hatchery
4536 Kernersville Rd.
Kernersville, NC 27284
(919) 788-6770

Bowerman Distributors
1442 N. Summers Rd.
Imlay City, MI 48444
(313) 724-2185

Bradshaw Farms
204 W. Bowles St.
Dumas, AR 71639

Catfish Acres
P.O. Box 260
Winnie, TX 77665

Catfish Unlimited
Route 1
Girard, IL 62640
(217) 627-2389

Cedar Creek Fisheries
Route 2
Osgood, IN 47037
(812) 675-1783

Cedar Lakes Catfish Farms
Route 1
Villa Rica, GA 30180
(404) 942-3735

Cen-Tex Hunting & Fishing
Route 1
Rogers, TX 76559

Clark Fish 'N Ranch
Route 1
Kingman, KS 67068

Clear Creek Fisheries
Route 4, Box 60
Martinsville, IN 46151
(317) 342-2973

Cleveland Fisheries
P.O. Drawer 460
Cleveland, MS 38732
(601) 843-8174

ConAgra Fish Products
P.O. Box 9367
Jackson, MS 39206

Billy D. Cooper Inc.
4426 Lemas St.
Houston, TX 77035
(713) 729-1105

Cottonwood Game & Fish Farm
Route 1, Box 101C
Norman, OK 73069
(405) 321-2287

D & B Catfish Farm
Route 2
Crockett, TX 75835
(713) 544-7465

Danbury Fish Farms
P.O. Box 528
Danbury, TX 77534
(713) 922-1561

Dover's Fish Hatchery
Route 1, Box 70
Havana, FL 32333
(904) 539-6754

East Third Fish Place
Route 2, Box 97M
Amarillo, TX 79101
(806) 335-1418

Eden Fisheries
Route 2, Box 79
Yazoo City, MS 39194
(601) 746-5085

Elk Grove-Florin Catfish Farm
8046 Elk Grove-Florin Rd.
Sacramento, CA 95823
(916) 682-3936

Edgar Farmer & Sons
Route 2, Box 290
Dumas, AR 71639

H. O. Fields
Route 2, Box 123
Weiner, AR 72429
(501) 252-3250

Fish Breeders of California, Inc.
P.O. Box 918
Niland, CA 92257
(714) 348-0547

Fish Breeders of Idaho, Inc.
Route 3
Buhl, ID 83316
(208) 543-6645

John B. Fitzpatrick
214 E. North St.
Dwight, IL 60420
(815) 584-2545

Flowers and Jones Fish Farm
RFD
Dexter, MO 63841
(314) 624-3376

Fountain Bluff Fish Farm
Route 1
Gorham, IL 62940
(618) 763-4387

4-Corners Catfish
920 N. Kansas St.
Topeka, KS 66608
(913) 234-8582

Gena Lakes Fish Farm
Route 1, Box 191D
Augusta, KS 67010
(316) 733-1843

Giesler Live Fish Co.
Route 1, Box 53
W. Columbia, TX 77486
(713) 345-3577

Greenfield Fishing Lakes &
Hatcheries
Route 8, Box 127
Greenfield, IN 46140
(317) 326-2496

Greenhope Farms
Route 1, Box 76
Morrisville, NC 27560

H. K. Hammett & Sons
P.O. Box 556
Greenville, MS 38701
(601) 332-1832

Hickory Ridge Fisheries Inc.
5922 N. Douglas Blvd.
Spencer, OK 73084
(405) 771-3705

Leon Hill Catfish Farms
Route 2
Lonoke, AR 72086

Hurricane Hill Fish Farm
Route 6
Ripley, TN 38063
(901) 635-1347

C. E. Jewett
Star Route, Box 55A
Mineola, TX 75773

K & W Fish Farm
Route 2
Haven, KS 67543
(316) 465-2359

Ken's Channel Catfish
Route 1
Alapaha, GA 31622
(912) 532-6135

King Mountain Hatchery
P.O. Box 321
Thomaston, GA 30286
(404) 648-2062

Krehbiel Fish Farm
P.O. Box 145
Pretty Prairie, KS 67570
(316) 459-6586

Kurtz's Fish Farm
Route 2, Box 155
Elverson, PA 19520
(215) 286-9250

Lake Ecology Control, Inc.
9205 S. Hardy Dr.
Tempe, AZ 85284
(602) 839-4210

Lake View Ranch
Route 1
Dewitt, MO 64639

Larson's Catfish Farm
Route 1
Mulberry Grove, IL 62262
(618) 326-8675

Moore Fish Farm
Route 2
Inola, OK 74036
(918) 341-4194

Robert Mutter
Route 2, Box 84
Glasgow, KY 42141

Alfred Nabholz
P.O. Box 122
Conway, AR 72032

James A. Noe
7301 Hampson St.
New Orleans, LA 70118

Northup's Fish Hatchery
Route 6, Box 88
Columbia, MO 65201

Nutricultured Products
P.O. Box 428
Plains, KS 67869
(316) 563-7566

Oak Valley Fish Farm
Route 2, Box 279
Stroud, OK 74079
(918) 968-2955

Opel's Fish Hatchery
Route 1, Box 51
Worden, IL 62097
(618) 459-3287

Osage Catfisheries Inc.
Route 1, Box 222
Osage Beach, MO 65065

E. A. Owen
P.O. Box 144
Williston, TN 38076
(901) 465-3343

Peterson Trout Farm
Peterson, MN 55962

Pickering Brothers Farm
Route 2
Taylorsville, MS 39166

Plains Fish Ranch
P.O. Box 101
Davenport, NE 68335
(402) 364-2122 or
        364-2186

Frank R. Pope
P.O. Box 2504
Opelika, AL 36801
(205) 749-9742

Raccoon Valley Fish Farm
Route 2
Pleasant Hill, MO 64080
(816) 987-3488

Ragsdale Fish Farm
P.O. Box 254
Dumas, AR 71639
(501) 382-5245

Roland Fish Farm
Route 2, Box 208A
Whitesboro, TX 76273
(214) 564-5372
        564-3812

Ross Fish Farm
Star Route 1, Box 46
Mountain Pine, AR 71956

Ruder's Fish Hatcheries
Route 1, Box 349
Millstadt, IL 62260
(618) 476-1388

Russell Gro. & Sta.
Moscow, TN 38057
(901) 465-8170

Schulty's Place
Route 3, Box 103C
Troy, MO 63379

Seminole Tribe of Florida, Inc.
Route 6, Box 588
Okeechobee, FL 33472
(813) 763-8453

Staway Ranch
Route 1, Box 66
Murchison, TX 75778
(214) 469-3318 or
        469-3630

Taylor Fish & Farms Inc.
Route 1, Box 91A
Dudley, MO 63936
(314) 624-3858

Thompson-Anderson
Enterprises, Inc.
764 E. Jefferson St.
Yazoo City, MS 39194

Triple M. Catfish Farm
Route 3, Box 362
Georgiani, AL 36033
(205) 376-2866

Twist Fish Farm
P.O. Box 144
Twist, AR 72385

Billy B. Veath
Route 1
Evansville, IL 62242

Water Resources
P.O. Box D
DeQueen, AR 71832
(501) 584-2944

Wilson Fish Farm
Route 1
Ramsey, IL 62080

Zetts Fish Farm & Hatchery
Drifting, PA 16834
(814) 345-5357

Bullhead Catfish

Avis Lake
RFD 1
Caruthersville, MO 63830
(314) 333-1819

Bowerman Distributors
1442 N. Summers Rd.
Imlay City, MI 48444
(313) 724-2185

Clear Creek Fisheries
Route 4, Box 60
Martinsville, IN 46151
(317) 342-2973

Hoeft Enterprises
Route 1, Box 237B
Milton, WV 25541
(304) 743-9806

Krehbiel Fish Farms
P.O. Box 145
Pretty Prairie, KS 67570
(316) 459-6585

Kurtz's Fish Farm
Route 2, Box 155
Elverson, PA 19520
(215) 286-9250

Moore Fish Farm
Route 2
Inola, OK 74036
(918) 341-4194

Opel's Fish Hatchery
Route 1, Box 51
Worden, IL 62097
(618) 459-3287

Ragsdale Fish Farm
P.O. Box 254
Dumas, AR 71639
(501) 382-5245

James B. Short
12141 Weaver St.
El Monte, CA 91733

Troutdale Ranch, Inc.
P.O. Box 68
Gravois Mills, MO 65037
(314) 372-6100

Sunfish Family

Largemouth Bass
(*Micropterus salmoides*)

Aquatic Control, Inc.
P.O. Box 100
Seymour, IN 47274

Bowerman Distributors
1442 N. Summers Rd.
Imlay City, MI 48444
(313) 724-2185

Brown's Trout Hatchery
Route 362
Bliss, NY 14024
(716) 322-7322

Calala's Water Haven, Inc.
Route 60, Dept. CFF
New London, OH 44851
(419) 929-8052

Cedar Creek Fisheries
Route 2
Osgood, IN 47037
(812) 675-1783

Billy D. Cooper, Inc.
4426 Lemac St.
Houston, TX 77035
(713) 729-1105

D & B Catfish Farm
Route 2
Crockett, TX 75835
(713) 544-7465

Danbury Fish Farms
P.O. Box 528
Danbury, TX 77534
(713) 922-1561

Fish Breeders of California, Inc.
P.O. Box 918
Niland, CA 92257
(714) 348-0547

Fish-Gro Fisheries
P.O. Box 87
Everett, PA 15537
(814) 652-2319

John B. Fitzpatrick
214 E. North St.
Dwight, IL 60402
(815) 584-2545

Greenfield Fishing Lakes &
Hatcheries
Route 8, Box 127
Greenfield, IN 46140
(317) 326-2496

Hoeft Enterprises
Route 1, Box 237B
Milton, WV 25541
(304) 743-9806

Ken's Channel Catfish
Route 1
Alapaha, GA 31622
(912) 532-6135

Krehbiel Fish Farm
P.O. Box 145
Pretty Prairie, KS 67570
(316) 459-6586

Kurtz's Fish Farm
Route 2, Box 155
Elverson, PA 19520
(215) 286-9250

Lake View Ranch
Route 1
DeWitt, MO 64639

Moore Fish Farm
Route 2
Inola, OK 74036
(918) 341-4194

North Star Fish Hatchery
RFD
Montour, IA 50173
(515) 492-3490

Northrup's Fish Hatchery
Route 6, Box 88
Columbia, MO 65201

Opel's Fish Hatchery
Route 1, Box 51
Worden, IL 62097
(618) 459-3287

Osage Catfisheries, Inc.
Route 1, Box 222
Osage Beach, MO 65065

Peterson Trout Farm
Peterson, MN 55962

Plains Fish Ranch
P.O. Box 101
Davenport, NE 68335
(402) 364-2122 or
        364-2186

Ragsdale Fish Farm
P.O. Box 254
Dumas, AR 71639
(501) 382-5245

Rose City Trout Farms
2646 N. Townline Rd.
Rose City, MI 48654
(517) 685-2200

Ruder's Fish Hatcheries
Route 1, Box 349
Millstadt, IL 62260
(618) 476-1388

Southern Fish Culturists, Inc.
P.O. Box 251
Leesburg, FL 32748
(904) 787-1360

Zetts Fish Farm & Hatchery
Drifting, PA 16834
(814) 345-5357

Bluegill (*Lepomis macrochirus*)

Aquatic Control, Inc.
P.O. Box 100
Seymour, IN 47274

Arkansas Fisheries, Inc.
P.O. Box 14
Fargo, AR 72049
(501) 734-3727

Bowerman Distributors
1442 N. Summers Rd.
Imlay City, MI 48444
(313) 724-2185

J. Buchanan
P.O. Box 1210
Picton, Ontario
Canada K0K 2T0
(613) 476-6284

Calala's Water Haven, Inc.
Route 60, Dept. CFF
New London, OH 44851
(419) 929-8052

Cedar Creek Fisheries
Route 2
Osgood, IN 47037
(812) 675-1783

Cedar Lakes Catfish Farms
Route 1
Villa Rica, GA 30180
(404) 942-3735

Chico Game Fish Farm
973-M East Ave.
Chico, CA 95927
(916) 343-1849

Clear Creek Fisheries
Route 4, Box 60
Martinsville, IN 46151
(317) 342-2973

Cleveland Fisheries
P.O. Drawer 460
Cleveland, MS 38732
(601) 843-8174

Danbury Fish Farms
P.O. Box 528
Danbury, TX 77534
(713) 922-1561

Fattig Fish Hatchery
P.O. Box 111
Brady, NE 69123

Fish Breeders of California, Inc.
P.O. Box 918
Niland, CA 92257
(714) 348-0547

Fish-Gro Fisheries
P.O. Box 87
Everett, PA 15537
(814) 652-2319

John B. Fitzpatrick
214 E. North St.
Dwight, IL 60420
(815) 584-3545

347

Woodrow Fleming
Route 4
Columbus, IN 47201

Giesler Live Fish Co.
Route 1, Box 53
W. Columbia, TX 77486
(713) 345-3577

Greenfield Fishing Lakes &
Hatcheries
Route 8, Box 127
Greenfield, IN 46140
(317) 326-2496

Hoeft Enterprises
Route 1, Box 237B
Milton, WV 25541
(304) 743-9806

Krehbiel Fish Farm
P.O. Box 145
Pretty Prairie, KS 67570
(316) 459-6586

Kurtz's Fish Farm
Route 2, Box 155
Elverson, PA 19520
(215) 286-9250

Lakeland Trout Farms
Route 1
Nunnelly, TN 37137
(615) 729-3731

Northrup's Fish Hatchery
Route 6, Box 88
Columbia, MO 65201

Opel's Fish Hatchery
Route 1, Box 51
Worden, IL 62097
(618) 459-3287

Osage Catfisheries, Inc.
Route 1, Box 222
Osage Beach, MO 65065

E.A. Owen
P.O. Box 144
Williston, TN 38076
(901) 465-3343

Peterson Trout Farm
Peterson, MN 55962

Schulty's Place
Route 3, Box 103C
Troy, MO 63379

Southern Fish Culturists, Inc.
P.O. Box 251
Leesburg, FL 32748
(904) 787-1360

3-R Fish Farm
Route 1
Lebanon, IL 62254
(618) 537-2343

Zetts Fish Farm & Hatchery
Drifting, PA 16834
(814) 345-5357

Hybrid Sunfish (male, *Lepomis macrochirus,* crossed with female green sunfish, *Lepomis cyanellus*)

Aquatic Control, Inc.
P.O. Box 100
Seymour, IN 47274

Bowerman Distributors
1442 N. Summers Rd.
Imlay City, MI 48444
(313) 724-2185

Clear Creek Fisheries
Route 4, Box 60
Martinsville, IN 46151
(317) 342-2973

Cleveland Fisheries
P.O. Drawer 460
Cleveland, MS 38732
(601) 843-8174

Danbury Fish Farms
P.O. Box 528
Danbury, TX 77534
(713) 922-1561

Fish-Gro Fisheries
P.O. Box 87
Everett, PA 15537
(814) 652-2319

John B. Fitzpatrick
214 E. North St.
Dwight, IL 60420
(815) 584-2545

Fountain Bluff Fish Farm
Route 1
Gorham, IL 62940
(618) 763-4387

Ken's Channel Catfish
Route 1
Alapaha, GA 31622
(912) 532-6135

Krehbiel Fish Farm
P.O. Box 145
Pretty Prairie, KS 67570
(316) 459-6586

Opel's Fish Hatchery
Route 1, Box 51
Worden, IL 62097
(618) 459-3287

Ruder's Fish Hatcheries
Route 1, Box 349
Millstadt, IL 62260
(618) 476-1388

Zetts Fish Farm & Hatchery
Drifting, PA 16834
(814) 345-5357

Trout Family

Brook Trout
(*Salvelinus fontinalis*)

Bar X Bar Ranch
P.O. Drawer 2
Pecos, NM 87552
(505) 757-8500

Beitey's Resort
Route 2
Valley, WA 98181
(509) 937-2154

Big Sky Trout Ranch
3654½ N. Montana Ave.
Helena, MT 59601
(406) 442-4575

Black River Trout Ranch
Forestport, NY 13338
(315) 391-3511

Bowerman Distributors
1442 N. Summers Rd.
Imlay City, MI 48444
(313) 724-2185

Brown's Trout Hatchery
Route 362
Bliss, NY 14024
(716) 322-7322

Cedar Springs Trout Hatchery
Route 2
Mill Hall, PA 17751
(717) 726-3737

Cedarbrook Trout Farms, Inc.
1543 Lakeshore Dr.
Harrisville, MI 48740
(517) 724-5241

Fernwood Trout Hatchery
Gansevoort, NY 12831

Fresh-Flo Corp.
Route 1
Adell, WI 53001
(414) 528-8236

Green Walk Trout Hatchery
36 North 5th St.
Bangor, PA 18013
(215) 588-1421

Harriman Trout Co.
P.O. Box 173
St. Ignatius, MT 59865
(406) 745-3113

M. T. Linttner
Route 1
Sutton, Quebec
Canada J0E 2K0

Jan L. Michalek
P.O. Box 408
St. Louisville, OH 43071
(614) 745-2187

Paradise Brook Trout
Route 1
Cresco, PA 18326
(717) 629-3422

Peterson Trout Farm
Peterson, MN 55962

Pisciculture St. Mathieu
71 1st Ave., W.
Amos, Quebec
Canada J9T 1T7
(819) 732-5236

Seven Pines Trout Hatchery
Lewis, WI 54851
(715) 653-2271

Brook Trout
(*Salvelinus fontinalis*)

Spring Creek Trout Hatchery
Route 1, Box 9A
Lewistown, MT 59457
(406) 538-3538

Trout Brook Farm
Route 2
Barneveid, NY 13304
(315) 896-2753

Zetts Fish Farm & Hatchery
Drifting, PA 16834
(814) 345-5357

Brown Trout (*Salmo trutta*)

Bowerman Distributors
1442 N. Summers Rd.
Imlay City, MI 48444
(313) 724-2185

Brown's Trout Hatchery
Route 362
Bliss, NY 14024
(716) 322-7322

Cedar Springs Trout Hatchery
Route 2
Mill Hall, PA 17751
(717) 726-3737

Green Walk Trout Hatchery
36 North 5th St.
Bangor, PA 18013
(215) 588-1421

Harriman Trout Co.
P.O. Box 173
St. Ignatius, MT 59865
(406) 745-3113

Jenkins Trout Hatchery
Route 1, Box 167
Utica, PA 16362
(412) 376-2887

M. T. Linttner
Route 1
Sutton, Quebec
Canada J0E 2K0

Jan L. Michalek
P.O. Box 408
St. Louisville, OH 43071
(614) 745-2187

Mount Lassen Trout Farm
Route 5
Red Bluff, CA 96080

Paradise Brook Trout
Route 1
Cresco, PA 18326
(717) 629-3422

Peterson Trout Farm
Peterson, MN 55962

Seven Pines Trout Hatchery
Lewis, WI 54851
(715) 653-2271

Spring Creek Trout Hatchery
Route 1, Box 9A
Lewistown, MT 59457
(406) 538-3538

Zetts Fish Farm & Hatchery
Drifting, PA 16834
(814) 345-5357

Rainbow Trout (*Salmo gairdnei*)

Bar X Bar Ranch
P.O. Drawer 2
Pecos, NM 87552
(505) 757-8500

Beitey's Resort
Route 2
Valley, WA 99181
(509) 937-2154

Big Sky Trout Ranch
3654½ N. Montana Ave.
Helena, MT 59601
(406) 442-4575

Bitterroot Trout Farm
P.O. Box 1158
Hamilton, MT 59840
(406) 363-3598

Black River Trout Ranch
Forestport, NY 13338
(315) 392-3511

Bowerman Distributors
1442 N. Summers Rd.
Imlay City, MI 48444
(313) 724-2185

Brown's Trout Farm
Route 3, Box 233
Tazewell, VA 24651

Bucksnort Trout Ranch
Route 1, Box 156
McEwen, TN 37101

Caribou Trout Ranch
P.O. Box 67
Soda Springs, ID 83276
(208) 547-3960

Cedar Springs Trout Hatchery
Route 2
Mill Hall, PA 17751
(717) 726-3737

Cedarbrook Trout Farms, Inc.
1543 Lakeshore Dr.
Harrisville, MI 48740
(517) 734-5241

Colo Mountain Trout Farm
Route 2, Box 17
Saquache, CO 81149
(303) 655-2294

Fernwood Trout Hatchery
Gansevoort, NY 12831

Fox Islands Fisheries
P.O. Box 427
Vinahaven, ME 04863
(207) 863-4321

Fresh-Flo Corp.
Route 1
Adell, WI 53001
(414) 528-8236

Garrapata Trout Farm
P.O. Box 3178
Carmel, CA 93921

Green River Trout Farm
Route 1, Box 267
Mancelona, MI 49659
(616) 584-3486

Green Walk Trout Hatchery
36 North 5th St.
Bangor, PA 18013
(215) 588-1421

Greenfield Fishing Lakes &
Hatcheries
Route 8, Box 127
Greenfield, IN 46140
(317) 326-2496

Harriman Trout Co.
P.O. Box 173
St. Ignatius, MT 59865
(406) 745-3113

Lakeland Trout Farms
Route 1
Nunnelly, TN 37137
(615) 729-3731

M. T. Linttner
Route 1
Sutton, Quebec
Canada J0E 2K0

Long Island Oyster Farms, Inc.
Eatons Neck Rd.
Northport, NY 11768

Macon Springs Fish Hatchery
Lanes Valley Rd.
Paynes Creek, CA 96075
(916) 474-3595

Jan L. Michalek
P.O. Box 408
St. Louisville, OH 43071
(614) 745-2187

Mount Lassen Trout Farm
Route 5
Red Bluff, CA 96080
(916) 597-2222

Nisqually Trout Farm
5780 Martin Way
Olympia, WA 98506
(206) 491-7440

Opel's Fish Hatchery
Route 1, Box 51
Worden, IL 62097
(618) 459-3287

Paradise Brook Trout
Route 1
Cresco, PA 18326
(717) 629-3422

Peterson Trout Farm
Peterson, MN 55962

Pisciculture St. Mathieu
71 1st Ave., W.
Amos, Quebec
Canada J9T 1T7
(819) 732-5236

Plains Fish Ranch
P.O. Box 101
Davenport, NE 68335
(402) 364-2122 or
        364-2186

Price Creek Trout Farm
Route 1
Talking Rock, GA 30175
(404) 273-3765

Rainbow Ranch
Route 8
Cumming, GA 30130

Rainbow Springs Trout Ranch
1157 County Road 214
Durango, CO 81301
(303) 247-2939

Rangen, Inc.
P.O. Box 706
Buhl, ID 83316

Rose City Trout Farms
2646 N. Townline Rd.
Rose City, MI 48654
(517) 685-2200

Rose Springs Trout Hatchery
LA Creek Route
Martin, SD 57551
(605) 685-6133

Rowledge Pond, Inc.
Route 1
Sandy Hook, CT 06482

Rushing Waters Trout Farm
Route 1, Box 149
Palmyra, WI 53156
(414) 495-4517

Seven Pines Trout Hatchery
Lewis, WI 54851
(715) 653-2271

Shenandoah Fisheries, Inc.
P.O. Box 276
Lacey Spring, VA 22833

Shive Springs Trout Ranch
P.O. Box 236
Pagosa Springs, CO 81147
(303) 968-5669

Spring Creek Trout Hatchery
Route 1, Box 9A
Lewistown, MT 59457
(406) 538-3538

Spring Valley Trout Farm
Route 2
Petersburg, Ontario
Canada N0B 2H0
(519) 696-3222

Stover Mountain Trout Ranch
Route 5
Ellijay, GA 30540
(404) 635-7649 or
        273-3179

Trophy Fish Ranch, Inc.
Glenwood Rd.
Richfield, UT 84701
(801) 896-4922

Trout Lodge
4008 Pioneer Way
Tacoma, WA 98443
(206) 922-5241 or
        922-6298

Troutdale Ranch, Inc.
P.O. Box 68
Gravois Mills, MO 65037
(314) 372-6100

Valley Head Trout Farm
Monterville, WV 26282
(304) 339-2569

Whitewater Trout Co.
P.O. Box 131
Whitewater, CA 92282

Tilapia Family

Java Tilapia
(*Tilapia mossambica*)

Fish Breeders of California, Inc.
P.O. Box 918
Niland, CA 92257
(714) 348-0547

Fish Breeders of Idaho, Inc.
Route 3
Buhl, ID 83316
(208) 543-6645

Oakland Bio-Aquatics
1840 Thunderbird St.
Troy, MI 48084
(313) 362-3199

Blue Tilapia (*Tilapia aurea*)

Southern Fish Culturists, Inc.
P.O. Box 251
Leesburg, FL 32748
(904) 787-1360

Nile Tilapia (*Tilapia nilotica*)

Hickory Ridge Fisheries, Inc.
5922 N. Douglas Blvd.
Spencer, OK 73084
(405) 771-3705

Oakland Bio-Aquatics
1840 Thunderbird St.
Troy, MI 48084
(313) 362-3199

SOURCES OF EQUIPMENT

Aerators

Aeration Industries, Inc.
50 South 9th Ave.
Hopkins, MN 55343
(612) 933-6313

Air-O-Lator
8100 Pasco St.
Kansas City, MO 64131

Aquatic Control, Inc.
P.O. Box 100
Seymour, IN 47274

Aquatic Environmental
Controls, Co.
44625 Tonopah St.
Newberry Springs, CA 92365
(714) 257-3588

Astra Chemicals Ltd.
1004 Middlegate Rd.
Mississauga, Ontario
Canada L4Y 1M4

BEHPCO Supply
1410 N. U.S. 71
DeQueen, AR 71832
(501) 584-3620

Beitey's Resort
Route 2
Valley, WA 99181
(509) 937-2154

Boatcycle Co.
P.O. Box 494
Henderson, TX 75652
(214) 657-3791

Bowerman Distributors
1442 N. Summers Rd.
Imlay City, MI 48444
(313) 724-2185

CCN Inc., Enertech Corp.
P.O. Box 420
Norwich, VT 05055
(802) 649-1145 or
        649-1350

Crescent Mfg. Co.
P.O. Box 3303
Ft. Worth, TX 76105

Delta Net & Twine Co.
P.O. Box 356
Greenville, MS 38701
(601) 332-0841

Environmental Management
and Design, Inc.
P.O. Box 493
Ann Arbor, MI 48107
(313) 995-0548

John B. Fitzpatrick
214 E. North St.
Dwight, IL 60420
(815) 584-2545

Florida Soft Crab Co.
P.O. Box 6585
Hollywood, FL 33021

Fresh-Flo Corp.
Route 1
Adell, WI 53001
(414) 528-8236

Hinde Engineering Co.
654 Deerfield Rd.
Highland Park, IL 60035
(312) 432-6031

J.S.C. Mfg. Co., Inc.
P.O. Box 471
Fordyce, AR 71742
(501) 352-2749

Kembro, Inc.
P.O. Box 205
Mequon, WI 53092
(414) 242-2630

L&M Aqua-Fab
1853 W. Commonwealth Ave.
Fullerton, CA 92633
(714) 525-0315

Limnological Associates
1024 Moreno Dr.
Ojai, CA 93023

McCrary's Farm Supply
114 Park St.
Lonoke, AR 72086
(501) 676-2766

McGee Mfg. Co., Inc.
6158 Fulton Ave.
Van Nuys, CA 91401
(213) 780-3008

Mel-Bro Hatcheries
Route 3, Box 149
Blountville, TN 37617
(615) 323-5579

Micro-Por, Inc.
P.O. Box 278
Colwich, KS 67030
(316) 796-1234

Monterey Bay Hydroculture
Farms
512 Columbia St.
Santa Cruz, CA 95060
(408) 423-3809

Getting Food from Water

Nylon Net Co.
P.O. Box 592
Memphis, TN 38103
(901) 525-8616

Opel's Fish Hatchery
Route 1, Box 51
Worden, IL 62097
(618) 459-3287

Peterson Trout Farm
Peterson, MN 55962

Rodale Resources, Inc.
576 North St.
Emmaus, PA 18049
(215) 965-6019

Schramm Inc.
901 E. Virginia Ave.
West Chester, PA 19380
(215) 696-2500

Schulty's Place
Route 3, Box 103C
Troy, MO 63379

Southern Farmers Assoc.
4200 Woodlawn St.
Little Rock, AR 72205

John L. Stengl
P.O. Box 2858
Kenai, AK 99611

Twin Island Lake
Route 2, Hwy. 40 & 61
St. Charles, MO 63301
(314) 623-3408

Wholesale Bait Co.
1405 Pleasant Ave.
Hamilton, OH 45015

Xodar Corp.
Powder Hill Dr.
Lincoln, RI 02865
(401) 333-0100

Cages

Act One Supplies
1530 MacArthur Blvd.
Oakland, CA 94602
(415) 530-0323

Aquatic Control, Inc.
P.O. Box 100
Seymour, IN 47274

Astra Chemicals Ltd.
1004 Middlegate Rd.
Mississauga, Ontario
Canada L4Y 1M4

Becker Industries, Inc.
P.O. Box 1028
Newport, OR 97365

ConWed Corp.
770 29th Ave. S.E.
Minneapolis, MN 55414
(612) 378-0030

Cottonwood Game & Fish Farm
Route 1, Box 101C
Norman, OK 73069
(405) 321-2287

John B. Fitzpatrick
214 E. North St.
Dwight, IL 60420
(815) 584-2545

Florida Soft Crab Co.
P.O. Box 6585
Hollywood, FL 33021

Fox Islands Fisheries
P.O. Box 427
Vinalhaven, ME 04863
(207) 863-4321

Greenhope Farms
Route 1, Box 76
Morrisville, NC 27560

Ken's Channel Catfish
Route 1
Alapaha, GA 31622
(912) 532-6135

L & M Aqua-Fab
1853 W. Commonwealth Ave.
Fullerton, CA 92633
(714) 525-0315

Marinovich Trawl Co., Inc.
P.O. Box 294
Biloxi, MS 39533
(601) 436-6429

McCrary's Farm Supply
114 Park St.
Lonoke, AR 72086
(501) 676-2766

E. L. Pennington
712 Third St.
Vienna, GA 31092

Salmon of the Ozarks
P.O. Box 245
Decatur, AR 72722
(501) 752-3969

Schulty's Place
Route 3, Box 103C
Troy, MO 63379

C. E. Shepherd Co.
P.O. Box 9445
Houston, TX 77011
(713) 928-3763

John L. Stengl
P.O. Box 2858
Kenai, AK 99611

Veldmaster, Inc.
34 S. Broadway St.
White Plains, NY 10601
(914) 761-1234

Dipnets

Crescent Mfg. Co.
P.O. Box 3303
Ft. Worth, TX 76105

Delta Net & Twine Co.
P.O. Box 356
Greenville, MS 38701
(601) 332-0841

Duraframe Dipnet
Route 2, Box 166
Viola, WI 54664

McCrary's Farm Supply
114 Park St.
Lonoke, AR 72086
(501) 676-2766

Nylon Net Co.
P.O. Box 592
Memphis, TN 38103
(901) 525-8616

Feed, Cold-Water Fish

Agway, Inc.
P.O. Box 1333
Syracuse, NY 13201
(315) 477-6289

Astra Chemicals Ltd.
1004 Middlegate Rd.
Mississauga, Ontario
Canada L4Y 1M4

Getting Food from Water

Bioproducts, Inc.
P.O. Box 429
Warrenton, OR 97146
(503) 861-2256

Greenfield Fishing Lakes &
Hatcheries
Route 8, Box 127
Greenfield, IN 46140
(317) 326-2496

Inter Home Fish Assoc.
12005 Highwater Rd.
Granada Hills, CA 91344

Jungle Laboratories Corp.
P.O. Box 2018
Sanford, FL 32771
(305) 322-8313

Rangen Inc.
P.O. Box 706
Buhl, ID 83316

Simpson & Co.
P.O. Box 1418
Colorado Springs, CO 80901
(303) 635-3501

Zeigler Brothers, Inc.
P.O. Box 95
Gardners, PA 17324

Feed, Warm-Water Fish

Aquafarms International, Inc.
P.O. Box 157
Mecca, CA 92254
(714) 393-3036

Bioproducts, Inc.
P.O. Box 429
Warrenton, OR 97146
(503) 861-2256

Dixie Mills Co.
P.O. Box 351
East St. Louis, IL 62202

John B. Fitzpatrick
214 E. North St.
Dwight, IL 60420
(815) 584-2545

Kordon Corp.
2242 Davis Ct.
Hayward, CA 94545
(415) 782-4058

McCrary's Farm Supply
114 Park St.
Lonoke, AR 72086
(501) 676-2766

Mountaire Feeds, Inc.
P.O. Box 5391
North Little Rock, AR 72119
(501) 376-6751

Oakland Bio-Aquatics
1840 Thunderbird St.
Troy, MI 48084
(313) 362-3199

Siler City Mills, Inc.
P.O. Box 249
Siler City, NC 27344
(919) 742-2166

Spring Valley Trout Farm
Route 2
Petersburg, Ontario
Canada N0B 2H0
(519) 696-3222

Wardley Products Co.
1 Aquarium Dr.
Secaucus, NJ 07094
(201) 348-4040

Zeigler Brothers, Inc.
P.O. Box 95
Gardners, PA 17324

Seines (Nets)

Aquatic Control, Inc.
P.O. Box 100
Seymour, IN 47274

Commercial Fishing Supplies,
Inc.
Creamery Rd.
East Haddam, CT 06423
(203) 873-9500

ConWed Corp.
770 29th Ave. S.E.
Minneapolis, MN 55414
(612) 378-0030

Crescent Mfg. Co.
P.O. Box 3303
Ft. Worth, TX 76105

Delta Net & Twine Co.
P.O. Box 356
Greenville, MS 38701
(601) 332-0841

E. I. duPont deNemours & Co.
1007 Market St.
Wilmington, DE 19898

Duraframe Dipnet
Route 2, Box 166
Viola, WI 54664

John B. Fitzpatrick
214 E. North St.
Dwight, IL 60420
(815) 584-2545

Florida Soft Crab Co.
P.O. Box 6585
Hollywood, FL 33021

Kahl Scientific Instrument
Corp.
P.O. Box 1166
El Cajon, CA 92022
(714) 444-2158

Marinovich Trawl Co., Inc.
P.O. Box 294
Biloxi, MS 39533
(601) 436-6429

McCrary's Farm Supply
114 Park St.
Lonoke, AR 72086
(501) 676-2766

Nylon Net Co.
P.O. Box 592
Memphis, TN 38103
(901) 525-8616

O.K. Corral
Highway 57 E.
Moscow, TN 38057
(901) 877-9804

Willard Rolow
Route 3, Box 98-R
Alsea, OR 97324
(503) 487-4674

John L. Stengl
P.O. Box 2858
Kenai, AK 99611

Veldmaster, Inc.
34 S. Broadway St.
White Plains, NY 10601
(914) 761-1234

Tanks

Aquaculture Eng. & Supply Co.
P.O. Box 25126
Houston, TX 77005
(713) 527-8817

Dura Craft Boats, Inc.
Hwy. 4 West
Monticello, AR 71655

En-West Corp.
P.O. Box 335
North Salt Lake City, UT 85054
(801) 533-0108

Red Ewald, Inc.
P.O. Box 519, S. Hwy. 181
Karnes City, TX 78118
(512) 780-3304

Florida Soft Crab Co.
P.O. Box 6585
Hollywood, FL 33021

Fresh-Flo Corp.
Route 1
Adell, WI 53001
(414) 528-8236

Paul Mueller Co.
P.O. Box 828
Springfield, MO 65801
(417) 865-2831

Neilsen Metal Industries
3501 Portland Rd. N.E.
Salem, OR 97303
(503) 581-7111

Pacific BioMarine Labs, Inc.
P.O. Box 536
Venice, CA 90291
(213) 397-9702

Peterson Brothers Boat Works,
Inc.
P.O. Box 158
Shell Lake, WI 54871

Peterson Trout Farm
Peterson, MN 55962

Sea Life Supply
740 Tioga Ave.
Sand City, CA 93955
(408) 394-0828

Spring Valley Trout Farm
Route 2
Petersburg, Ontario
Canada N0B 2H0
(519) 696-3222

S S Filtration & Dev. Co.
1429 Speers Rd.
Oakville, Ontario
Canada L6L 2X5
(416) 827-3171

Test Kits, Ammonia

Hach Chemical Co.
P.O. Box 907
Ames, IA 50010
(515) 232-2533

Test Kits, Carbon Dioxide

Carolina Biological Supply Co.
2700 York Rd.
Burlington, NC 27215
(919) 584-0381

Hach Chemical Co.
P.O. Box 907
Ames, IA 50010
(515) 232-2533

LaMotte Chemical Products Co.
P.O. Box 329
Chestertown, MD 21620
(301) 778-3100

McCrary's Farm Supply
114 Park St.
Lonoke, AR 72086
(501) 676-2766

Test Kits, Dissolved Oxygen

Carolina Biological Supply Co.
2700 York Rd.
Burlington, NC 27215
(919) 584-0381

Delta Net & Twine Co.
P.O. Box 356
Greenville, MS 38701
(601) 332-0841

Florida Soft Crab Co.
P.O. Box 6585
Hollywood, FL 33021

Hach Chemical Co.
P.O. Box 907
Ames, IA 50010
(515) 232-2533

LaMotte Chemical Products Co.
P.O. Box 329
Chestertown, MD 21620
(301) 778-3100

McCrary's Farm Supply
114 Park St.
Lonoke, AR 72086
(501) 676-2766

Sea Life Supply
740 Tioga Ave.
Sand City, CA 93955
(408) 394-0828

Test Kits, pH

Carolina Biological Supply Co.
2700 York Rd.
Burlington, NC 27215
(919) 584-0381

Dyna-Pet Inc.
1110 Florence Way
Campbell, CA 95008
(408) 379-9339

Hach Chemical Co.
P.O. Box 907
Ames, IA 50010
(515) 232-2533

LaMotte Chemical Products Co.
P.O. Box 329
Chestertown, MD 21620
(301) 778-3100

McCrary's Farm Supply
114 Park St.
Lonoke, AR 72086
(501) 676-2766

Wardley Products Co.
1 Aquarium Dr.
Secaucus, NJ 07094
(201) 348-4040

Test Kits, Water Hardness

Carolina Biological Supply Co.
2700 York Rd.
Burlington, NC 27215
(919) 584-0381

Hach Chemical Co.
P.O. Box 907
Ames, IA 50010
(515) 232-2533

Jungle Laboratories Corp.
P.O. Box 2018
Sanford, FL 32771
(305) 322-8313

LaMotte Chemical Products Co.
P.O. Box 329
Chestertown, MD 21620
(301) 778-3100

McCrary's Farm Supply
114 Park St.
Lonoke, AR 72086
(501) 676-2766

INDEX

Page numbers in italics represent illustrations.

Abandoned Farms, Maine
    commercial mussel raising at, 116
Acidity–Alkalinity. *See* pH
Acriflavin, 253
Aerators
    in coastal enclosures, 132
    in lakes, 100
    in ponds, 194-95, 265, 286
Agitation
    to control pond scum, 176
Algae
    benthic, eaten by tadpoles, 74
    Cladophora in streams, 27
    control of in ponds, 169-78, 195
    culture tanks for, 109
    domesticated for food, 321-22
    in garden pools, 306
    increased by fertilizing pond, 189
    protecting small fish, 208
    as result of pond aging, 169
    in solar-heated fish tanks, 261-62
    from tidal wetlands, 108-9
Alligator, for aquaculture, 330
Alum feeder, for filtering pond water, 197
Aluminum sulfate, for muddy water, 191
Ammonia, 221, 239, 289
Anacharis canadensis. See Elodea
Anchor worm, 255
Animals, population near creek, 44-46
Aquaculture
    definition of, *ix*
    types of, *ix-xi*

Aquatic life, increased in creek, by dam, 39-46
Arrowhead, 66, *67*, 174, 317
Artesian spring, *8*
Azolla. See Fern

Bacteria
    causing disease in fish, 251
    in spring water, 18
Banks
    of ponds, 166
    of trout stream, 31-33
Bass, largemouth, 249
    analysis of pond population, 205-6
    bait for, 215
    growth rate of, 215
    harvesting to maintain population of, 204
    stocking artificial pond with, 202-8
Beaver
    dams built by, 58-60
    hunted for pelts, 57-60
    population of, 58
Beaver pond, 57-62
    ducks on, 60, 62
    fee-fishing and hunting on, 60
    log drain for, *59*, 60
    sowing millet on, 60-62
Benzene hexachloride, 255, 256
Birds, population near creek, 44-46
Blackspot disease, 253-54
Bladderwort, 178
Bluegills, 240-41
    analysis of pond population, 205-6
    bait for, 215
    eating leeches, 197

363